T0288346

WHO BY
FIRE
WHO BY
SWORD

THE JOURNALS OF FOUR
COURAGEOUS JEWISH WOMEN
IN TURBULENT TIMES

TOBY ORLANDER

URIM PUBLICATIONS
Jerusalem • New York

Who By Fire Who By Sword:
The Journals of Four Courageous Jewish Women in Turbulent Times
by Toby Orlander

Copyright © 2013 by Toby Orlander

Book design by Ariel Walden

Printed in Israel

First Edition

ISBN: 978-965-524-134-1

Urim Publications, P.O. Box 52287, Jerusalem 91521 Israel

Lambda Publishers Inc.
527 Empire Blvd., Brooklyn, New York 11225 U.S.A.
Tel: 718-972-5449 Fax: 718-972-6307

mh@ejudaica.com

www.UrimPublications.com

וְהִיא שֶׁעָמְדָה לַאֲבוֹתֵינוּ וְלָנוּ. שֶׁלֹּא אֶחָד בִּלְבָד, עָמַד עָלֵינוּ לְכַלּוֹתֵנוּ. אֶלָּא שֶׁבְּכָל דּוֹר וָדוֹר, עוֹמְדִים עָלֵינוּ לְכַלּוֹתֵנוּ. וְהַקָּדוֹשׁ בָּרוּךְ הוּא מַצִּילֵנוּ מִיָּדָם

"THIS COVENANT THAT REMAINED CONSTANT for our ancestors and for us has saved us against any who arose to destroy us in every generation, and throughout history when any stood against us to annihilate us, the HOLY ONE, blessed be his name, rescued us from their hands."

For my dear father, R' Oyzer Chaim Orlander, *a"h*, a giant of a man, who in his charismatic way, taught me the meaning of honesty, integrity, and Chassidus.

*

For my dear mother, Necha Lamet, *a"h*, a powerhouse who set super-human limits for herself, and guided us, her children, with love to achieve to our fullest and to never give up.

Contents

Prologue

*T*HEY'RE COMING. I CAN HEAR THEM IN THE DIS-
tance, rumbling closer and closer, the Russian liberators in
their tanks. These past few weeks, the mortars and bullets
have been whizzing past our hiding place, and by one of the many
miracles, we haven't been hit.

Just beyond the farmhouse I hear the feeble "shouts" of joy from
the "walking dead" – the few skeletal remnants of European Jewry,
the few remaining Jews in the city of Sambor. It's over; this ghastly
war is finally over.

I watch from the little split between the bricks – the window, as
we call it – as the Russian army heads toward the city, their vehicles
rolling over the worn stones. Soldiers, pouring out of their tanks
and trucks, bewildered at what they are seeing, are recoiling in shock
and disgust. Their minds are having a hard time processing that
those scantily clad ghosts, those "sub-humans" crawling out from
their hiding places, stretching out their emaciated hands, begging
for a scrap, those "things" are real people. I watch from my vantage
point, and the tears course down my own sunken cheeks uncontrollably. They have finally come, and I have survived. Why me?

So many dead, so many haven't made it, why me?

No reason . . . perhaps just so that the story be told, just so
that the dead are remembered. Perhaps it's for Dina, for Freya and
Tonya. For all Jewish girls, through all the centuries, whose lives
were thrown into turmoil by monsters trying to eradicate the Jewish
people. Those monsters are long gone and mostly forgotten . . . yet
we are here; we've been here for the last 5700 years, and we will be
here till the coming of Moshiach. "Am Yisroel Chai."

Necha

Sambor, August 1944

· BOOK I ·

Dina's Story

Chapter 1

*M*Y NAME IS DINA. I WAS BORN IN LONDON IN the year 1170. I am the eldest in our family of four, all of us girls, and much to my mother's distress. Mama has tried so hard to present Father with a son, but after the last of so many stillbirths, her physician has informed her there will be no further pregnancies. Mama is distraught at the verdict, and however much Father tries to calm her by complimenting his four wonderful daughters, Mama remains inconsolable. She hasn't produced a son and heir. Father is indeed very pleased with his girls, and the more so, as he himself comes from a long line of only sons, and daughters are a rarity and novelty.

I'm seventeen, and very aware that I'm not like other girls my age. That is not to say that I'm any better, nor am I any worse than my peers, I'm just . . . different.

Since my youngest years, I've always tagged along one step behind my Father. I'm his shadow and I follow him everywhere. His friends and associates have been very patient with me, and have always allowed me to sit quietly in a corner, be it during prayers, learning times or just social occasions. I have picked up habits that are normally reserved for a son. I can daven better than most girls, and can follow deep Talmudic discussions, sometimes even interrupting the men's discourse with questions of my own. I speak and write in four languages, and Father says I have an amazing talent with ciphers.

Mama is less excited with my "accomplishments." I am not very good with the cooking nor baking, and even less so with the sewing and mending. This would be a calamity in itself in any other household; however, we are all so lucky that my sister Sarah, who is barely a year younger than I, is a master in the kitchen and an absolute genius with the needle. Sarah is my exact opposite: she has ink black hair and large onyx eyes. Her skin is the like most luscious honey, and lips the color of berries. I, on the other hand, have hair the color of harvested straw; blue eyes; and pale, milky skin.

*

Sarah enjoys all the things I find burdensome, and never thinks to question anything. I love Sarah dearly, and I love her doubly for taking the pressure off me, keeping Mama happy, and picking up the slack, so that our household can run smoothly.

Our household is far from a simple one to run. Living in the center of London, Father is always inviting travelers to join us for meals and lodging. On any given day, you can hear French, German, and even Latin spoken in our home. Father's family originates in Rouen, Mama's family come from Mainz, so guests feel at ease, able to converse in their native tongue. I am the in-house Latin expert, having picked up the language from overhearing the many clergymen, who are regular customers of Father's.

My Father, Aaron ben Yoseph Montague, is one of the most successful commercial advisors to King Henry II, monarch of all England. This position was originally awarded my grandfather Yoseph by William the Conqueror. King William was convinced that the commercial skills of the Jews, combined with an injection of fresh Jewish capital, would make England more prosperous and mightier than all of Europe. He brought Jewish merchants from Rouen in Normandy, and appointed these "invitees" as the moneylenders and coin dealers for the Crown. Jewish merchants were needed if the King was to collect taxes, which he used to build castles throughout the land. Money-lending for interest is considered a sin for Christians by the Catholic Church, whereas Jews are able to engage in this type of transaction with non-Jews. The King solved his own problem, and created an honorable means of income for his new Jewish citizens. As the masses could not afford to pay the high sums levied at them, borrowing money to meet the royal demands was imperative. Thus, grandfather Yoseph became the first administrator for the King, keeping a record of all transactions, loans, and property ownerships in the Domesday Book.

For the past one hundred years, we English Jews have became "Royal serfs" owned by the King, who holds the power of life and death over us. Yes, we've flourished under the King's protection, but have had to pay a heavy price for this privilege; we are taxed more heavily than anyone else.

While the commoners are quite happy to have reliable and honest moneylenders, we've incurred the wrath of the King's powerful barons and retainers, as well as the clergy. They have come to hate us, for, more often than not, they too are forced to borrow from the Jews in order to cover their debts and taxes, and they resent the King's relying on "Jews" to control His Majesty's finances.

*

Since my twelfth birthday, I have been accompanying Father on his trips to the Exchequer. This is where the Domesday Book is kept, and where Father keeps track of all revenue paid to the Monarch, and all monies still owed. This book is of special importance, as it contains a record of all land ownership, and facilitates determining the amount of tax levied at the landlords, according to the size of the property.

Last year, Father finally acquiesced to my demands of assisting him at work. After five years of carefully observing what Father was recording, which ledger he was using, in what columns he was making an entry, how the tallies worked, I've been allowed to carefully enter my first "tax receipt" from one of the sheriffs. I can feel Father looking over my shoulder, but not once does he interfere in the transaction while I am recording it. The sheriff has come to pay taxes as well as take out a loan. This means recording the correct amounts on the tallies. The tallies are sticks, approximately eight inches long, on which I must carve the right-sized notches. The size of the notch determines how much is owed, and the stick is then broken in half.

One half is saved as a record in the Exchequer, the other half given to the sheriff as proof of payment. I see a twinkle in Father's eye as I go about the transaction, and collect from the sheriff. I sense a spark of pride in Father; his daughter has learned her lessons well.

Chapter 2

I'VE DONE IT AGAIN; I'VE CAUSED MAMA GREAT DIS-
pleasure, and it's certainly not my intention. From my
private corner in the solar,* I can hear the clatter and bang
of the pots as Mama exasperatedly vents to Sarah, "Dina has made
herself scarce again. What am I going to do with your sister? Who
will marry her; she has none of the skills required of a wife, and
hasn't any inclination to learn. Her only interests lay in reading and
writing, and I tell you this, Sarah, it can't be healthy. Men are not
interested in educated women. A woman's place is in the home and
in the kitchen, not writing silly journals."

My "journal" is a bone of contention. It's my best friend and
confidant.

*

I've been making entries on these bound parchment pages for the
past few years and this so-called journal has become very important
to me. In fact, these pages were a gift to the king from one of his
lords, who had traveled all the way to China and returned with hundreds of sheets of parchment. Not having any use for it, the king
generously passed it down to his trusted bookkeeper, Father. As this
innovation had no place in the Exchequer, I was the recipient of this
wonderful treasure. This journal, which Father bound for me, has
become my mind, my heart, and my soul. It's absorbed my tears
and my laughter, my trials and triumphs. I'm so thankful to Father;
without actually voicing his approval of my keeping a journal, aware
of Mama's displeasure, he keeps me in good supply of quills and ink,

* Sleeping quarters; so named as there was always a light source

· 16 ·

and has never discouraged me. Father even helped me procure a velvet etui to protect it, and a niche to place it in for safekeeping. I write in German, for the practice, but mainly for the privacy. I wouldn't feel comfortable having Sarah, nor Maryam or Tzipa, the younger ones, reading my innermost thoughts. Although Maryam and Tzipa are disinterested, Sarah is always asking me what I'm writing about. I share some of my musings with her, but I'm glad her German is non-existent, and she isn't able to read the entries.

*

For this, I am so grateful to Mama. She took pains to make sure that my German was of the highest order, teaching me to read and write from a very young age. Mama, Yehudis bas Zecharia, is descended from one of the most prominent families in Mainz – Torah scholars and also very educated people. The family barely survived the First Crusade, most of the adults ruthlessly killed, although my mother's grandfather and some of his younger siblings were able to hide and escape to Britain. Mama is a very beautiful woman, hair black as pitch, eyes the color of heather, and although small of stature, she is as forceful as a battering ram. It is never a good idea to cross swords with Mama; she runs the house with an iron fist.

The clatter and bang continue in the kitchen. The servants have been prodded into action, as Father is expecting visitors. I've come down from the solar just in time to help the servants gather some wood from the pile stacked against the outer wall of our house. There's a fire roaring in the hearth, but Mama has us add some more wood so that the many pots are all resting on a heat source.

I'm feeling nauseous from the intermingling of the cabbage, leeks, and meats, but I daren't leave now. Mama is already scowling at me, I can't move fast enough, and I keep dropping things. Luckily the bowls are copper, and already dented from my previous mishaps. I am normally given the job of laying the table, and this shouldn't be a difficult task, but somehow I'm always letting things fall or spill. Sarah has her hands in the kneading bowl, almost up to her elbows, and the aroma of the first batch of breads is now rising from the baking furnace, mingling with the other foods and neutralizing the smells of the cabbages. I'm thankful to her, as she has asked Mama for some further instruction, thus distracting her, and I can get on with my chores at my own speed. Sarah is a great ally; just a wonderful sister.

We must be getting a very important visitor, as Father, too, is rushing about, overseeing the preparations. When everything is to his liking, he retires to the solar to change into his Shabbat clothing, leaving instructions that we are all to do the same. Sarah, quick as a rabbit, finished her chores, and is now hustling Maryam and Tzipa up to the solar ahead of me. I'm about to join them, having put the final touches on the table, when I hear a carriage pull up at the front of the manor, followed by the clang of the door knocker.

I'm torn between running upstairs and trying to make myself presentable, or showing the person in so that he doesn't have to wait in the cold. I choose to open the door, even though I know my woolen tunic is spotted and snagged, and my hair, in disarray, flying out from under my cap. Big mistake. I open the door to find four men on the doorstep, instead of just the one I thought Father was waiting for. The eldest of the group, and obviously the most prominent, cleared his throat and asked if Father was home. Remembering my good manners, I ushered them into the great hall, but remained mesmerized by the older man. His eyes could have been javelins, so piercing were they, that in the few moments it had taken me to settle the group, the man was already haunting me. I left them seated around the table with a jug of ale and went in search of Father.

By the time I'm "presentable," and not looking like a bedraggled mongrel, Father and the entire family were assembled in the great room. Mama, Sarah, and the servants were busy at the hearth, while the two younger ones, Maryam and Tzipa, were playing a new game called 'jacks.' I made my way over to the table, where the men sat engaged in animated conversation, trying to overhear what they were talking about. To my great delight, French was being spoken and I tried to busy myself behind Father's chair in the hope of following the conversation. Father was addressing the older man as Reb Shmuel ben Tibbon, who, I was to learn, is from Fustat, in Egypt. I'm not sure where that is and will have to remember to look up the location on one of the many maps in the Exchequer.

Reb Shmuel tells Father that he has come such a long distance on the behest of Reb Moshe of Fustat to lecture at the Torah center in Lincoln, and to mediate any scholarly disagreement. So engrossed was I in what Reb Shmuel was saying, I didn't realize that I was just standing, immovable, clinging to the heavily laden platter that Mama had put into my hands for placing on the table. I stood, just listening, while the food got cold. Father had to clear his voice twice before I snapped into attention and remembered what was required of me. In fact, I should have left the platter on the table and stepped away, but I was so anxious to hear every word, I chose to serve each of the men individually. I was getting annoyed stares from Mama, and Father was looking at me with his usual twinkle. I kept moving around the table, piling more and more food on everyone's dish, when, to my embarrassment Reb Shmuel turned toward me and asked my name. I muttered, "Dina," ready for a quick retreat, but Reb Shmuel arrested me with his next question.

"Have you heard of the Mishneh Torah of our great Rabbi?"

I was shaking my head in the affirmative, not knowing if I should let on that I knew things that only men should have knowledge of. What would he be thinking of me, admitting to such knowledge – and worse still, what would he think of Father?

"Very impressive; Reb Aaron, you have done well in teaching your daughter. Women are the real cement of our families and future generations, and they should, indeed, be educated."

Turning to me again, "Why don't you pull up a stool and sit next to your Father."

I was back in two blinks of an eye, having rushed to Mama with the almost empty tray of food, and grabbing the stool from the hearthside. I set myself down quietly just behind Father's elbow and in time to catch Reb Shmuel's opening thoughts on the Mishneh Torah, and its importance to understanding the Jewish laws. From there he went on to recounting the story of Reb Moshe ben Maimon's life, and lifeworks. So fascinated were we that we were unaware of how late the hour. The women had already gone up to the solar for the night. The servants had prepared straw matting in the great room for our guests, and Father and I thanked Reb Shmuel, took our leave, and left our guests to retire for the night.

*

Reb Shmuel and his entourage stayed with us for two more days, during which time I was allowed to join their Torah discourses. Reb Shmuel was extremely knowledgeable, and listening to him was pure pleasure. My curiosity was especially piqued when he recounted the horror stories of atrocities inflicted on our brethren during the Crusades in France and Saxony. I had previously heard stories from Mama and Father, but never in such detail. I was left with one strong impression; the Church had the power to organize the lords, and they, in turn, incited the rabble into a frenzy of anti-Semitism whereby the Jewish communities on the Continent were a free-for-all, for their looting and killing. Woe to the communities that were in the Crusaders' line of march toward the Holy Land. It served the Church well, getting rid of the Jews, to whom they were heavily in debt, having borrowed extensively from Jewish moneylenders to finance the Holy Wars, and to build their churches.

I was sorry to see Reb Shmuel and his entourage leave, but I was grateful that he left me with many, many points to ponder.

Chapter 3

ARAH HAS INTERCEPTED ME AT THE DOOR, AND shoved me back outside, all the while giggling uncontrollably. It takes all my patience to wait for her to stop stammering and tell me what's so exciting. Sarah finally comes out with it. She's overheard Mama and Father discussing the merits of a certain Yehudah who has been proposed in marriage for me. I can't believe my ears. I'm not anywhere near ready to get married, and I was hoping to do more cerebral things with my life before settling down with a husband and eventually a family. I was sure that Father was sensitive to my feelings and that he would be able to sway my mother. Sarah is prodding me, all the while tickling me and trying to get a celebratory reaction out of me.

"Sarah, cut it out! I know this must seem exciting to you, but I am far from happy about this turn of events."

"You can't mean that, Dina," she replies. "Marriage is what all girls dream of, and I heard this Yehudah is very learned and very special. I'm sure that if Father and Mama are considering him, he's perfect."

I'm not sure that remaining outside with Sarah will get me anywhere, so we slip quietly back into the great room. Not wanting to be seen by Mama and Father, I motion to Sarah that I'll be going to the solar, and quietly make my escape. This is an unbelievable turn of events for me, and I'm going to need some time and solitude to process it.

*

It's taken me two days to get up the courage to approach Father.

I finally cornered him in the great room, alone, milling over the

Talmud. Careful not to interrupt him, I sat down at the table and waited for a signal to speak, which came just a few minutes later, as he closed the tome.

"Father, I know I shouldn't be questioning you and Mama, but don't you think I should be consulted about my future, and surely when it comes to the issue of marriage."

Father is studying me from under his heavy brows, his expression the same as when he is worrying a difficult passage in his learning. I'm almost exploding, holding my breath. Have I overstepped the boundaries of respect? I'm relieved when Father smiles, extends his hand and asks, "Dina, do you think I'm not sensitive to your wishes? Do you think I'm unaware that you have many dreams to fulfill before settling down? In fact, your mother and I were waiting to speak with you about Yehudah. We think he would be perfect for your sister Sarah."

I am laughing and crying and singing for joy. I manage to make so much noise that the rest of the family come running to see what the commotion is about. Rushing over to Sarah, I swing her in the air and plant a million kisses on all the surfaces of her face and hands.

"Stop it already, Dina, what's this all about?" I pull up short realizing that Sarah is unaware of what is going on around her, so I steer her in the direction of Father and Mama, and I, together with the two smaller ones, make a hasty retreat.

Back in the solar, I have time to examine my true feelings, and nothing makes me happier right now than knowing this is right for Sarah. I scramble to get out my journal and record what has been happening to our family the last few days. Between the visit of Reb Shmuel, and Sarah's impending engagement, my quill flies over the pages filling in all the details. What would I do without this journal?

*

A thought has been trying to work its way to the forefront of my mind, almost in the same way a chick tries to break its eggshell to get out. After days of incessant head pains, I am finally able to process the thought.

Reb Shmuel was very specific about the role of the Church in the tragic saga of the French and German Jews. I know that in England, King Henry II is particularly careful to see that his Jewish money-lenders are not persecuted, he doesn't want to kill the bird that is laying the golden egg. What was causing my head pains was thinking of what would happen once Henry II was dead and replaced by a less sympathetic monarch.

How would we fare at the mercy of the Church and its Crusaders? How would we fare under Henry's unscrupulous sons? Was there anything I could do to protect my family and community? I resolved to be on the lookout for any telltale sign that the tide was turning against us.

Chapter 4

*C*ALDRONS BUBBLING, SERVANTS RUSHING TO AND fro, our home is buzzing with activity in preparation for Sarah's engagement. Dear Sarah, she keeps asking for my forgiveness in getting engaged first. I try to explain how relieved I am, that I am not mentally or emotionally ready to accept the yolk of married life yet, but Sarah, who is so blissfully happy, doesn't seem to get the message. Sarah, so beautiful and so good; I have yet to meet Yehudah, but I hope he will be kind to my little sister.

Sarah has a new dress for the occasion, and Mama insisted that I have one too. Mama has been a lot more accepting of my "un-domestication" since Sarah's acquiescence to wed. She is less harsh with me, more forgiving when I bungle one of the chores. I guess this is her way of commiserating with me on my "spinsterhood." I think she is convinced that I will remain "on the shelf." Adding the last touches to Sarah's hair, we both hurry down to the great room and wait for our guests.

The first to arrive are Yehudah and his parents, arriving on foot from the poorer Jewish neighborhood. Although Yehudah's father is a doctor, and wealthy, he chooses to live among his patients. This is the first time Sarah and I get a glimpse of Yehudah.

Father, being sensitive to Sarah's feelings, has created a corner in the great room where she and Yehudah can sit and get to know each other. From the corner of my eye, I see them talking and laughing and I have a feeling that everything will be alright. The rest of the guests arrive in dribbles. Our Rabbi, Yonasan ben Chia; our neighbors; the various moneylenders; and some of Father's non-Jewish acquaintances and business associates. Some of the King's deputies, sheriffs, and knights and a handful of clergymen are also here.

There are lots of people milling around greeting each other; there is laughter and cheer while a mass of food is being consumed. Funny how the non-Jewish guests are only interested in the vats of ale.

I try to help Mama by seeing to the guests' needs, passing around cakes and sweetmeats. Everyone is stopping to wish me well, and speed in finding my own husband. I can detect pity in some of their expressions; little do they know that my single state is of my own choosing. I work my way around the outer perimeter of the room and come face to face with Abbot James. I've met him previously at the Exchequer, and I'm not at all taken by his slimy compliments and jaundiced eye. He reminds me of a lizard, with his scaled cap and hooded robe. My skin crawls whenever his gaze passes over me, and he's looking at my family and my home in the same poisonous way. I hold my breath hoping someone will divert his attention away from everyone and everything I hold dear. I have no such luck, as he slowly turns back toward me, examining me from top to toe.

"So, young lady, how is that your sister has usurped your place on the marriage line? Is there not a young man around that is ready to offer for your hand?

I'm sure that if you can't find a Jew boy, I'd happily find you a candidate."

He is repulsive, this Abbot, as he continues, "Might it be that you aren't even sisters, you so fair and she so dark?"

Having made this statement, the Abbot is so amused by his own ingenuity and witticism that he rushes off to share the joke with some of the sheriffs and knights.

I feel a migraine coming on and I slip away to the solar. The party lasts into the wee hours and in a fog, I hear Sarah coming up, undressing, and I feel her slipping into our bed. Her sigh of contentment lulls me back to sleep.

*

The morning brings all kinds of camaradie, as the family sits around the table in the great room recalling details of last night's party. My parents are beaming, feeling lucky that they've snared the most eligible boy as their son-in-law. Father reminds all of us to be extra thankful to the Almighty for His generosity.

Chapter 5

*I*T'S BEEN DECIDED THAT SARAH AND YEHUDAH WILL wed during the next "spring fair," which gives us almost a year to prepare for the event. Sarah is busy with her trousseau, embroidering every piece of linen and silk she can get her hands on. Yehudah is determined to move to Norwich, where there is a very large Jewish community, and an important learning center. Mama is not very keen on the idea, but I think Sarah and Yehudah have managed to win Father over, and they will be moving east.

Father has commissioned the sheriffs of Norwich to keep their eyes open for a stone house in the Jewry. This is the neighborhood adjacent to the market square that is most heavily populated by the Jewish community. It is close to the market and guildhall and, of course, the Shul and Yeshiva. Father is adamant about a stone structure, as the timber houses are too often destroyed by fire, as are the wattle and daub huts. These huts are for the poorer people, made of a mixture of straw and manure, then whitewashed with lime. Besides being a fire hazard, these huts are always damp and smelly. Most of the houses in the Jewry are made of stone, and a source of jealousy for the non-Jewish public. So far, the sheriffs have returned with a handful of suggestions, but nothing has been finalized yet.

*

Spring is turning to summer, the days passing so quickly, before we know it Rosh Hashanah will be here. Father keeps me busy at the Exchequer, giving me more freedom with the accounts and less supervision. I've had a few encounters with Abbot James since Sarah's engagement, and I am more convinced than ever that he needs watching. I've seen him whispering to various other clerics and sheriffs as they come to settle their accounts, and he is always there, just in the background, when a disagreement arises. I've asked Father to observe him, but we haven't been able to catch him out at anything. I warn Father that there are so many different intrigues that one doesn't know the truth about who is allied with whom. These are dangerous times, and I fear that shortly, things will become much more so.

I've so often heard Father tell stories about the turbulent times during the 60s. King Henry was keen on securing the Crown's dominance over the Catholic Church, by establishing the Royal Magistrates Court. The king wanted secular law to be uniform, obeyed by all, including – or especially including – the clerics, thus reducing the influence of Rome and the Papacy.

He advocated a more just legal system whereby 'trial by ordeal' and 'trial by combat' were replaced by a panel of 'twelve lawful men.' This turned into a major dispute between Henry and his very close friend Thomas Becket, Archbishop of Canterbury, advocate of the Church. When the latter refused to ratify Henry's proposal, argument ensued, and Becket fled to France, fearing for his life. Things came to a head in 1170 when the Pope threatened to excommunicate all of Britain, unless Becket was assured safe re-entry to Britain and reinstated to his cleric duties.

Thomas Becket returned, but a provocative statement made by King Henry – "Who will rid me of this turbulent priest?" – was enough to spur some of his knights and barons into setting things right. Thomas Becket, Archbishop of Canterbury, was murdered in the Cathedral on the stairs leading to the crypt on December 29, 1170.

Since that dark moment, King Henry's reign has been fraught with sadness. His best friend estranged and dead, and his own children plotting the takeover of his throne.

I keep at it; I'm persistent in cautioning Father to beware of Richard, Henry's eldest son, heir to the throne and commander of his armies. I've overheard Abbot James and some of the knights and barons aligning themselves on the side of Richard. I fear that, should there be an attempt to overthrow King Henry, this quasi-peace that reigns is soon to end in war. Father assures me that he has his finger on the pulse, and anyhow, there is not much that can be done at this point.

*

Today has turned out to be an exceptionally mild and sunny day, and Father has dismissed the driver so that we can walk home from the Exchequer. It's such a pleasure walking alongside Father. He is an extremely tall and good-looking man, unusual in that his hair is the color of bleached corn, and he turns heads wherever he goes. We hardly have the occasion to walk home, as after or during the rains, it is practically impossible. Trying to negotiate the streets in the mud is like wading through a tub of butter. The earth squishing underfoot, and sinking almost up to one's knees; people have been known to lose their shoes in the quagmire. The last few days have been dry, and today is glorious. Our route takes us through the maze of twisting streets and lanes that comprise the city. Father pulls up short as we come out of a lane onto one of the market squares. There is a large crowd gathered, shouting and jeering, and at that moment, the crowd parts just a bit to afford us a view of two men in the stocks. They are being bombarded with rotten vegetables and horse droppings, being ridiculed in the most horrible fashion. Father asks the man next to him if he knows what crime these two blokes have committed, and is told they were caught stealing bread. We make our way quickly past the square, into another lane. I am feeling sorry for the two men, and now I know what the term means to be a "laughing stock."

Stealing is indeed a sin, but I am imagining all kinds of situations that induced these men to steal. I wonder if there are families with dozens of children waiting at home to be fed, or perhaps old parents, or sick wives. Enough! There is really nothing I can do at this point.

Chapter 6

SOMETHING IS AFOOT. I WOKE UP THIS MORNING TO loud banging at the front door and by the time I arrived downstairs, Father had already let a messenger in. In Father's hand, an opened envelope, the King's seal broken, and a letter, again with the King's seal on it. I saw Father's worried expression. "Dina, this is not good. The King has written demanding 60,000 pieces of silver from the Jewish community for the financing of his next Crusade."

"The first two Crusades have been unsuccessful in capturing the Holy Land from Saladin, so now our King is preparing to march again, and is in need of funds."

"Oh, Father, how are our people going to amass such an amount? We are still reeling from the levy the King put on us when he built the Palace of Westminster. Doesn't he realize that there is just so much you can milk the cow?"

"Tell your mother that I'll be out the entire day. I'm going to be speaking with Reb Yonasan and the community elders; this is not a simple situation."

Indeed, not simple, 60,000 silver pieces is a 'king's ransom.' The Jewish community is drained. Father was gone the entire day, and most of the night. I waited up for him, anxious about his safety, but also curious as to the outcome of his meeting with the elders. When he finally did come home, he was too exhausted to recount at length what transpired. What he did manage to tell me before going to bed was that everyone would be putting their hands deep into their pockets, and that we would meet the King's demand. As

I mentioned early on in my journal, we are lucky to have the King's protection, but it comes with an enormous price tag.

*

I was busy attending to Friar Peter, one of the King's more trusted clerics, when one of the sheriffs of Norwich came into the Exchequer looking for Father. Sheriff Geoff is a little, rotund man, with whiskers covering most of his lower face, and veins in a cobweb pattern decorating his cheeks. In spite of his bizarre looks, he's always wearing a smile, and always polite.

"Master Montague, I've brought some news of a very interesting house in Norwich, newly on the market. It's down a lane, a few yards past the Jewry, yet close enough to be considered part of the same neighborhood. The house is stone with a large great room, a separate kitchen with its own cooking oven and a separate smoking oven. There is a staircase leading to a very large solar with southern exposure. The price seems interesting and the house is unoccupied for the moment."

Father thanks Sheriff Geoff, and they arrange to meet next week in Norwich to view the house.

*

Both Sarah and I, along with Father and Yehudah, are travelling to Norwich to see what Father deems a "bargain of a house, and too good to be true."

It is now or never, for soon we will be celebrating Rosh Hashanah and until after Succot, it's impractical to set out. After that, the rains set in and the highways are rivers of mud. Not to mention the highwaymen. Their "activities" increase with the bad weather; being that there are fewer travelers on the roads, the constables are less likely to venture out.

Just over one hundred miles, the trip shouldn't take us longer than a day. Father made sure that we start out at the crack of dawn, in order to arrive before nightfall. I've never been outside of London, and we leave town in a holiday mood, Mama, and even Maryam and Tzipa, waving us off at this early hour. Mama prepared a hamper that is enough to tide us over for the journey and then some. I saw her packing up a few of her delicious blueberry cakes and I think, if I were ever to be stranded on an island with nothing else to eat but Mama's blueberry cakes . . . I could survive forever.

The two days we spent in Norwich were very productive. Father was very excited with the house, and had a hard time believing what a bargain it was. Sarah and Yehudah were both walking around as if on air. Father asked me to check out the more practical details, see if the rooms were bright and airy enough, make sure that the kitchen had the right dimensions and that the ovens would work. I made it a point to look at the 'privy' and was pleased to see that it was usable. Sheriff Geoff did his best to smooth out the transaction with the owner of the property, and a handshake closed the deal.

Our return trip was swift and uneventful, and to my delight, Mama had more of her blueberry cakes waiting for me.

Chapter 7

I HAVE NEVER UNDERSTOOD THE MACHINATIONS OF the House of Plantagenet, King Henry's royal line. I know that the king married at a relatively young age, he was only nineteen, and that his wife, Eleanor of Aquitaine, presented him with eight children. As the children grew older, King Henry, hoping to avoid dispute over succession, had his eldest son, Henry the Young, crowned the Young King, much to his other sons' displeasure. Eleanor, stuck in an unhappy marriage, hating her husband the King, plotted against Henry, inciting her sons against their father.

The younger Henry, in spite of all the advantages his father bestowed on him, spurred on by his angry mother, launched a revolt against Henry II in 1173, with the aid of his father-in-law, the reigning monarch of France. Realizing his disadvantage, fleeing from Henry II's strength, and fearing Henry's wrath, he escaped to France, where he was joined by his angered brothers, Richard and Geoffrey.

As Eleanor, the instigator of it all, tried to flee and join her sons in France, Henry II gave orders for her arrest. She was held prisoner for the next fifteen years, and Henry's sons never forgave him for that. The intrigues did not end there. Still in France, Young Henry and Richard quarreled over the building of a castle, and Richard turned and allied himself with his father. A short while later, Young Henry died of dysentery, and Richard became heir to the throne.

There continued terrible disputes between the remaining brothers. Henry II, hoping to settle the matter, ordered his sons back to England. By this time, Geoffrey had been killed at a tournament, leaving only John. Phillip Augustus of France, seeing the chance to bring down the House of Plantagenet, convinced Richard that Henry was planning to disinherit him in favor of John.

Nothing has been settled, yet there is hatred between father and son, brother and brother. This is a terrible situation, for the king, for the family, and for the country. At every corner, burghers assemble to politicize, to voice opinions on how to run the country, and about which of the blue-bloods are best equipped to be king. The clergy are very happy with this turn of events, as it weakens the king's power, all the while strengthening that of the Church.

If all goes according to plan, King Henry will be off to France, organizing a Crusade, joining most of the other European monarchs trying to recapture Jerusalem from Saladin. I'm not sure if leaving England unattended – or, to be more precise, in the hands of Richard and the clergy – is such a wonderful idea. I'm also afraid that any consolidation with Phillip Augustus of France, even if it is for a Holy War, does not bode well for our king.

*

I am engrossed in some of the entries in the Domesday book, when I hear raised voices in the antechamber. Father is busy with a collection, and concentrating on the tallies. I'm not sure what to do, when I overhear the following conversation in Latin: "It won't be long now, before the king will be dead, and Richard will be crowned Monarch of England. We must be patient, and diligent; the right moment will present itself shortly."

Could I have heard correctly? Were people plotting against the king? What did they mean by "the right moment would present itself shortly"? I inch closer to the antechamber and come face to face with . . . Abbot James.

"Hoy, little Jewess, are you lost? What have you come in search of? Are you unaware of your place, and station? How dare you roam so freely in places reserved for the highest personages and the clergy. You shouldn't be seen anywhere other than at your table with your tallies and books. You know something, little Jewess? Your days in the Exchequer are numbered.

"You Jews have had a free ride for too long, but that will soon change, and when the time comes, I have some special plans for you."

His words still, and will forever, reverberate in my head. It takes all my self-restraint not to rush over to Father and blurt out what happened. I wait patiently until Father has packed away the Domesday Book, the tallies, and other ledgers before I commence telling him that something awful has happened to me. Father signals me by humming a song, "Oznayim la'kotel," and in a wink, I understand the danger of saying too much in such a public place.

I am even careful not to speak in front of the carriage man, and control myself until we reach the house. Once inside and behind closed doors, everything flows, like a torrent of water gushing out of a broken dike. My entire family sits spellbound, almost unable to absorb the meaning of the Abbot's tirade.

"Dina, you've done well to control yourself, and refrain from responding to the Abbot's words. I'll have to call an emergency meeting with Reb Yonasan and the elders, and see how we are to proceed with this information."

In fact, there wasn't much anyone could do about what I had overheard. Approaching the king's advisors would be too dangerous, not knowing who was loyal or who was "turned." The Rav and the elders decided to discretely spread the word among the Jews of London and ask everyone to be on the alert, and report any other incidents.

*

Although we live a relatively protected life under King Henry's rule, English Jews can never forget what happened on this very soil to our brethren. Not very many years ago, in 1144, charges were brought against a Jew from Norwich of a blood libel against a Christian child. This man was accused of using the child's blood for the Passover Seder, killing and burying him. The image of a murderous Jew, out to hurt Christians, developed in the public mind, spurring Christian attacks on Jewish settlements. These murderous rampages occurred in Gloucester in 1168, in Bury St Edmunds 1181, and in Bristol 1183. As comfortable as we get, as high as we climb on the ladder of success, as much as we are accepted into a secular society, and however much money we amass, we are strangers in a strange land, and The Almighty has His own ways of reminding us.

The Rav has called together a community meeting, and announces that paying the king's tax demand has now become imperative. Father and some of the other moneylenders have been able to negotiate paying the tax in installments, but it is of utmost importance not to incur the king's wrath.

Chapter 8

PREPARATIONS FOR THE WEDDING ARE AT FULL speed; the house seems to be on a twenty-four-hour, non-stop schedule. Sarah has been keeping me busy the last few weeks with the geese. Not my favorite bird, especially now that I must have helped pluck what seems like thousands of the 'beasts' so that Sarah will have a pair of down coverlets and pillows. I'm more than happy for Sarah to be warm; I wish, however, that there would be a different way to relieve the geese of their fluffy down.

To do the plucking properly, one must remove the feathers from the slaughtered goose, and then gently peel away the fluff at the tip of the quill. The regular part of the feather is then either sold or used for ordinary feather coverlets. I might be exaggerating when I say thousands, but I'm sure you can imagine that very many geese are needed to create just one pillow, let alone a set of pillows and a set of coverlets. Feathers removed, the birds are soaked, then salted, left to drain and, then rinsed and rinsed and rinsed again. The servants take over smoking the flesh so that the meat will keep until the wedding.

Mama and a team are busy at the hearth. We were fortunate this autumn to have had a very good harvest. Fruits were in abundance, and extra sweet from their exposure to the sun. Mama has all the preserving pots out, and they are bubbling away with a variety of the most delicious stewing apples, pears, plums, and all kinds of berries. Once cooled, the preserves will be put into vats and stored in the cellars. I enjoy helping Mama with the clean-up, scraping out the delicious remnants of the sugared fruits from the bottom of the copper pots. At the back of my mind, I shudder as I think what the house is going to smell like once Mama begins with the leeks and the turnips, the cabbages and parsnips.

Father is busy with the wine. He has some of the young Torah students of the community helping with pressing the grapes in the cellar. They arrive every morning, and leave in the evening, their feet and legs stained, almost the exact color of King Henry's robes, a deep royal purple. The smell of the fermenting grapes permeates the house, adding to the festive air.

*

London is whirling with activity. King Henry's knights are here from every corner of the realm, preparing to depart on the Third Crusade. The army will be joining King Henry in France, where he has gone to LeMans to join with the European forces. Richard is also leaving for the Continent, via London, so the knights loyal to him are also present on the streets.

Father has warned us to stay indoors, as the knights and their entourage tend to frequent the taverns and then wander the streets and lanes in an inebriated state. Sarah is more than happy to stay home and sew the remainder of her trousseau, all the while adding more and more embroidery to her linens. I, however, am bored and itching to get out. I'd be interested to see some of the pageants, which herald the departure of the army. The city is teeming with jesters, troubadours, and jugglers, while the knights, covered head to toe in armor, prance around on their horses – those, too, covered in chain mail. It's an exciting but dangerous time; the knights have their own laws, and privileges, and when drunk, nothing and no one can stand in their way. They have been known to pillage, and even kill, on a whim, just for the revelry. Reb Yonasan has cautioned the community to stay out of the way of the army, and keep a low profile.

Father's presence is required in the Exchequer, but he says that for the moment, he is happier for me to stay home with Mama and the girls. He can deal with the work on his own, and I have to be patient and wait for the armies to leave London.

I've decided that I've been neglecting Maryam and Tzipa, seven and six years old, respectively. They are such a pleasure, keeping each other company and busy, that I tend to forget that they are in the house, and they are certainly not a burden on Mama. I thought that now, as I can't go out anyway, it might be a good opportunity to teach the younger ones to cipher.

I've collected my old abacus from the cellar and some loose beads and I'm all set to give them their first lesson.

Maryam, seven, is a natural student. She catches on immediately to the addition and subtraction, and tomorrow I'm going to teach her to write the numbers. Tzipa is not as quick, but that is not to say that she has less of a capacity to learn, only that she is a bit slower than Maryam. I'm just sorry that I haven't thought to teach the girls before. I never imagined that teaching would be this gratifying. At the end of our "lessons," the girls hug and kiss me with such enthusiasm that I have resolved to try and teach them every day, even on those days that I am out working with Father.

Chapter 9

*T*HE DRESSMAKERS ARE IN THE HOUSE, AND I WISH I were elsewhere. I am not very interested in clothing; the only thing I am particular about is that the wool doesn't itch. They've arrived with laces and silks and linens, with baskets of needles and notions. Sarah is the first to be measured and also the first to choose from the array of fabrics. She finally settles on a pale butter colored silk, which does wonders for her complexion. It's to be trimmed with a ribbon in multicolored glass stones, and repeated on her turret hat. The hat sits on a wimple, made of the same butter colored silk as the dress. I watch in fascination, so happy for Sarah and the way she looks.

Mama is pressing me to look through the fabrics and make my choice, but I tell Mama I'll be very happy to wait and see what's left after she and the two little ones are settled. Mama's chosen pale, blossom-green brocade for Maryam and Tzipa, and they will be having slippers made to match.

For herself, Mama's chosen a midnight blue wool, spun so fine as to be almost weightless. The seamstress has suggested a corsage in white lace, and a wimple in simple white silk.

My turn, and I'm not excited about the assortment. I don't very much care for the brocades, and the silks are too impractical. I'd much rather have a more simple dress that can be worn daily until it falls apart. Mama is having none of it, and neither is Sarah. She wants me to look absolutely beautiful at her wedding and starts rummaging around through all the bales. She comes up with a warm raspberry colored silk, and, holding it up against me, "ohhs and ahhs" and "ohhs and ahhs" – she's got Mama, the little ones, and even the dressmakers delighting in her find. I know when I'm defeated, but at least I have some say over the wimple, and I've chosen white linen with a bit of embroidery.

The dressmakers will remain in the house from now until all of the sewing is done, which means more people underfoot and more people to be fed. Under normal circumstances I'd be going mad, confined to the house with so many people twenty-four hours a day, but I've just heard that the armies will be leaving London in two days; miraculously, everything is bearable now.

The snows are thawing, the weather is milder, and I am so happy to be back at work. I'm careful to remain in Father's presence, not wandering off on my own, nervous about meeting Abbot James. I see him weaving his way in and out through the archways, and when he catches me looking his way, he sneers, and bursts out in a wild laugh. I'm convinced he's deranged, but I'm sure, surer than anything else ever, that he's dangerous.

*

With just days remaining before the wedding, activity has accelerated at home. The ovens are blasting nonstop, baking an assortment of cakes and breads, their delicious aroma spreading through the entire house. The meats have been brought in from the smoking room, and are being cut and prepared. All the vats with preserved fruits and vegetables, the wines – everything is coming up from the cellar and being laid out for the banquet.

The servants have set up tables all along the border of the great room, and these are covered with heavy linen cloths; all this activity in anticipation of the wedding meal for about one hundred guests. Father has invited the Rav, all the elders of the Synagogue, and all the congregants. He has made the hard decision of not inviting any of his non-Jewish business associates, as he did for the engagement, remembering the commotion that Abbot James created, and not wanting a repeat performance.

The big day has arrived, and I admire how calm Sarah is keeping – Mama less so. She's rushing around, giving instructions to all the servants, tasting all the food, and just generally worrying that everything should run smoothly. Sarah is up in the solar helping dress Maryam and Tzipa before getting ready herself.

Father has gone to Yehudah's house to accompany him here for the Chuppah, and knowing Father, he will be back punctually for the start.

I'm not in any hurry to get into my own dress; I know I'll be in it for long hours today, but I had better go up to help Sarah.

Dressed, combed, and ready, Sarah is a beautiful bride. Indeed, the buttermilk silk gives her an incomparable glow, and her shining eyes are sparkling brighter than the colored gems in her headdress; she is radiant. Mama arrives together with Yehudah's mother to escort Sarah to the Chuppah. I must quickly rush to dress myself, otherwise, I'll miss everything.

I'm in time to see Sarah making her last rotation around Yehudah under the Chuppah. Yehudah, standing so tall between both fathers, is very handsome in all his finery, and very serious looking. He must be thinking of the huge responsibility he is undertaking, a wife, and hopefully a family. I see him closing his eyes and softly praying, and together with him, I softly ask The Almighty to grant them long and happy years together.

The seven blessings, the placing of the ring, the breaking of the glass, the Mazal Tov wishes, guests, and more guests, and food, so much food, and wine . . . L'Chaim.

I had to find a quiet corner, just to catch my breath and rest my feet. I should never have let Mama talk me into these new shoes. The points alone are weapons, never mind the heels. I would have been very happy in my old black shoes, but Mama was not giving in. She absolutely insisted I have raspberry colored calf shoes, to match my raspberry dress. I have to admit, they do complete the outfit beautifully, if they would only not pinch . . .

Maryam and Tzipa are the sensation, stealing the show in their brocaded dresses, they've prepared a little song and dance for the bride and groom. They are not shy, repeating the sketch when everyone calls for an encore, and running giddily through the room when they're done. I slip back into the "pinchers" and make my way around, seeing to the guests. Everyone is stopping to tell me how beautiful I look, and to wish me a bridegroom before the month is out. I accept their wishes graciously, hoping that my relief at not being the bride today is not visible. I hope with all my heart that my dear Sarah and Yehudah will be blissfully happy, but I couldn't see myself getting married in such turbulent and unsure times.

Chapter 10

HOW I MISS SARAH. SHE AND YEHUDAH LEFT FOR Norwich straight after Pesach, and our house is not the same. I try to keep Maryam and Tzipa busy with lessons and games, but everyone misses Sarah's sweet and happy presence. Mama most of all misses Sarah's help. I try as hard as I can, and Mama is very encouraging, but I do know that housework is not my forte. The weather has turned warmer, and the days are longer. Perhaps we can convince Father that a trip to Norwich in a few months would be very nice for the entire family.

*

Tragedy has befallen England. King Henry II is dead; he died in France. He was trying to defend his crown against his own sons, and they tricked him; Richard and John, together with Phillipe of France, ambushed him and forced him into surrender. Our king has died of a broken heart, abandoned and betrayed. Long live King Richard.

There is sadness on the streets, as well as revelry celebrating Richard's succession. Richard has strong support from the Church, and Abbot James is one of his trusted men. I fear that the tide will turn for the Jews of London, and I share this with Father.

"Dina, I think you're right. I think hard times are coming for us, and we are in danger. I will discuss with Reb Yonasan what can be done to protect our community, but I fear it is very little."

Indeed, Reb Yonasan is just as worried as we are, but sees no way out of the dilemma. He does suggest that there be a fast day, and a day of prayer, and hopefully we will be heard in the heavens.

London is preparing for a coronation, to take place next month, in September, at Westminster. Richard will be returning home to be crowned before leaving again on the Crusade. I am very nervous about the coronation. I witness all kinds of degrading incidents against my fellow Jews, most of them very subtle, yet still degrading. I think London is a very dangerous place, and again I speak to Father about going to Norwich for a few weeks. To my surprise, I don't have to use too much persuasion. Father has already made plans, and we're to leave next Sunday.

What a happy group we are, going to visit with Sarah and Yehudah in Norwich. We've packed enough to last us a month, as Father says we will have to return mid-September, in time for the High Holy Days. Maryam and Tzipa have brought along the abacus and beads, as well as their game of jacks. I haven't packed too many things, besides my special case where I keep my quills, ink, and of course, my journal. Father still stopped in last night after Shabbat was out to tell Reb Yonasan that we would be leaving for Norwich for a month, or until things became more stable in London. Mama is just so happy to be seeing Sarah, she hasn't once complained of all the effort of closing up the house for that extended period. Father has taken the precaution of hiring two sheriffs to accompany us, and we are all more relaxed about the journey.

Norwich, home to Jews since William the Conqueror, and the Norman conquest of 1066. As in London, some of the early settlers began to work as moneylenders, and the Jewish population grew and flourished. Norwich is the center for the wool trade, and has trade links with all of the continent. Being a port city, Norwich has prospered, and with it, her Jews. As in London, the Jews of Norwich – some 200 strong – found protection with the Crown and her agent, the local sheriff. In spite of the tragedy that befell Norwich Jews during the blood libel of '44, the Jews have since had a peaceful coexistence with their neighbors.

*

We've arrived, and Maryam and Tzipa have to be lifted out of the carriage, as they've fallen asleep. Sarah and Yehudah greet us at the door, and usher us into the great room, where a table is set. Sarah has outdone herself, cakes and fruits all laid out on her finest linen. There are straw mats on the floor for me and the two little girls, while our parents have a space in the solar.

I leave Mama and Father to catch up on the news of the last few months with the young couple, and join Maryam and Tzipa on the mats. Before my head hits the straw, I'm dreaming.

Something has woken me. I'm drenched in sweat, shivering. I think it has something to do with my dream, yet I can't remember what it was. All I do know is that I'm terrified. I remain on the mat, not wanting to wake the girls, but my heart beats wildly in my body, and I can't fall asleep again. The hours drag and finally, I hear Father coming down to begin his day. He's surprised to see me awake this early, yet when I tell him about my terror, he pulls up short. "Dina, I too had a dream last night, and I too woke in a sweat, not knowing what I had dreamt. I have an uneasy feeling that there is bad news coming."

We pass the days quietly and in peace. Nothing untoward happens to remind Father and me of our nightmares. The days pass swiftly as we enjoy Sarah and Yehudah's company and are introduced to the community at large. Maryam and Tzipa have both found friends, and there are daily visits to and fro, bringing life and laughter to Sarah's humble home.

The peace is shattered by banging on the door, and Mama, who is the nearest, opens to find Sheriff Geoff on the doorstep. Something is amiss, as all color is drained from his face, and the sweat is pouring down his ruddy cheeks. "I must speak with your husband, please, and in private." Father, who's heard the exchange, presents himself to the sheriff, and steps outside with him, closing the door behind himself. It's not long before Father re-enters, falling into a chair, barely able to whisper, "Tragedy has befallen our brothers in London."

Chapter 11

HE THIRD OF SEPTEMBER 1189, CORONATION day, and Richard the Lionhearted, in all his regalia, is to be anointed King of England, the ceremony to take place in Westminster. Not knowing that Richard had barred women and Jews from the ceremony, many Jews arrive at the Cathedral to present gifts to the new king. Angered at this blatant disrespect of the king's orders, Richard's courtiers strip and flog the Jews, then throw them out of court.

Word spreads like wildfire, the message twisted by some sly clergy, that Richard's ordered all Jews killed. So began the massacre of the Jews of London. Some are burnt alive in their homes, others are mutilated. Many, out of fear, have agreed to be baptized. One thing is sure: very few escape unscathed. Richard, realizing that this chaos could destabilize his realm and interfere with his departure for the Crusades, calls a halt to the rampage. Our friends, our entire community, decimated.

Hearing the details recounted, I realize that that was what I saw in my dream. I saw houses, along with their occupants, burning. I saw gutters overflowing with Jewish blood. I saw all the horrors. How fortunate that we weren't in London. What merit does Father – do all of us – have to be spared this butchery? Will it end there?

There is no going back. We have lost our home in London and all our belongings. We are just very thankful we haven't lost our lives. We are, however, extremely concerned about Yehudah's family. We have had no news from them, and fear the worst. Father has asked Sheriff Geoff to see if he can find out anything from his contacts in London, but the prognosis isn't good. In this case, "no news is *not* good news."

*

There is a silver lining to our cloud; there is a new life on the way. Sarah is with child and the baby is expected in the spring. The news helps uplift everyone's spirit and eases our pain. We mourn not our material losses, but the loss of Yehudah's parents, the loss of all the men, women, and children that we knew so well.

Father again calls on Sheriff Geoff, as we are going to need a house. Not a large one, Father warns, nothing on the scale of our home in London. We will need approximately the same sort of house that Sarah and Yehudah have, and something that is unoccupied so that we can move in immediately. Within days, Sheriff Geoff has come up with four different suggestions.

Father has been out the entire day going from one house to the next with the sheriff, inspecting the cellars and the roofs. He's settled on one, but has Mama and all of us come to give our approval. The house pleases me for two reasons: it is about one hundred yards from Sarah and Yehudah, and there is a wonderful view of the marketplace and castle from the solar. The house pleases Mama too, as well as the little ones, so that's decided. We will be moving in for Rosh Hashanah.

*

> Blessed are You, our G-d, Sovereign of the Universe,
> Who has granted us life, Who has sustained us,
> and Who has enabled us to reach this festive occasion.

*

"*Shehechiyanu*" – It's Rosh Hashanah and Mama softly whispers the blessing over the candles. On his return home from Shul, Father loudly proclaims the same blessing over the Kiddush wine. During the new year holiday, the "Shehechiyanu" will be said for the newly harvested fruits, over a new article of clothing, and for our new home. We are all gathered around the Rosh Hashanah table, together, yet I think we are all lost in our own thoughts. Yehudah is surely thinking of his parents; Father, Mama, and I about all our friends; and the little ones . . . and Sarah, dear Sarah, I'm sure she is thinking about this terrible, dark world that she will be bringing her child into.

Almost everyone in Norwich has a family member or friend that perished in the London massacre. Over all the High Holy Days, bits of news trickle in about the fate of those people. There was no specific warning to this rampage, although Father and I did feel the animosity and threat oozing from the Church and many of the knights. Father had warned the Rav to be careful and caution everyone to lay low since, with King Henry's death, the community was no longer protected. We have also been told that Abbot James was at the head of the column raining destruction on the Jews. The terrifying sound of his maniacal laugh still reverberates in my mind.

*

The Autumn rains do no let up, and most of my days are spent indoors. Father has found solace in the Yeshiva and together with Yehudah, he spends most of his waking hours there, poring over the holy books. I know he misses his days at the Exchequer as much as I do, and hopefully when we are more settled, Father will find a new business to keep us both busy. In the meantime, as I am indoors so much, I have created a learning schedule for Maryam and Tzipa. They are so grateful for all the time I devote to them, kissing and hugging me; they've even surprised me with some embroidered handkerchiefs, their own handiworks. They've promised to give me lessons on the finer art of needlework, but I've warned them that I am beyond redemption.

Chapter 12

A CRY HAS GONE UP. THERE ARE TWO FAMILIES missing. Two Jewish families living on the outskirts of the castle have vanished into thin air. Sarah knows one of the women personally, as she is a very competent midwife and has been attending to Sarah from the beginning of her pregnancy. In total, seventeen people have vanished – five adults and twelve children – disappeared without a trace. The Rav has organized various search parties, but the snows have begun falling and it is hindering the effort.

Lord Neville, the nobleman in control of Norwich, has offered some of his men to help trace the whereabouts of the families, but to no avail; there is no lead and the worst is feared.

Sheriff Geoff is again the bearer of more bad tidings. He was at the ale house and overheard some of the knights in their drunken state boasting about the Jews that they killed and threw into the well. In the darkness of night, the sheriff went to check, sliding down on a rope to almost the bottom of the well, and indeed, found the bodies of many men, women, and mostly children.

Sheriff Geoff cautions us not to make the knowledge public, as this could have terrible repercussions on him as well as on us. Is there no place that a Jew can find peace?

Father has started spending his days at the trading rooms, speaking to the captains and traders of the many carvel arriving from France, Spain, and Portugal. I'm hoping that this means we will be going into some kind of business, even if it might be only selling wool, the most popularly traded item in Norwich. All this activity has revived Father's spirit, and the sparkle in his eyes has returned.

I am not allowed to accompany Father, as the trading rooms are an inappropriate place for a woman, let alone a Jewish girl. Just recalling the last days at the Exchequer, and the Abbot's lecherous stares, are enough to make me bite back my protests. We have been told that Abbot James headed one of the deadly onslaughts against the Jews of London, may his name be forever erased.

*

Sarah has gone into labor, but it's months too early. Mama and I tend to her, helping her as best we can, while Yehudah is out, frantically searching for a doctor. Mama has always been very strong, but I marvel at how she doesn't lose her head or become hysterical when Sarah starts hemorrhaging and expels a dead baby. Mama's only concern at the moment is to stop the bleeding and save Sarah's life. On his return with the local doctor, Father has to tell Yehudah that the child is dead, but that miraculously, Sarah has survived. The doctor takes over from Mama and sedates Sarah, while the rest of us wait impatiently downstairs to hear what he has to say.

The doctor softens the blow, "Sarah will pull through, and will be able to bear other children."

The Almighty in His mercy has not hit us with both hands. It's taken Sarah a week to regain her strength and get back on her feet. I so admire her courage; not a word has she said, not a complaint has she made. Her only thoughts are for Yehudah, and restoring his spirit. She is truly an amazing woman.

*

Father has returned from the trading rooms much earlier than usual, and is greatly excited. He has us all gathered around the parlor table before he removes a chamois bag from his tunic. We huddle around, curious to see what it is that has Father so buoyant. With a bit of fanfare, Father upends the sac and out spill eight colored gems. I, with nil knowledge of precious stones, can see that these aren't the glass variety such as were sewn on Sarah's wimple cap for the wedding. These stones are absolutely glowing, and have a life of their own, almost dancing on our table.

All eyes turn to Father as he places the gems back into a pouch, then into a secret pocket in his tunic, and announces, "I am preparing for our move to Spain. It has become too dangerous for us to remain in England since our protector, King Henry, has died. Richard the Lionhearted is just that, a cold, cruel heart, and to remain here is almost certain death. I've exchanged most of our silver and gold for these gems. It will be much easier to leave, less obvious of our intent, if we do not remove coffers heavy with coins. I ask you all to prepare yourselves, we will be leaving within the next few months."

Chapter 13

*I*T WASN'T MONTHS AT ALL; IT WAS BUT A FEW DAYS. Sheriff Geoff has been in and out of the house daily and yesterday, he arrived with the news. An entire band of Knights Templar was assembling for departure to the Holy Land from the port of Norwich. In a state of drunken stupor, they were overheard telling one innkeeper that their plan was to relieve the Jews of their gold and silver, kill them all, and finance the "Holy Crusade" with the booty.

This news spurs us into immediate action. Father has gone to warn the Rav and the community elders of this impending tragedy. Mama has started filling hampers with food and clothing. I run up for my journal, quill, and inkpots. Sarah has only taken some of Yehudah's Talmudic writings, and Maryam and Tzipa have the abacus and their jacks. By the time Father returns, we are all nervously assembled near the door, waiting for further instructions.

Father explains that we cannot all leave together, as this would signal anyone watching that we were going for good. Mama and the two little ones would go by carriage with Sheriff Geoff, departing as if on a short trip to London, with only the two hampers.

Sarah and Yehudah would leave a few minutes later, as if on a stroll, and Father and I would be the last to leave. We were to meet at the docks, where Sheriff Geoff would be waiting with Mama, the girls, and the captain, who was going to smuggle us on his carvel, for a very hefty sum of gold.

As planned, Sheriff Geoff pulled up to the front door with the carriage, and helped pile in the two hampers, Mama, and the little ones. Their departure was uneventful, and within twenty minutes, they would have arrived at the port.

The next to leave were Sarah and Yehudah. They left, going in the opposite direction, and doubling back a bit further on, so for anyone observing, they were not headed in the same direction.

Twenty minutes later, Father and I were just about to open the door when we heard the pounding of hoofs and a terrible war cry go up. Knowing what was about to happen, we ran to the rear of the house and slipped out onto an alleyway, running in the direction of the port. Behind us, houses were torched, and the Jewry was turning into an inferno. We could hear the shrieking of the injured and the dying, but there was little we could do to help. The king's knights hampered our advance, destruction in their hearts, roaming the lanes and streets looking for fleeing Jews. We had some close calls, but finally arrived at the designated spot where Sheriff Geoff and the captain were waiting. To our great consternation, Sarah and Yehudah were not there.

The captain was adamant, "Master Montague, there is no way that we can remain here much longer, without endangering everyone's safety. I will only be able to smuggle you on board for another hour. For the moment, it is safe, as the crew are all eating and drinking in the local tavern, but they should be returning by midnight, and we set sail almost immediately after. We must make haste."

"No! I'm not moving a step without them." I can't believe I've said that. But I feel very strongly; I will not leave and abandon Sarah.

Father, who's been pacing back and forth, stops in front of the captain. "Please give us fifteen more minutes. If by that time my daughter and son-in-law are not here, you can leave. We will not be going with you, and you will receive a forfeit amount of gold from me."

I think those were the longest fifteen minutes of my life. As the seconds ticked by, I could only imagine what would happen if the knights found us.

I started imagining all kinds of horrors done to Sarah and Yehudah, when suddenly, Father started running toward the dark alley near the dock, and into the light came Sarah and Yehudah, dirty and scratched, but alive. Alive.

At this point, I feel I have to deviate from recording my personal story, because it would not be fair to any future reader of this journal, perhaps in generations to come, not to be informed of what happened to the Jews of Norwich.

On the sixth of February 1190, twenty-first of Shvat 4950, local peasantry revolted against the local lords, attacking the Norwich Jewish community. Many escaped to the local castle and the rest of the Jews were slaughtered in their respective villages. Those Jews who did escape to the castle committed mass suicide.

This rampage against the Jews in Norwich followed the same pattern as the terror in London, York, Oxford, and Lincoln. May their blood be avenged. The extent of calamity visited on the Jews of Norwich was only later made known to us.

*

Father bids farewell to Sheriff Geoff, and I see a bulging purse exchange hands. It is the least Father can do to repay the sheriff's putting his life on the line for us. The captain, in the meantime, helps us all up the flimsy, corded gangway, onto the deck, and into the hold. He opens the trapdoor and we descend, one by one, into the bowels of the carvel and a safe hiding place.

I steel myself; I have always been terrified of dark, closed spaces, and this is by far the darkest I've ever seen. I have to be strong, I'm the oldest, and I have to be a good example for Sarah and the little ones. If I become hysterical, the hysteria will spread, and we will all be discovered.

We've hardly had time to make ourselves comfortable, when we hear the first treads on deck of the returning sailors. They sound in a good mood, singing and shouting and laughing. They have filled their bellies with food and drink and are ready to sail down the river and into the sea.

In a very short time, we hear the creaking of the winches, and the vessel begins to move. I am floating on a cloud of wool, as is everyone else. We are not uncomfortable, just nauseous from the smell of the wool. This mingles with the decaying smell of the skins and has us all choking down our bile.

A week. The journey to Spain will take a week, and I'm not sure that we are going to survive the "wool." Can you imagine, surviving the marauding army just to succumb to "wool." It is so absurd that I start giggling and have to be shaken by Father to stop. I hope I haven't endangered all of us, but the thought of perishing because of some wool was just too much.

The slight swaying of the carvel turns into heavy rolling, as we are tossed around on the mounds of wool, the waves buffeting the sides of the vessel; I'm assuming that we must be out at sea already. We are all moaning in unison, hoping not to be heard by the deck-hands. Father is forcing all of us to sip just bits of water, as going without for too long is very dangerous. Solid food just doesn't come into question, and I'm afraid that by the time we dock, whatever we have with us will be rotten. I'm very optimistic, thinking that we will dock; it's never crossed my mind that we won't make it.

Chapter 14

*L*IGHT — SOMEONE HAS OPENED THE HATCH. I SEE the captain peering down at us, "Has anyone survived the trip?" he asks. We've arrived, and we'll be docking at Gigia in a short while. Behind the captain, I see the faces of some of the deckhands staring down at us, surprised at this extraordinary cargo. I'm sure all they were expecting was wool and sheepskins, not reckoning on finding a human cargo in the hold. 'Human' is stretching it more than just a bit. By the light of the open hatch, I see what my family look like and can imagine how frightening I, too, must seem.

We all have white fuzz in our hair and attached to our brows. Our clothing is extremely wrinkled, stained, and smelly, and our skin tones are all a different shade of green. "Human" is not a word I would have used to describe us.

The vessel has come to a full standstill as we leave the hold and come up on deck. None of us are steady on our feet, and we hold onto each other for support, squinting into the harsh daylight. The captain is shouting orders to the sailors, ordering the lowering of the sails and the placing of the gangplank. He then turns to Father, extends his palm, and asks for his payment. Father is more than happy to give him the agreed sum of gold, thanking him for the risk he had taken, and wishing him farewell. One by one, we descend the gangplank onto a rotting dock. The docks seem to be abandoned, as we pick our way carefully off the jetty and onto solid ground.

We arrive at the huts bordering the wharfs, but we have yet to encounter anyone. We make our way past the shacks, past more huts and lean-tos, and still not a soul to be seen. Gigia is a ghost town, and turning a full 360 degrees, we can now see the carvel that was our home for a week, already miles out at sea.

My first thought is to look into Mama's hampers and see if we can salvage any of the food. Unfortunately, as I had predicted, everything is rotten.

Father was peering into the huts to see if there was anything that could be used as a weapon. We would also be urgently needing water, shelter, and food. In our exhausted, weakened state, we would be prey to anyone with bad intentions if we didn't have the energy or tools to defend ourselves.

I keep wondering if this is not some kind of bad joke that the captain of the ship has played on us, abandoning us here in this forsaken no man's land. Hut after hut – empty, with not even a scrap of firewood. Father suggests that we choose one of the less dilapidated huts, as the sun is setting and with night falling soon, we will be in need of a safe place to sleep. I wonder how safe any of these huts can be; I cannot envision them as a protection against beast nor man.

Each of us has found a space, and we settle in for the night, even though our stomachs are growling after a week of fasting. Father soothed the two little ones with promises that there would be some food tomorrow. I have never known Father to make a promise that he can't keep and I hope this won't be the first time.

*

The sun shining in my face awakens me, and at first, I'm not sure where I am. I see a blue sky overhead, where a roof should be, and am aware of sea gulls squawking. It takes me a minute to remember where I am and what's happened. Sitting up, I see everyone is still asleep, everyone except for Father – and he is not in the hut. Quietly making my way to the doorway, I don't want to wake anyone; I slip outside to the morning stillness, broken only by the squealing sea gulls. I am determined to find Father, I just don't know where to start looking. I'm sure he's about somewhere scavenging for food or water, but should I go left or right?

I choose right and head in the direction of a cluster of trees. They seemed only a minute or two away from the hut we are sleeping in, but it has taken me about fifteen minutes to arrive at the perimeter. And it is not just a cluster of trees, it is a dense forest. I can't see around it, and I can't see through it; that is how close one tree is growing to the next. I work up the courage to call out for Father, but I don't get any response. Just as I'm about to turn back, I see some berries growing among the moss of fallen tree trunks. In my excitement to get to them, I trip over my own feet, landing smack in middle of the berry patch. Never mind, it's worth getting my clothes stained, and I gather in all the berries, making a pouch out of my tunic. Laden with the precious find, I make my way carefully back the way I came, to the hut.

From a distance I see Yehudah is already up and about, as are Maryam and Tzipa. They see me coming and run to help me with my load. The excitement mirrored in their faces when they see what's for breakfast; this is a real treat. Father shows up just behind me with some wild apples, but more important, he's found a freshwater stream a ways off. He's done some reconnaissance, but hasn't yet seen any humans.

We've eaten and bathed, and restored our spirits; now what? We all agree that we can't remain here, but where are we to go, and how are we to get there? We've lost actual count of the days, but Father is almost sure that it is almost Shabbat. We collectively go out to the forest edge and bring back berries and apples to sustain us for two days. The water will be another problem, as we haven't any receptacles to store it in, so we'll just have to do without for a day.

Father and Yehudah spend most of the Shabbat day singing and chanting prayers, while Mama keeps us busy with reminiscences of her youth. She has some wonderful stories, and we all chime in with memories of our own younger days. The Shabbat passes too quickly, and with the sighting of the three stars, we all wish each other good tidings for the coming week, and snuggle down to sleep.

The following morning, Father has us all all gather 'round and commences to draw a map in the dust with a twig. We are in the northern part of the Castile and a long way off from Toledo. Getting to Toledo is a long and treacherous journey southward over unknown terrain. Our goal, Toledo, is home to a large and prosperous Jewish community and most importantly out of the path of the Crusaders.

Father is saying that there is no way we can make the journey on foot, and a means of transportation is vital. Father wants to go alone in search of a wagon, but I will not hear of it. I convince everyone that I will accompany Father, and Yehudah will remain behind to protect the others. I say a silent prayer that they will not need protecting, for, should the circumstances warrant, I do not know how or with what Yehudah will protect anyone.

Father cautions them to remain together, going out as a group for water, and to pick berries and fruits. He takes Yehudah aside and impresses on him the danger of anyone going out on their own.

We are ready to leave, Father and I, early the next morning, and head eastward along the shore. We've taken along some of the apples, and hope we will be finding other food on the way, although I am not as worried about the food as I am about water. Under the strong midday sun, we start to feel parched, and Father suggests that we stop for a while in the shade of some trees. For the moment, the apples are our only source of nourishment and liquid. What happens when we run out of apples?

Father has set us a limit. We will walk for three days. If during that time we haven't found a village or a city, we will turn back. Father doesn't want to be away from the rest of the family over Shabbat.

Chapter 15

*P*RAISE TO THE ALMIGHTY. WE ARE INTO OUR SEC-
ond day heading east, our supply of apples almost
gone, when Father sees some fishermen out in small skiffs.
We hurriedly follow the shoreline and arrive at a very small village
with some huts. There are three peasant women about, all busy
with a different chore; but when they see us arrive, they stop all
activity. I'm sure that the fact that Father has come in the presence
of a female is the reason they're not panicking and running for
shelter. A woman whose skin is sun darkened and lined, who
seems to be the oldest of the three, steps forward, shooting questions at us. Father is trying to calm her in English, but the woman
keeps shrieking. When I try some of my French, it brings the tirade to a standstill, as the woman understands some of what I am
saying. Father, realizing that the dialect spoken here is similar to
the French of his youth, reverts to that language and slowly explains to the woman that we are in search of food, water, and a
carriage.

As we speak, more women and children have joined the little
group, pouring out of the huts to see what's happening. By now
there is a pretty large gathering of only women and children; I'm
assuming all the men are out fishing. One of the younger women
has brought out a gourd of water and a cup formed from a shell.
It's probably the most delicious drink I've ever had, this water. The
older woman, she tells us her name is Maria, and is speaking what
I imagine is Castillian. With our knowledge of French and Latin,
both Father and I are able to follow and converse with these people.
Maria has told us to sit down, the men will be back soon with their
catch. Sure enough, it doesn't take long before the first skiff sails

into the little harbor and the children run out to greet the rower, waving toward us, the unexpected guests.

Within minutes, all the little boats are back, and the men are making their way in our direction. The most senior of the men, in the forefront, stops to have a word with Maria, then turns to us.

"Maria tells me that you are in need of food, water, and a wagon. We can sell you some of our fish, we can tell you where to find water, but we don't have a wagon. The nearest place that you will find a wagon is the next town over, in Colunga, almost a day's travel eastward."

Father takes a moment to think and then extends his hand, "My name is Michael and this is my wife, Juliet. We are part of a larger group that landed a ways west of here and we could really use a wagon. If any of your men would be interested in journeying to Colunga and bringing the wagon to us in Gigia, he will be paid in silver by our headman. I have a small amount of silver on me and would be happy to pay for some fish, and perhaps a gourd for carrying water.

The men were more than happy to sell some of their catch, and not one, but two gourds for carrying water were offered. One of the younger men volunteered to make the journey to Colunga for the wagon, and some silver coins exchanged hands. He was promised an important sum for delivering it to us in Gigia. The women brought out some roots, some sun-dried fruits, and a flat bread made of flour and water, dried in the sun – not unlike the matzot that Father bakes for Pesach.

"Oh yes," Father has remembered something else; "do you have any sharp knives, or cutlass? I lost mine walking along on the shore, and daren't make my way back without some protection." That, too, was for sale and Father paid for both a knife and a saber.

Taking our leave, Father and I both thanked the group for their help and hospitality. I was relieved once we were on our way back, and questioned Father about his introduction of himself and me.

"Dina, I learned from the story of our forefather Avraham. He claimed his wife was his sister, and though that was certainly the best option in their case, I applied Avraham's wisdom and thought it would be most prudent to say that we are husband and wife, and not advertise that we are Jews. I thank the Almighty that we are safely away and returning to our family, and hopefully they will be coming with a wagon in a few days.

"It was risky to trust them, paying in advance, but I'm thinking that human nature will induce the fellow to want more of our silver, and show up with the wagon."

I've noticed this before, but today it seems more so than ever: the way back from a journey always seems shorter thank the trip out. As we approach Gigia, I ask Father about it, but he just chuckles and says that he has noticed the same thing, but it is improbable that the distance is shorter; it's only an illusion.

Maryam sees us first and raises the alarm. We are met by everyone with such enthusiasm and joy, they are just happy to have us back safely. When they see the water gourds and fish, the joy turns to celebration.

Mama now has a knife with which to clean the fish, we have water for rinsing, and the men have gone in search of wood and flint to start a fire. Before long, the fish are sizzling over some stones and we are waiting around for our first serious food in the last few weeks.

Father is happy to recount our adventure, and our little surprise. We are hoping to get a wagon within the next few days, and true to his word, the young fisherman arrives three days later with an open-bed wagon. We are ready to go south, south to Toledo.

Chapter 16

W E ARE FORTUNATE, OUR JOURNEY SOUTHWARD takes us along some of the tributaries of the Tagus river, and we will have a good source of water for drinking, washing, and perhaps, with some luck, fish. Father insists that Sarah sit up top next to him, as she is not completely recovered from the birth and sitting in the rickety wagon can be harmful to her body. Mama, Maryam, Tzipa, and I each have found our own little corner where the bumping is less of a shock. Yehudah is happier walking alongside the wagon, he claims it's more peaceful, as he isn't very much interested in the girlie talk taking place in the back of the wagon. Our progress is slow, but we thank the Almighty every moment for our good fortune in surviving the various misfortunes that have come our way.

Father is a bit concerned, and shares his worry with us during one of the evening "meals." I can actually call this one a meal seriously, as we have some mushrooms that Mama and Tzipa gathered, fish that Yehudah caught, and Father has found a very strange berry that grows on trees. Father has heard about these berries, and says they are called olives, and grow in abundance in the Holy Land. They are usually pressed for their oil, and in Jerusalem, this oil was used for all the different services that the Kohanim preformed in the Temple. "Beware," Father cautions, "they have large pits in their centers."

I'm very content with our meal, but Maryam and Tzipa are less so. They're not interested in the olives, with their special, strange aroma; so I'm more than happy to eat their leftovers.

As I was saying, Father is worried. We are down to the last of the silver and gold coins that he brought from London. Soon we will have to sell one of the gems, and that will be a problem unless we arrive at a city quite soon. For the moment, we can manage with the water, fish, and different fruits and plants that we find along the way. But we will not have anything to barter with if we can't sell one of the gems soon.

*

Something has disturbed my sleep; I'm not sure what it is. Laying here in the straw, I have the feeling something just isn't right. I'm about to move when I see Father sitting up and signaling to me to remain still. He moves over to Yehudah quietly, hardly disturbing a straw, and places his hand gently on Yehudah's mouth. By the light of the moon, I see Yehudah's eyes fly open and Father signaling to him; there is someone approaching our wagon in the dead of night. Father passes the saber to Yehudah, and armed with only the knife, he jumps up and out of the wagon in one agile movement. Yehudah is not far behind him, and they surprise a man rummaging around in our campfire. Grabbing him by the scruff of his neck, they turn him around, pointing both the saber and knife at him. I've also jumped out of the wagon and at this point, Mama, Sarah, and the girls are all peering over the sides of the wagon with terrified eyes.

The man, the thief, is but a boy, hardly into his teen years, and he is more terrified than we are. Father is speaking French, asking the boy what he is looking for, but he just shakes his head, points to his ears and makes some kind of animal sound. By now Mama, Sarah, Maryam, and Tzipa have joined us at the campfire and we are all standing around the boy in a circle.

Our thief is deaf, and I think very hungry. Seeing him in the moonlight, he has sunken cheeks, and hollow eyes, and looks as if he hasn't eaten in weeks. Mama picks up on this and has disappeared into the wagon to retrieve some of the leftover fish. She hardly has the chance to come down from the wagon when the boy grabs the fish and devours it, almost choking on one of the fish bones. Maryam has come back with the water gourd, which she hands the boy. He is gentle as he takes it from her hands and gulps down the liquid. Sated, the boy bobs his head up and down, and again forms some animal sounds that we take as a thank-you. We all head back to the wagon, hoping to get some more sleep, but the boy isn't leaving. He lays down very close to the campfire, curls into a fetal position, smiles, and goes to sleep.

The boy's adopted us, and we him. Father's given him the name Adam, and he's made himself indispensable. The first morning, and Adam has already gathered wood for the fire and filled the gourds with water. Our morning meal normally consists of berries and water, our evening meal, fish and whatever roots and berries we can gather. I know we're lucky to have these, I'm just getting tired of the fish.

When I sigh as a piece of grilled fish is handed to me, Father reminds me of harder times; the hardships and tragedies during the destruction of our Temple and our Babylonian captivity; I remember everything I've read in the Book of Eichah, and accept my fish gladly.

Adam has taken to walking alongside the wagon, just a few steps behind Yehudah. He helps forage for food and wood, and yesterday he somehow managed to catch a wild goose. He returned from the woods with such excitement carrying the squawking bird. Father took the bird from his hands and tossed it skyward as we all watched the bird flap wildly and take flight.

Adam stood in stunned silence, and it was useless to try to explain in sign language that the bird would have needed ritual slaughter, and Father was not studied for the role, nor did he have the right knife to perform the killing the correct way. Father, however, was careful to pat Adam on the back and give him an extra large piece of fish at the evening meal.

We've come to a fork in the road, and as Father guides the wagon toward the right, Adam is gesticulating that we take the road on the left. Father has brought the wagon to a halt and Adam keeps up his pantomime, and through his gesticulating, he brings us to understand that the road on the right is smooth and level, while the road he wants us to take is hilly and rocky, but the road on the right is known to be the home of different bands of marauders, while the road to the left is safer. It is no contest, we are going to take Adam's advice and turn left. Father has no wish to clash swords with thieves and, perhaps worse, murderers. Adam is pleased that Father has listened to him, as we recommence, taking the left-hand fork.

Progress is slow; the road is, indeed, very rocky and uphill. On the first day, we came across a waterfall and were able to refill the gourds, but there has been no sighting of water today, and our supply is diminished. The rivers are in the valley and we are headed toward a plateau. I know we've done the right thing avoiding confrontation with the thieves, but will we be able to survive without water?

Day four of this difficult leg of our journey, and we are thanking the Almighty that He has sent us Adam. Tzipa was walking alongside the wagon this morning when Adam burst past her and started banging on the ground with a stick he had fashioned into a spear. Tzipa, surprised and scared, started crying, and Adam was gurgling at the highest pitch. We all rushed over to see what the commotion was – a poisonous snake, speared and dead, lying in the dust at Tzipa's feet. If not for Adam, Tzipa would have been bitten, and I shudder to think what would have happened.

The trail is starting to take a downward incline and Father is sure we will soon find some water. Indeed, toward evening of day four, we are again on a flatter part of the road, which is running parallel to a river. We are happy to soak our weary feet, have something to drink and do some fishing. Sarah is splashing the little ones, and we haven't been this lighthearted in a long time; we again bless the Almighty for all His kindness.

Chapter 17

ARLY MORNING AND WE ARE ON OUR WAY, AND again the road is curving upward, but on this part of the trail, we are surrounded by hills covered with pregnant grapevines, and olive trees; surely, we won't go hungry on this stretch. As we reach the top of the next rise, Father pulls the wagon to a halt. We've arrived at a fortress, a city enclosed by a high wall. Father stops the wagon, ever cautious, he is unsure of how to proceed; do we enter the gates? are the citizens welcoming to travelers, especially foreigners? or do they have the habits of the Sodomites? As Father pauses, Adam is gesturing, but I can't make out what he is saying. Yehudah thinks he is trying to guide us further down the road past the walls, toward something or somewhere else.

It's been decided. Father will accompany Adam on foot, and see where he's leading him to. We are to remain here with the wagon and wait; it is mid-morning and the idea is that Father must be back before sundown, otherwise we will all come looking for him.

We settle down to wait, looking for some shade, as, at this elevation, the sun is very strong. Father's left the water gourds behind, and we stuff ourselves with grapes and olives, rinsed down by some water. Before long, we see Father returning with Adam, and we all gather 'round to hear what he has to say.

"Just over the rise, there is a monastery, the Santa Maria la Real De Las Huelgas. I spoke to the Abbess, who is proficient in French, and she has assured me that it is safe to enter the city. She's given me directions to the home of Todros ben Meir Abulafia, who she says is a very prominent Jew."

Hearing this, we collect our meager belongings, and are about to get back into the wagon to head toward the gates, when Adam embraces first Father, then Yehudah, and bids us farewell. Before any of us can react, he is gone.

For months afterward, I always wondered who Adam really was, and if he wasn't a special angel sent to help us get through some difficult times; for no one in this city of Burgos knew of a deaf boy, and we never saw him again.

*

Todros ben Meir, what a splendid home he has – almost a palace – and we are royally accepted and made welcome. The servants are fussing about preparing food and putting out matting to sleep on. Father is sequestered with Rav Todros – surely, I am assuming, working out a plan for our future.

For the moment I am just happy that there is a roof over our heads, delicious food, and that we are not needing to escape from anything. Rav Todros's wife, Chana, is so kind; she has brought clean dresses for all of us. I'm sure she has emptied all her chests of their finery. Being that there aren't any children in this household, Maryam and Tzipa will have to make do with a tunic.

I've eaten, and quenched my thirst, and helped Mama settle Maryam and Tzipa, who were ready to go off and explore this wonderful house – but that wouldn't be the correct thing to do, not having been offered to be shown about. I'd like to be a fly on the wall in Rav Todros's study room, but no one has invited me to join, so I do the only thing I can, I lay down to sleep.

*

I haven't slept this well since . . . what seems a lifetime ago in London. I wake to the smell of baking bread and boiling milk. That is a luxury I have been dreaming of a long time. Doña Abulafia has the same idea about starting the day with something warm, and she hands me an enormous bowl of hot goat's milk.

The aromas have awoken Mama, Sarah, and the girls, and they all converge in the kitchen, happy and rested. Our hostess is plying everyone with breads and milk, and refilling the bowls as necessary. The men, just coming in from their morning prayers, are welcomed with plates filled with more of the same breads and lots of hot milk.

Father is very excited; Rav Todros had found a buyer for one of the gems, and he was able to make a very nice profit. Rav Todros is also trying to convince Father to remain in Burgos, where there is a nice Jewish community and most of the Jews are making a reasonable living. Alfonso VIII, King of Castile, is very generous with his Jewish subjects, entrusting tax collecting throughout the Castile to Jewish agents. Rav Todros himself is an Almojarifazgo, or collector of revenues.

Seeing as Father has had the experience of being head of the Exchequer for King Henry II, Rav Todros is sure he will succeed in business in this bustling town of Burgos.

It's been decided; we are all tired of traveling and Burgos is as good a place as any to settle. Within days Father has found us a reasonable house, which we can move into immediately. We are anxious to be in our own home, as Pesach is in a few short weeks, and although both Rav Todros and his wife, Chana, are wonderful hosts, Pesach is a time when families like to honor their own traditions. Sarah and Yehudah will be staying with us, until we get our bearings and are sure we want to stay in Burgos permanently. It is important for Yehudah to find the right study group, and that will be a determining factor.

Father has been very busy trying to procure wheat kernels, a pestle and mortar with which to grind them, and water that has "cooled." This water has to be drawn from a clean well, and must rest, or "cool" overnight before being mixed with the flour for the eighteen-minute process of the matzoh-baking. Mama is busy instructing the servants on how best to scrub the wood-burning stove so that not a speck of flour remains, after which Yehudah has been prodding the fires so that they reach maximum heat, and at such a high degree that there is no question that any crumb of dough has survived.

Sarah and I have been sent to the market place to buy cooking pots and eating utensils, as well as cloths for the table. We've also been rummaging around at the fabric stalls, looking for materials for our clothing. We've been very successful in our purchases, and make our way home, laden with all the various items.

I have yet to discover how Mama has managed to put together such a royal holiday table in so short a time. Matzos, fish, chicken, carrots, and greens – all the familiar and traditional foods. There's even wine that Rav Todros sent over as a gift in honor of the Yom Tov, and he and his lovely wife will be joining us for the "Seder."

As Father takes his place at the head of the table, Rav Todros to his right and Yehudah to his left, I am overwhelmed with emotion, and when Tzipa begins the "Ma Nishtana," I turn to see that I am not the only one whose tears are streaming down their cheeks. We are most fortunate to have survived the massacres in London, and in Norwich; massacres that claimed the lives of most of those communities. As the evening draws to a close, and I open the door for Eliyahu, I turn heavenward and make a special wish that our prayers reach the celestial court, and that Mashiach ben David make a speedy appearance, and bring the Almighty's children to the Promised Land.

Chapter 18

I'M AWAKENED BY THE SOUND OF RETCHING. I FIND Sarah doubled over a basin, green as mold and retching bile. "I'm with child," she gasps even as she doubles over again. I'm trying to think what Mama's remedy is for this condition, when Mama herself appears and gives Sarah a sip of some potion that she's concocted for just such a malaise. As I see the color returning to Sarah's cheeks, I feel pretty bad for the way she's feeling, but at the same time, I'm very happy and thank the Almighty, that the stillbirth didn't affect her chance of having more children.

Yehudah is hovering in the background, as is Father; men are helpless in situations such as these. I wonder why it is said that men are stronger than women; I don't see any men that would be able to deal with childbirth.

*

Burgos is glorious in the springtime. So many different flowers and fruits, it's like an artist's paint box. The countryside just beyond the fortress walls reminds me of an oriental carpet. The Burgos market attracts people from far and wide in search of olives, grapes, and the assortment of local fruits.

So many of our Jewish neighbors are involved in the oil guilds, as pickers, as pressers, or as traders. Father has been commissioned as an *Almojarifazgo* or bookkeeper, and will be working in close association with Rav Todros. He has told Father on many occasions that working with him is almost like having a son. He and his wife never had children, and they have "adopted" all of us.

I am going to have to find some kind of occupation, as I'm not sure accompanying Father and Rav Todros on their revenue collecting will be appropriate. Perhaps I can assemble some of the children and teach them ciphers, as I have done with Maryam and Tzipa. Sarah, heavy with child, is again busy with handworks, embroidering every piece of linen she can lay her hands on. Before we know it, it will again be Rosh Hashanah, and Mama is trying to store as much food as possible in the cellars, in anticipation of the winter months. One of the servants has shown us how to transform the sheep's milk into cheese, which will keep a few weeks due to the very moderate climate in Burgos that will preserve it. We are avid students as she demonstrates just how to curdle the milk, strain and dry it, and then just how to store it. I thought that after our voyage on the carvel, smothered in wool, I'd never want to hear the word "sheep" again, let alone eat a by-product; but wonder of wonders, I have become very fond of the cheese.

Our stocks have been replenished, our cellars full, and we are now ready to usher in the New Year, 4951. We meet with many members of the Jewish community in the home of Rav Todros, as it's the only space large enough to accommodate such a large gathering, and Rav Todros is the only Jew in possession of a Torah Scroll. I stop to reflect how lucky we are that although the prayers are being sung with a different melody than the melodies I am accustomed to, the prayers themselves are the same; the world over, Jews can pray together petitioning the heavenly courts as one.

Aren't we an amazing people?

Rav Todros has been telling Father that the months just after our Succot will be a very busy time for them as revenue collectors. King Alfoso is adamant that all taxes be paid up before the end of the year, and citizens have to be reminded that their taxes are due. Just as he promised, Rav Todros keeps Father busy from sunrise to sunset, yet I haven't seen Father so happy or animated in a long time. How I wish I could join them; keeping the books and calculations is something I love.

The winter has set in, but it is much milder than the one I remember in England, and although we have had a light snow, it was only the once, and the temperatures were barely freezing. Sarah's time is nearing, and Mama has installed a midwife in the house. Those terrified visions of that other time, thinking that should the baby come quickly, there will be no help on hand, has spurred Mama to have the midwife on call. Maryam and Tzipa have been whispering in a corner of the kitchen, working on some kind of surprise for Sarah, and no one is allowed to peek.

Yehudah has settled in nicely with a group of Torah scholars, and is happy to keep his mind occupied with thoughts other than that of the impending birth. All in all, I think we have settled in beautifully to our life in Burgos, and our home resonates in contentment, in spite of the fact that Father is careful that we do not live on too high a standard.

Of the eight original gems that Father traded in Norwich, he has only had to sell two. It gives Father, and all of us, a sense of security, and should the necessity ever arise and we again have to take flight, the gems are readily available and transportable.

Chapter 19

AMA IS SHAKING ME AWAKE. "DINA, QUICK, the baby is coming and the midwife needs masses of boiled water. Wake up the servants, give them instructions, then come upstairs. We might need your help."

I run downstairs to do as Mama has asked, and together with the servants, we put the large copper pots up to boil. I'm torn between staying to wait for the water, or going upstairs to assist. I've never done this before, and just hearing Sarah moaning is keeping me rooted to the safe spot in the kitchen.

I've never thought of myself as a coward, but there is something about Sarah's innocent yelps; the sound has touched a raw nerve.

Moans have turned into screams, and I can't remain downstairs forever. I head up with an urn of boiled water, which Mama relieves me of. Sarah is on the bed, with the midwife bent over her and blocking my view. I'm pleased, as I'd rather not see what is going on. Father and Yehudah are pacing just outside the door, and seeing as I can't be of help in the room, I join them in their pacing. Not a minute too soon, as Sarah utters a blood-curdling screech, and we hear the cry of a baby. Seconds, or is it minutes, elapse and Mama is in the doorway holding a swaddled baby, and beaming from ear to ear. "Yehudah, mazal tov, you are the father of a beautiful little girl."

Mama hands me the little bundle and returns to help the midwife see to Sarah. Indeed, this little girl has the most startling black eyes, and she is already eyeing me curiously. Washed and settled down, Sarah is ready to hold her baby, and Mama comes to retrieve her.

Naomi – just days old and she has already stolen everyone's heart. I've been busy tending to her and giving Sarah a chance to get back on her feet, and I'm completely smitten. Even the little ones, Maryam and Tzipa, are doing their best to help in the household now that Sarah is laid up. They've completed their surprise and it's been unveiled: a doll, made of cloth remnants and rags – something for Naomi to play with once she's a bit older.

Naomi is turning out to be a very easy baby, content to sleep between feedings, and with a very happy disposition.

*

Something serious must be afoot; Father has summoned me to the great room. I arrive to see Father in discussion with a fine-looking gentleman, if a bit foreign looking. They are speaking in French, but the man's French has an underlying accent, and I can't place it.

Father introduces me to R' Eliezer ben Gvirol, who is an emissary of R' Shmuel ben Tibbon, the man who visited us in London, what seems so many years ago. R' Eliezer is saying that after the massacres in London and Norwich, Jews worldwide learned of the fate of their brethren and R' Shmuel feared that our whole family, too, was wiped out. He was happy to learn from some traders that had arrived in Alexandria that a family survived intact and escaped to Spain. More questioning of the sailors revealed that it was, indeed, our family that was set ashore in Castile.

R' Eliezer has been sent to locate us.

I listen to the entire story, with an uneasy feeling that this is leading to something quite different than just a happy reunion. I didn't have to wait long before I heard the essence of R' Eliezer's visit.

If he finds this family to be, indeed, the family of Aaron ben Yoseph Montague of England, and if, indeed, the eldest daughter, Dina, has not been promised in marriage to anyone, he, R' Eliezer, was to be the agent and propose a union between Dina and the son of R' Shmuel.

"He is a young man in his twenty-sixth year, already heading one of the great yeshivos in Alexandria," recounts the agent; "a man with fine character traits, and if I may add, very pleasing to the eye."

Having said that, R'Eliezer whips out a small miniature from his breast pocket and presents it to Father. He studies it for a moment and then passes it on to me.

I've never before held such a precious piece in my hands. The miniature is enamel, framed in gold, and executed in the most vivid colors. Indeed, the young man in question is very handsome.

I hadn't noticed, but while I took my time studying the miniature, R' Eliezer has left the room and I am alone with Father.

"Dina, I think that you, yourself, are aware that the time has come for you to wed. I was always hoping to find someone for you that could match your intellect and appreciate your knowledge. I'm sure you will recall how taken R' Shmuel was that you could keep up with us during his Torah discourses. I was starting to get apprehensive as I looked at the possible candidates here in Burgos, and found them not well suited to you. I feel very comfortable with the suggestion of R' Shmuel's son, Zecharia. Just think about it . . .

"I don't expect an answer immediately, as R' Eliezer will be with us for a few more days, but I want you to consider it carefully, weigh the pluses against the minuses."

*

The travelling chest is almost full, and standing here with mixed emotions, I remember so many scenes, so many memories, all flashing by in my mind. I see Sarah on my lap, being pulled through the snow on a sled by one of the servants, her high-pitched laugh echoing off the stone houses in our lane. I can see Father sitting with me over the Talmud, explaining an intricate calculation. I see Mama, bending over me as I pretend to sleep, kissing my cheek, even though I've burnt the food I should have been stirring. I am remembering Maryam and then Tzipa as infants and toddlers, following me around with blind adoration. Those were the happy times, the times before London's Jewry was decimated, before Norwich and York and cities east were devastated by mobs of angry citizens incited by the Church and the Crusaders. My emotions are jumbled; I am happy, yet sad, excited, yet wary, I have decided to accept this marriage proposal. Have I jumped in at the deep end, again?

I will be leaving tomorrow, the first leg of the journey will be by carriage in the company of two maidservants, R' Eliezer, and four mercenary soldiers that have come with R' Eliezer from Alexandria. As was explained, we will be traveling overland until we reach Valencia, and there, we will board a carvel to bring us to Alexandria. Father has assured me that this trip will be a lot more comfortable than the previous one, wrapped in oil-smelling wool, at the bottom of the hold. My marriage will take place almost immediately upon arrival, and as newlyweds, we will be living with R'Shmuel until we find our own home.

*

Father's come to get me; it's time. The moment has arrived and my traveling trunk is already being loaded onto the carriage; the maidservants are seated and R' Eliezer is patiently waiting for me to get in.

Father places both his hands on my head, and blesses me, "Yivorechecha Hashem veYeshmerecha . . ." – no tears but a break in his throat as he completes the Bracha. Mama isn't crying, but she's having a hard time blinking back the tears, as she gathers me to her, kissing me and hugging me. Maryam and Tzipa have their arms wrapped around my waist, entreating me to stay, until Father pries them away. Sarah, my dearest Sarah, hugging Naomi to her chest as though Naomi were me, and she wasn't going to let go. I embrace them both, wrapping them in my arms, and slip Sarah my journal in its special wrapping. "Sarah, when Naomi is older, please give her this journal. Hopefully she will have learned German and can follow the story of our family. It's the only thing I have of value, and I leave it for her; in fact, it's her legacy."

Our carriage moves off, southward bound, but a part of me will forever remain in Burgos.

· BOOK II ·

Freya's Story

Chapter 1

"*F*REYA, FREYA, WHERE ARE YOU, CHILD?*"*

That's Luiza, our maid, and there is no way I can manage to hide from her. She has eyes at the back of her head and a real Castilian temper. Any minute now, she'll find me and lament over my misdeeds.

"Ah, here you are, Freya! Haven't I told you at least one hundred times to keep away from the window? You know it displeases your parents."

I turn with a sigh, drop the sheer curtains back in place, and get up from the window seat. I'm starting to hate this "house arrest," and the walls of my gilded cage are slowly strangling me.

I'm only twelve, but I'm old enough to know that things are not right. Not at home, not in our neighborhood, and not in the city. I try to sneak a peek out the window sometimes when Luiza isn't watching, and what I see has me baffled and concerned.

The streets are deserted. The Abadis from across the way, Sara and her family, have disappeared overnight without a trace. Days later, their house was occupied by a very important-looking Catholic family. Where is Sara? Where has her family gone? Why are all our Jewish friends not around anymore? I don't see them on the street, or rushing to their businesses.

What has happened to the Shul? Why is it boarded up? What is that cloud of smoke hanging in the air, and that awful stench? Why have my parents' friends and their children stopped coming around? Why are all Pere's seforim packed up in crates and stacked in the library?

No one to answer my questions, I get relegated to my bedroom when the adults have important "issues" to discuss. Mere spends most of her time with baby Emanuel, Manu for short, and escapes to her room to avoid Pere's strange visitors, men in uniform, always questioning and arguing with my gentle father. I try to hear what the shouting is about from my perch at the top of the staircase, but the ever-vigilant Luiza always seems to be right there to march me back to my room.

I've started writing. Mere has given me an old journal that she's had since she was a child. It tells the very exciting story about a girl called Dina from England, and takes place about three hundred years ago. Mere said I could use the empty pages to write on, so I've begun keeping my own journal. It will never take the place of Sara, or any of my other friends. It's a poor replacement for Pere and Mere's attention, but I'm starting to realize that something very serious is underfoot and I will have to satisfy myself with my writing.

I am Freya, daughter of Don Salamon HaLevi and Doña Yachet, born in the year 1480 in Toledo, Kingdom of Castile. My earliest recollections are of a serene household cared for by a dozen servants – maids and butlers, upstairs and downstairs – cleaning and polishing our magnificent home, and seeing to the family's every need.

My room was once my own little paradise. Pere and Mere had it filled with every doll and toy imaginable, and I even had my very own nana, Tzipi, a Jewish girl from Worms. How I loved her. She sang to me in her soft voice, songs about our people in Galus. Songs about our nation's love of the Creator. Happy songs, melancholy songs, no matter, they were always beautifully sung.

She taught me the Alef Bet, to read, write, and pray, and she did it all while showering me with love. She taught me to read and write German, the language Mere spoke at her home when she was growing up. Tzipi left after my tenth birthday. Pere said I had outgrown a nanny, and it was time for Tzipi to return to her home and get married.

I remember fireplaces stocked with wood and burning bright to keep out the winter chill. Those wonderful aromas wafting out of the enormous below-level kitchen, friends and dignitaries forever visiting and being fed an array of delicious foods, fruits, and vegetables, served up in such abundance on the most beautiful, delicate dishes imported from some far-off lands, over many seas in the east.

The carriage house: Pere kept a beautiful ebony wood carriage that he used when he left home to conduct business, and the white one that Mere and I used on our outings. I was always fearful of the horses and never dared venture as far as the stables, although my most special memories are of the sorties I took with Mere in the wonderful white carriage.

Most of the horses are gone, the white carriage too. We no longer go out on sorties, Mere and I. Our fireplaces are no longer lit, and friends have stopped coming. Pere has developed worry lines on his forehead, and Mere spends her time rocking and soothing Manu. Mere has been very uncommunicative these past months, in fact, these past few years. She has suffered one miscarriage after another and two stillborn births. Mere, once happy and spirited, has become a walking shadow of herself. The only time I see a light in her eyes is when she is fussing over Manu.

Luiza, the downstairs maid, is one of the only servants still working for us. Once a very busy and prosperous household, our home has become a ghost of its old self.

The days are gone when the rooms resounded with interesting conversation and laughter. Our magnificent home has the feel of an old, abandoned woman, once beautiful, once the center of attention, now totally forgotten.

I feel lucky to have this journal, a quill, and a pot of ink.

Chapter 2

I'VE AWOKEN TO THE NOISE OF FRENZIED ACTIVITY in the hallway. I slowly open my bedroom door and am aware that something is happening. Pere is rushing about, stuffing documents into a travelling chest. Mere has Manu all swaddled and is packing a wardrobe with our clothes. Luiza has been sent off to the kitchen to assemble hampers with provisions. I just stand to one side, helpless and concerned. Pere notices my distress and tweaks my cheek. "Not to worry, Freya, we are going on a journey." I would have liked to ask him a few questions, but he is already outside giving instructions to the carriage men.

Mere has come down the staircase, and hands me Manu. He is really the sweetest baby, and the light of Pere and Mere's eyes. His bris eight months ago was a royal event. Those were happier days, and the house was filled with guests bearing gifts for the "HaLevi" son. How the situation has changed so radically in such a short time. Mere is standing in the great hall with tears streaming down her cheeks as she looks around and says her goodbyes.

They are calling for us from outside, and we quickly make our way out and into the carriage. I barely have the chance to make myself and Manu comfortable, when the doors are shut and the carriage starts to roll.

Pere and Mere both sit in silence, staring out the window, forlorn. Pere shakes himself out of his reverie and begins to recite the Tefilas Haderech, prayer of the traveller. That completed, Pere turns to me and begins to translate word for word. Never before have I paid such attention to the words and their meaning. All of our previous trips were happy occasions, holidays to the coast or trips to the mountains, and I mainly repeated the prayer by rote. Now, however, the words take on a different meaning.

" . . . lead us toward peace, emplace our footsteps toward peace, guide us toward peace, and make us reach our desired destination for life, gladness, and peace."

Mere is softly crying in her seat as she rocks Manu to and fro. He must be feeling her angst and he starts to wail. I'm also having a hard time controlling my emotions. We are leaving our home for a destination and destiny unknown. What does the Almighty have in store for us? Please, please Hashem, bring us safely to a place of serenity and peace.

It has just dawned on me why Pere's good friend Don Izak Ababrbanel has not visited of late. A constant visitor to our home, he and Pere spent many hours sequestered in Pere's library. I'm just remembering a conversation I overheard between him and Pere. Don Abarbanel was saying that he was winding up all his business affairs and leaving for Portugal. He cautioned Pere to do the same, and as quickly as possible. Was this what he meant, to pack in such haste, abandon our home, and flee as thieves to places unknown?

I get jolted out of my reverie as crowds rushing in the general direction of the city square overtake our carriage. We are moving in that direction, as it is the only way out of town. Our carriage stops to give way to an open-bedded wagon carrying bound men, women, and children in the direction of the square.

"Pere, what are those large stacks of wood for, and where are they taking those people? What are they doing with them?"

Before I can ask another question, Pere has pulled down the shades, and knocked on the carriage roof, signalling the drivers to proceed. We are underway again, Mere still rocking baby Manu, still weeping. Pere looks at me with concerned eyes, studying my face in the dimmed cabin.

"My child, we are embarking on a dangerous journey, but to have remained in our home would have been even more dangerous and is no longer an option.

"We are living in terrible times, in a country that has been home to Jews for the last 300 years. We have contributed so much to all facets of the country's economy, sciences, medicine, and art. It has been a golden age.

"Today, Queen Isabella has taken on a religious advisor,

Torquemada the Inquisitor, who is in his own way is just as wicked as the infamous Haman of Persia. He has ferreted out many Conversos, and has arrested anyone suspected of not entirely being loyal to the Catholic Church."

Pere sighs, and takes my hand in his, "I wish the times were different, I wish I wouldn't have to burden you with this.

"The Abadi family. They were given the choice of converting or being sent off on a ship, westward across the great seas. They have chosen resettlement and have departed on this treacherous journey. May the Almighty guide their every step.

"Many of our friends were not given the option of resettlement, and when they refused conversion, were burnt at the stake. Hashem yakum damom, may their blood be avenged.

"I know that you've seen things that have baffled you, that you have many unanswered questions about what has been happening these last few months. All I can say is that I tried to spare my family the heartache of abandoning our home, and I have not been successful. I have categorically refused conversion, and our arrest was imminent."

I squeeze his hand, and as a tear escapes his eyes, "Pere, I'm sure all your goodness will be repaid, and the Almighty will keep us safe."

"Dear child, so many good people have perished . . . ah, but let's try to keep a positive outlook. I see you've managed to bring your journal along, and the pages are starting to fill up. I hope you'll have many happy moments to recount and joyous occasions to celebrate in our new home. We are on our way to Portugal, where a Jew is more welcome."

At that moment, Pere closes his eyes and starts to nap. I didn't dare ask him the million questions that were buzzing in my head. I sat back and soundless formed the word . . . Portugal. As the wheels of the carriage churned and took us westward, they churned to the rhythm of Portugal . . . Portugal . . . Portugal.

Chapter 3

MERE HAS FINALLY COME OUT OF HER STUPOR and gets busy with the food hamper. Luiza has packed all the remaining fruits, vegetables, and breads, along with pastries from the pantry.

Food is being passed around, but Pere is refusing to eat.

"Freya, do you know what today is? It is the Ninth of Av. It is the day we commemorate the destruction of our Holy Temple in Jerusalem, a day of fast. It is the day that marks the beginning of our Diaspora, and our suffering as a nation is not over. We have left so many to the mercy of the Inquisitors. May our cries and prayers reach the heavens, and may we be worthy to be returned to Zion, and the rebuilding of the Temple."

I take the food forced on me by Mere, but my appetite has left me. Pere has again made me aware of our precarious situation: homeless, and travelling on treacherous roads to the unknown. I raise the shade of the carriage window and am shocked to see hundreds of people travelling in the same direction we are. Old and young. Some on wagons or donkeys, but most of them on foot, carrying what seem to be all their worldly possessions. Pere is also surprised by the masses of people, and calls for the driver to halt the carriage. The carriage stops and Pere alights to speak with some of those nearby. I'm half hanging out the window, trying to follow their conversation, when Mere pulls me back in.

"Freya, please, pull down the shade and try not to draw attention to yourself. One day your curiosity will land you in big trouble."

I'm not sure why Mere is making such a fuss, but I have to respect her wishes. On Pere's orders, the carriage has again started rolling, but he is outside, walking alongside and engrossed in conversation with a group of men. I wish I were a boy.

I bet if I were a boy I'd be allowed to walk at Pere's side. I wouldn't have to hide behind some shade; I could do anything and not "draw attention" to myself. On the other hand, writing a journal would probably be considered "girlie." I guess being a female has its advantages, but at this moment, I am downright frustrated.

Night is almost upon us, and I hear Pere telling the drivers to stop the carriage.

There is a large open field with a small freshwater stream, and it seems the perfect place to settle down for the night. Pere rejoins us and is now ready to break his fast and eat something. I have to keep myself from blurting out all the questions I have, so as to give him a chance to quench his thirst and satisfy his hunger. Hardly has he swallowed his first bite, and we hear a commotion just outside our carriage.

Pere puts his food down, opens the door and instructs us not to leave the carriage or open the shades. His stare penetrates my eyes, and I look away. He does know my inquisitive nature, and has guessed that I would very much like to follow him and see what the ruckus is about.

After ten minutes, and some raised voices, Pere returns to the carriage. It seems that while most of the men wanted to stop and rest for the night, a small group wanted to continue on. Pere, in his soft yet firm way, has convinced everyone that it would be in all our interest to stay together and not travel unknown roads at night. Pere helped everyone find a spot, and assisted in setting up an enclosure close to the stream so that the women could see to their needs. It was decided that Mere would go first while I watched Manu, and then it would be my turn. It didn't take long before she was back and there was a quick, hushed exchange between her and Pere.

Mere opened one of the trunks and removed one of her scarves. She takes the sleeping Manu from my arms and hands him to Pere, then proceeds to cover my hair and half my face. What could she be thinking? Why do I need to be covered?

We hop out of the carriage.

"Freya, go straight down this slope for fifty meters and you will find the other women. Come right back when you're finished with your toilet, and don't wander off exploring." Mere really knows me, and she has just clipped my wings.

Off I go, trying not to trip in the dark, and indeed, about fifty meters away, I find an assembly of women . . . all in some state of undress. This can't be for real. Am I expected to take care of my needs in front of all these women? Ah, maybe that's why my parents tried to camouflage me with the scarf; they are trying to save me some embarrassment. Oh well, I better make the most of an uncomfortable situation before it gets more uncomfortable. I manage to find an isolated spot behind a low bush and am able to do what needs being done. Then a bit of washing up in the refreshing stream, and back up the incline.

Most people have bedded down for the night. Some are on the wagons, some under the wagons, and very many just on the wayside, using their bundles as mattresses. Into the carriage, and I almost land on Manu. Mere has made a makeshift bed for him on the floor and he is fast asleep. I drop a kiss on Mere's cheek, get cozy on the seat, say the Shema, and am asleep before I know it.

I wake up with a start. Manu is gurgling. Light is creeping through the shades and there is the light tap, tap, tap of rain falling on the carriage roof. Mere is still asleep but Pere is not in the carriage. Dare I open the shades to look for him, or even better, do I go out and see where he is? I'm just about to move past Mere when the door swings open and Pere climbs in. He is very distressed. I can tell by the way his lips are pinched and his eyes are focused. He rouses Mere, waits till she is fully awake, and then tells us . . . the carriage-men have fled in the night.

With weeks of travel ahead, we are now left to our own devices. Poor Pere, he will now have to be the driver as well as the stable boy, taking care of the horses.

Although I have this terrible fear of animals, I offer to help Pere harness the horses for travel. Of course, neither Pere nor Mere will allow that, but at least the offer has brought a smile to his lips.

Before daylight fully breaks, our caravan is ready to roll. With people ahead of us and people behind us, in spite of the light rain, there is an air of excited anticipation. We are headed to a new home, renewed hope.

Chapter 4

*I*T WAS THE CALM BEFORE THE STORM. YOUNG AND old, men and women, march alongside the many wagons and the few carriages, in step to the churning of the wheels. One group began to chant and before long, the melody and words were picked up all along the column.

"And they that know Thy name will put their trust in Thee:
For Thou, HaShem, hast not forsaken those that seek Thee." (Psalms)

Over and over the chant went. The sun rises and the sun sets, and on we march in song.

It is day four of our journey, and so far the weather is holding up. Not too hot and we've only had just that bit of rain the first day. We are also lucky to constantly cross peasants on the road heading toward Toledo with their wares. We're able to buy fruits and vegetables to replenish our food supplies. Without fail, the peasants ask us if we wish to convert. Their tenacity amazes me. They circulate through the column and start up conversations with all the younger people. Always offering food and shelter, and of course forgiveness if they will just repent and return to Toledo for baptism. I don't think anyone has succumbed to their entreaties, but the adults keep an eagle eye out when the peasants are around.

Mere has become more relaxed with me and I'm allowed to ride up top with Pere, if I promise to keep my hair and some of my face covered with the scarf. She is more than happy to be left alone with Manu. He's really such a good baby, not any trouble at all. His teeth are starting to cut, and Mere says we can expect him to be in some pain and less content. I've given him an old rag doll that I salvaged from my room at home; it's to chew on, but so far, he's as cooperative as ever. Mere is animated only when she is busy with him, and

I'm hoping that this new place we are heading to will reawaken her old spirit, that she'll be her lively, talkative self again.

*

Everything looks different from up here next to Pere; I hadn't realized the mass of people that we are – surely thousands and thousands of travelers. Pere explains that we should be arriving in Merida in another ten days if all goes well. From there, another week to the border of Portugal, where a large group will be breaking away and heading for Algarve, while we will be continuing on (perhaps another week) till we reach our final destination of Lisbon.

I've made a friend, Sofia. She's travelling with her parents to Lisbon, too. I met her last evening when we stopped for the night and the men set up a spot for the women's "toilet." Sofia was there, trying to find some privacy behind a bush, when she happened on me. We both had a start, and then began to giggle. What with trying to juggle our clothing without exposing ourselves, and not falling into some prickly bush, we were a comic pair. She told me that her father was a merchant and had dealt in fine fabrics until they were expelled from Toledo. She is an only child, but has lots more freedom than I do. Her parents allow her to wander freely about the camp, and she doesn't have to wear a scarf. She keeps me amused as she describes some of the people on this caravan. She has me holding my sides in pain as she mimics the walk of one of the wagon drivers. He's a cross between a drunken sailor and a wooden rocking horse, and as Sofia continues on her way in this particular fashion, she bumps straight into her father, who's come to find her.

He is less than pleased with her shenanigans, and with a bit of a strong arm escorts her back to their carriage. I'm happy to go back to my own carriage knowing that tomorrow is another day, another day in the company of Sofia.

Day five, and I'm jolted awake by loud wailing just outside our carriage. Pere and Mere scramble to arise, but I'm already halfway through the door, where I'm confronted by the wailing woman. She is sobbing as she holds out the wrapped body of a small child. "She's dead, she's dead, the fire has consumed her," she shouts. Pere quickly pulls me back inside, warns me not to leave or even look out the window, and makes his exit. Mere and I sit quietly, with a sleeping Manu, as the sounds move further and further away.

Pere is back, and the storm has come in the form of "the dreaded plague."

Chapter 5

THE SHRIEKS ARE UNBEARABLE. EVERY FAMILY HAS someone dying or dead. We haven't moved onward for days, and Pere has been out most of the time helping the sick and burying the dead. Mere is keeping a vigilant eye on Manu and me; no one leaves or enters the carriage. Every hour she checks our foreheads and cheeks to see whether or not we are running a fever. I have to roll up my skirts and sleeves so that she can make sure there are no lesions on my body. I'm not even permitted out to see to my needs, Mere has organized a chamber pot.

Our food stocks are starting to run low, but the peasants are keeping away from our group. Bad news travels fast and the peasants have heard that we have been visited by the "black death."

I'm worried about Sofia, but Pere says he has seen her father, and the family is fine. I wish I could just get out for a few minutes, just to see for myself. I'd like to give Pere a hand; he has such black rings under his eyes, I'm worried for him. He has taken the well being of the entire group on his shoulders, seeing to their every need, and all in his quiet, unassuming way.

Shabbat has arrived, and an uneasy calm settles on the group; men, women, and children trying to settle the sick, and see that their own needs will be taken care of until nightfall tomorrow. While Pere settles the horses, sees that they are fed and given water, Mere has taken out two candles and her precious brass candlesticks, an heirloom from her grandmother. Luiza has remembered every detail and even the embroidered cover for the challah has been packed neatly in the trunk. Mere leaves it in its place, as we do not have challah.

The men gather not far from our carriage and begin their song, Shalom Alechem:

Peace unto you, ministering angels, messengers of the Most High, of the supreme King of kings, the Holy One, blessed be He.

May your coming be in peace, angels of peace, messengers of the Most High, of the supreme King of kings, the Holy one, blessed be He.

Bless me with peace, angels of peace, messengers of the Most High, of the supreme King of kings, the Holy one, blessed he He.

May your departure be in peace, angels of peace, messengers of the Most High, of the supreme King of kings, the Holy one, blessed he He.

For He will instruct His angels in your behalf, to guard you in all your ways. The Lord will guard your going and your coming from now and for all time.

A special peace reigns. The moaning and crying has diminished. Have our voices reached the heavens? Have our cries been heard?

We have a meagre Shabbat meal, but we are fortunate to have this much. Pere reminds me that some of our fellow travellers are making do with only radish and water. I keep getting flashbacks of our times in Toledo. The food-laden table, the shining brass and silver, the flowing wines, the wonderful clothing we all wore.

This is a far cry from those memories. I have been very spoiled, and I'm going to have to lock those memories away if I'm going to make a go of our new situation.

I have to look forward if I'm going to survive.

Shabbat day passes in relative peace; the angels are watching over us.

*

Day six, the calm that was Shabbat has passed. I try to pass the time playing with Manu and writing; it helps shut out the moans and anguished cries from outside.

The stench is beginning to permeate the carriage and Mere tries to conceal it with some of her fine perfumes. The relief is temporary.

Pere has gathered all the able men. They are going to gather twigs, light a fire, and burn all the dead, along with all straw, mattresses, and ticking. He is convinced that the insect-infested materials are keeping the plague alive. As with most leaders, and Pere is a natural leader, there are those who resist, and Pere has his work cut out for him in trying to make them see his view. After many hours of argument, and much lost precious strength, Pere is finally able to make the bonfire. Burning wood replaces the malodors of the last few days.

Manu is restless. It must be the smell, or his teeth cutting through. He's running a fever. He's developed swelling on his neck and in his armpits.

Manu has the dreaded plague.

Chapter 6

I WILL PROBABLY HATE MYSELF FOREVER AND EVER, but I am of no use to my parents.

I am terrified to look at poor Manu. He is swollen and black, and having a hard time breathing. I sit in my corner and try to tuck myself into the smallest ball possible. Mere has abandoned herself to hysteria, and Pere is having a hard time dealing with both a sick child and a wild wife. She is shrieking and tearing her hair, and I am starting to get caught up in this madness. I begin to cry, and then join Mere in her shrieking. Pere grabs me and shakes me till I stop.

"Freya, please, take control of yourself. I have enough on my hands what with Manu being ill and your mother in this state."

I'm desolate. I've caused Pere such pain. I am being selfish, and not helping the situation at all. I slouch back in my seat, trying to think of ways to be helpful without going too close to Manu. I am terrified by the thought of catching the plague. What will happen if Pere or Mere get sick?

I feel the hysteria returning, when Mere lets out a whelp and collapses to the floor.

Pere is bending over Manu and after a moment, he's wrapping him in a blanket, totally covering him. He opens the door to the carriage and leaves with this bundle that is my sweet, innocent brother, Manu. I raise the shade and watch as Pere heads into the trees, puts his bundle down and starts digging a hole with his bare hands.

Mere, on her hands and knees, is moaning. I stoop down to raise her from the floor and manage to get her up on the bench. She keeps pounding her chest and wailing.

I take her in my arms and try to calm her as one would an injured child. In a split second, our rolls have reversed; now I have to be the strong one. I don't know how long we've been sitting here rocking, but I have managed to quiet her.

Pere has returned. He takes my place next to Mere and begins, in his soothing voice, to tell Mere that he was fortunate enough to find a place where he could bury poor Manu. He has said the Kaddish, and marked the spot. I have never seen Pere so sad, yet there was relief in his voice. He would have been heartbroken to have had to burn Manu's little body.

Day twelve, and we have burnt or buried all the dead. Those of us that are still alive have been to hell and back, but we are here, breathing, and plague-free. Pere estimates that we have lost about 300 souls – men, women and children. Tomorrow, we continue on our journey.

Day thirteen, the sun coming through the window has woken me. Mere is already up and dressed, and staring out in the direction of the little grave. She barely answers my greeting, and makes no move to stop me leaving the carriage to see to my needs. I'm almost out the door when I remember I haven't taken the scarf. I quickly retrieve it from the bench, cover my hair, and step out. Pere is busy harnessing the horses and shouts a "good morning." The entire camp has come alive, and they are preparing to leave. I rush to make sure that Sofia is in her carriage and alright. We fall on each other like long lost sisters, crying and laughing, and promising to meet up this evening when our caravan stops for the night. I'm just about to head back when Sofia stops me.

"What's with the scarf, Freya; why do you constantly cover your hair and half your face?"

"I'm not sure; Pere and Mere have made it a condition of my leaving the carriage, but we'll talk more when I see you later."

Back in the carriage, Mere hasn't moved from her position. I prepare some of the vegetables and biscuits for her, but I can't cajole her to eat. I tell her all about Sofia, I tell her about the other people I've met these past few days, but I can't get her to react. She just sits and stares.

How can I help you, my dear mother? You have lost the light of your life, your dear little boy, but you still have me. How can I implore you to show me some love too? I may be just a poor second, I'm not a boy, but I love you, Mere.

I formulate all of that in my head, yet I can't come out and say it. Why is it that things are so much easier to write than to voice?

I think I have a big problem. My ink is running low, and with the extra days spent immobilized during the plague, we'll not be arriving in Merida for another week.

We might also have a shortage of our other supplies, although food shouldn't be a problem, as the peasants have returned with their wares in tow.

The caravan is slowing down; I wonder why. I check that our carriage has completely stopped before I open the door and exit. Pere has climbed down from his seat at the top and is headed for the front of the column. Dare I follow him?

My curiosity gets the better of me, and I follow a short distance behind. Seems Don Jozef is having trouble with his wagon. A wheel has fallen off, and luckily, it isn't broken. It means getting all the people off the wagon and getting a few strong men to lift it up while the wheel is reset. Off comes Doña Carla, Don Jozef's wife. She needs two men to help her out, and one of the younger boys has to bend over so that she can use his back as a step down. Off come two small boys and goat. Off come a very shy young couple, and it's refreshing to see the glint in their eyes as they control their mirth in order not to embarrass Doña Carla.

Before long, the wagon is repaired, and we are ready to roll.

I catch up with Pere just as he's about to remount the carriage and tell him that Mere hasn't had any food since yesterday.

"Pere, I've tried every way I know to get Mere to eat. She's refusing food and isn't responding to anything."

Pere's shoulders sag under the weight of what I've just told him, yet he opens the door and goes into the carriage. Mere is sitting in the semi-darkness, a blank stare on her face, and doesn't react to what Pere is saying. After some minutes he opens the canteen of water and forcibly makes her drink a few drops. Nothing he does will get her to swallow some solid food.

Finally, we're on our way, but so much time has been wasted and it's almost nighttime. I'm happy that we're stopping, as I wanted to catch up with Sofia. I find her on the way to the bushes, and we fall into step like old friends. She's heard about Manu, and commiserates with me about Mere's condition. How I wish she'll get the chance to know her as she once was; the "grand dame" of Toledo, so gracious and vivacious.

Sofia is babbling on about Don Jozef and Doña Carla. Sofia's carriage has been travelling just behind their wagon in the caravan, and it seems that Doña Carla is keeping everyone entertained. She has a hard time moving around; Sofia says she reminds her of a burlap sack full of cats, yet she knows everyone and everything going on around her. She knows just which women are with child, and which husbands and wives don't see eye to eye. She's never been in our carriage, but according to the way Sofia describes her, I'm sure she knows more about what is happening with Mere than I do.

I knew it, my ink is run . . .

Chapter 7

*I*NK! WHAT A COMMODITY. HOW FORTUNATE I AM that Don Juda Danush is travelling with us. He is an alchemist, previously employed at the royal court, but has been expelled like the rest of our group for his beliefs. Pere had made his acquaintance before at court functions and has asked him to help me out with the ink. He's shown me how simple it is to produce ink. We went out to cut some dry hawthorn branches. I was lucky, as this is the end of summer and the branches have been dried by the sun and heat. We then pounded and soaked the bark, boiled it in wine and water until the liquid was thick and blackened, then poured it into cloths to dry.

Once dried, it was again mixed with some wine and salt and . . . Voila – ink!

Day sixteen, we are almost in Merida, and it is almost Shabbat. I've been able to rouse Mere a bit and get her washed and changed. Just in time, as we have reached the outskirts of the city. Our diminished caravan slowly pulls to the side, meters from the entrance gates. Everyone is in a frenzy to settle in before sunset. Pere has tethered the horses, and makes sure they will have enough feed and water to last over Shabbat. I am left in charge of the "carriage" while he goes off through the gates in search of various supplies. He returns a while later with fruits and vegetables in a bucket, and of all things . . . a cow.

"Pere, what are we going to do with the cow?"

"Freya, I'm concerned for some of the infants. Without milk, they can't develop, and I'm not sure that their mothers are able to feed them. Why don't I quickly milk her and you can go up and down the column to see where the milk is needed."

Pere empties the bucket of the fruits and vegetables, and milks the cow. Living in a city, I'd never seen a cow being milked. As the bucket fills, I stare in fascination.

I'm not sure I will ever again drink this white liquid, streaming out of the cow's udder.

Pere hands me the bucket, sees to it that my scarf is knotted under my chin, and sends me on my way. Up and down the column. I'm so pleased at the excitement the milk is generating. Women are kissing my hands as I pour milk into their outstretched cups. It's a bit embarrassing, but I am so pleased that Pere thought about it, just to see the smiles on the children's faces. The bucket is empty, and I head back to the carriage; just in time, as Mere is about to light the candles.

Blessed are you, Lord our G-d, King of the Universe, Who has sanctified us with His commandments, and commanded us to kindle the light of the Holy Shabbat

Peace settles once again on our caravan.

*

Shabbat has passed without incident. The sun has set, the sky so clear that the stars, signaling the end of Shabbat, seem within reach. I can hear the men murmuring in prayer, and children running up and down the column playing and enjoying themselves. This is the first time in many days that the heavy cloud of sorrow isn't hanging in the air. Even Mere has had a good day, joining us for our meal, and contributing to the conversation.

"Freya, Freya, come on out. Doña Carla is organizing games and dancing for the girls." Sofia has pulled open the door to the carriage, "Come on, Freya," and then she stops. She's staring at me. She's not moving.

"Sofia, what's wrong? Why are you staring at me?"

"Your hair, it's white."

Mere gets busy rearranging my scarf, and ensuring all my hair and part of my face are covered. "Don't be silly, Sofia, the light is playing tricks on you. Freya's hair is just like anyone else's. Freya, you may go out for a bit with Sofia, but we will be retiring soon, as tomorrow we have an early start."

I'm more than happy to have Mere's permission to have some fun, and I race Sofia toward Doña Carla's wagon. There's music coming from behind the wagon and the girls are out front dancing.

Sofia joins the dancers, but I'm more interested in seeing where the music is coming from.

One of the passengers on Doña Carla's wagon, the young boy who helped her get down when the wagon wheel broke, is playing a flute. His music is magical, and he is so transported by his playing, he doesn't even notice me standing there listening. I could spend hours here, but I'd better get back to Mere and the carriage if I don't want to abuse the privilege.

*

I've lost track of the days, and Pere tells me we are going to have to make up some of the lost time. He is thinking of pushing longer in the evenings and starting out earlier in the mornings. He explains that we have to have passed the border within a week if we are to make it to Lisbon in time for Rosh Hashanah. No sooner has he said this when the heavens open and we are engulfed by a storm. In the blink of an eye, the sky has turned purple and black, and the clouds are emptying their load.

The winds have joined in wreaking havoc and our caravan is under attack. The men are rushing about, trying to anchor everything down, and getting the women and children as well as the livestock under some kind of shelter. Pere has barely seen to our horses and the cow, plunging into the carriage, when the crash and flash began.

Mere has drawn me close to her, and I bury my face in her shoulder trying to shut out the light. It's hopeless to cover my ears; the crashing sounds are like nothing I've ever heard before. The storm seems to go on for hours, when in reality, Pere tells me it hasn't been more than about twenty minutes. And it leaves, as suddenly as it came. One moment the sky is totally dark, the next moment the sun is out.

Pere opens the door to leave and I take a look out. Disaster! Large trees have crashed and are blocking the way, while the road itself is one glob of mud.

People are shouting that some of the wagons were in the path of the falling trees and have suffered damage. One of Don Jozef's horses has been hit by lightening and is dead. Pere turns back to me and says, "Freya, I think we are going to need a special miracle if we are to get to Lisbon for the High Holy Days."

Chapter 8

*I*T'S TAKEN US FOUR MORE PRECIOUS DAYS TO GET everyone ready for travel. We lost a full day waiting for the mud to dry. Most of the wagons and carriages can't be moved out of the mud, and so many need repairs. They have to be completely unloaded so that the men can do the work more easily. I'm happy to do my share and help the mothers keep the young children occupied and out of the way of the adults. Tomorrow is Shabbat, but it's been decided that we'll proceed as far as we can until just before the candle lighting.

We've stopped in time to settle in and wash up. Shortly before the men begin the Kabbalat Shabbat prayer, Pere gets up on a trunk and calls everyone to attention.

"We've seen these past few days what damage too much water can cause, yet without water, we can't survive. How fortunate we are that we will be travelling almost the entire way along side the Tagus, and we will have plenty of water.

When we raise our voices to the Almighty in prayer, let us not forget to thank Him for his great mercy in that we haven't been washed away and yet He sees to our needs."

A hush falls on the group as everyone contemplates what a close call we've had.

Pere doesn't let melancholy set in on the group as he begins the *Lechu Neranena* in a strong, melodious voice, inspiring everyone to join in. I'm so proud of Pere, although he is always berating me that pride is a very bad trait. I'm hoping that he means pride of oneself, and not selfless pride in another.

I've been meaning to ask Mere about my hair. What's so shocking about the color, and why was Sofia so astonished to see it? I'm anxious for an answer, but I'm not sure now's the right moment. Mere has been more animated these last few days, but I'm still fearful of pressing her.

What a wondrous thing Shabbat is. Fathers spending the day with their wives and children; everyone relaxed and doing their best to forget the unfortunate circumstances that have brought us here. The good mood is contagious and up and down the wagons and carriages, the same tune is picked up and sung until the entire caravan is singing, in their favored Ladino:

> Cuando el Rey Nimrod al campo salía
> miraba en el cielo y en la estrellería
> vido una luz santa en la judería
> que había de nacer Abraham Avinu.
>
> When King Nimrod went out to the fields,
> Looked at the heavens and at the stars,
> He saw a holy light at the Jewish quarter;
> A sign that Abraham, our father, was about to be born.

And the song goes on about the downfall of Nimrod and the rise of Abraham. Again and again the song is repeated, louder and louder and with more gusto. Some men are even starting to substitute Torquemada's name for Nimrod and wishing for his downfall. If only it would be that simple. I frequently listened as Pere was having a discourse with his peers upon their visits to our home in Toledo. I wasn't able to follow most of the intricate learning, but one theme always repeated itself. Our people have been expelled from Jerusalem, our lot, to wander and be persecuted; we will never be free until the time of the Moshiach. All the singing and all the wishful thinking won't change the situation. We are still homeless, with many more miles to go until we find some safety.

It's Sunday and we're trying to get an early start. Beside the disastrous time lost with the plague and the storm, we now have a traitor in our midst. The cow, which we've named "Red," is playing the prima donna. Red has been trotting along behind our carriage, but every so often, refuses to advance without a break. That means stopping the caravan while Red does her "thing." She's only happy when she gets everyone's undivided attention, taking her time grazing and drinking, before she's ready to get in line again. Her temper is what prompted us to give her her name.

Pere hopes that by some time tomorrow, we'll be at the junction where those who are continuing on to Algarve will part ways with us. The crackle of excitement is in the air. Everyone is anxious to reach his or her destination and begin anew. We are all doing our best to push on even though day is quickly turning to night.

I hear shouting; I look out the window and people are running to the rear of the caravan screaming, "Highwaymen" – we are being attacked by highwaymen.

Chapter 9

*M*ERE COMES TO LIFE. SHE GRABS ME QUICKLY and shoves me under the seat, arranging her hooped skirt to completely cover me. No sooner has she done that than the door is pulled open, almost being torn off its hinges. I can't really see what's happening, and I can barely hear, as my heart is beating so strong it's making me deaf. I do see the cabin is being lit up, probably by some kind of lantern, and a man is shouting. "Is there anyone else in this carriage, any young girls or boys?"

Mere keeps her wits about her, "Can't you see I'm alone? I've just lost my only son to the "black death" and I fear that our group is still infected, so I am keeping to myself."

Hearing about the plague, the man quickly calls to the rest of the highwaymen, telling them that the caravan is infested. In fear of catching the plague themselves, they rush to mount their horses, and gallop off in such haste that they leave behind all the hostages and goods they have been rounding up from the various wagons and carriages.

People are crying from fear and relief. I hear it from inside the carriage, I've crawled out from under the bench and Mere is watching me like a hawk, I'm not allowed anywhere near the window. Pere is outside helping resettle everyone, but pops his head in to tell me that Sofia is fine, as are the other young girls and boys the highwaymen were rounding up. Mere eyes me and sees my anxiety. She explains that there is a lot of gold to be made in the sale of slaves to the Sultan in the East. Boatloads leave weekly from the Castilian ports with children and young adults that will never see their home or families again, and are sold into slavery."

Mere is the heroine of the day. People keep stopping by to praise and thank her for having her wits about her, and coming up with an idea that saved us all from heartache. Now that we're stopped, we will be making camp here for the night.

Some of the men have secured the perimeter and made sure that the highwaymen have truly gone, and we are safe. Mere has again installed the chamber pot, and I'm again not permitted to leave the carriage. I should be thankful that Mere is so vigilant, but sometimes, I'd like to spread my wings and fly.

We've arrived at the crossroads. This is such a bittersweet moment. So many of the small ones I've become attached to are leaving. Don Jozef and Doña Carla, together with their passengers, all going on to the Algarve. I'm going to miss the comrade. Mere lets me put on my scarf, go out, and say my farewells. Tears are shed, over budding friendships, by the fact that so many hardships were shared; our lives have been welded together, and it is as if our family is being separated.

With Don Jozef leading the party, the caravan heading to the Algarve is underway.

"To life and peace and . . . to life and peace" – the cry goes up and follows them until they are but a mere speck on the horizon.

*

Our caravan has shrunk. Less than half of the original group are continuing on to Lisbon, a few in carriages, some in wagons, and the rest on foot. I can tell that the grownups are very concerned about another attack by highwaymen. None of the young adults are allowed to stray from the column, and some of the mothers are keeping their daughters in the carriages, taking example from Mere. The only thing the other mothers haven't done is tied their daughters' hair up in scarves.

Even Sofia, whose parents are so liberal with her, must stay in her carriage most of the time and is only allowed out for her toilet. We meet up at the riverbed each evening and try to catch up on "caravan news." The problem is that with everyone staying in, there is nothing to report.

We have been making good time these last few days, and are hoping to reach our destination next week. The countryside is dotted with farmhouses and vineyards, and that makes buying food supplies much easier. The peasants are friendly, and aren't trying to convert us at every stop. Pere says that King João II of Portugal is very kind to his Jews, thus his subjects take his example, and we have a bright future to look forward to. Mere seems to have a more pessimistic view, and says that she hopes the "Spanish wind" will not blow toward us.

"I'm tired, and I can't face more expulsion, and more autos-da-fé. I hope you are right, Salomon, and we will find refuge here with this king.

"I think the time has come to speak to Freya about being seen in public. Freya, you wonder why we insist on you covering your hair. You and I both have a very special hair color that some people call 'spun gold.' Mine is always covered, as I am a married woman, but your hair attracts a lot of attention. You don't realize it, as for the past years, you have led a very protected life, but 'spun gold' is so rare here in Spain and Portugal that people will kidnap women with this hair color, just to make a king's ransom selling them as slaves on the African coast or in Istanbul to the Sultan. You must always be careful to keep your hair covered."

So now I've finally learned what all the fuss is about. I am aware that my hair is light while everyone else's is dark or even black as coal, but I didn't realize up until now what the danger was about. I am thankful that my parents are treating me as an adult and confiding in me. I promise to be vigilant and never let my hair be seen, and am pleased to see the relief on their faces.

Pere's in a very good mood. "Another twenty-four hours and we should be at the entrance to Lisbon. Then all of this will be behind us, and we can start anew."

Pere, up earlier than usual, is out helping some of the others harness their horses so that we get on the road in time. There are many more wagons on the road all traveling to the big city; merchants with all kinds of goods, farmers with their produce, ranchers with livestock. Mere is more concerned than ever that I stay inside, and has agreed to let Sofia travel the rest of the way with us. I'm happy for this time with her, and we promise each other that no matter how far apart our homes will be, we'll stay in touch. If all goes as planned, we should be at our destination by midday tomorrow, and Mere unwraps some precious dried apricots that Sofia and I share in celebration and in anticipation. We all hunker down for the night, yet I'm not sure that any of us will sleep, the excitement is so palpable.

I wake up to a blazing sun, and the carriage is already underway.

How can that have happened? I couldn't fall asleep last night, tossing and turning. Sofia is chattering away with Mere, and looking out of the window, I'm amazed at how many people are on the move. It takes me a couple of minutes to get myself presentable, and before I can sit down again, a cry goes up outside. Men and women cheering, shouting, and dancing, hugging and crying; on the western horizon, drenched in golden light, the city of Lisbon, with a sapphire sea shimmering at its edge. We've arrived, Lisbon.

Chapter 10

*S*LOWLY, ONE BY ONE, OUR WEARY CARAVAN ENTERS
the city. Pere stops our carriage, descends, and in a voice so
powerful as to catch the attention of all the travelers, in-
tones the blessing for safe arrival:

*Barukh ata Hashem, Elokeinu Melekh ha-olam, Ha-gomel la-
hayavim tovot shegmalani kol tov.*

"Blessed are You, Lord our G-d, King of the Universe, Who be-
stows good things on the unworthy, and has bestowed on me every
goodness."

We are all rushing around, saying our farewells, and promising
to keep in touch. Everyone is anxious to get going and find their
new home. Pere is back in the driver's seat and checking the scrap
where he's written the street name of our new home. It's Rosário 12,
a house on the square. After asking some passers by, we are directed
to a small lane that will lead out onto the square. It's not so easy
manoeuvring our carriage through the narrow streets, especially
with "Red" still attached to the back fender. She is up to her antics
again and I hear laughter following us as we slowly thread our way
along. As we pass through the Alfama, Pere tells me that it is a
mainly Jewish neigborhood, and we see many of our fellow travellers unpacking their possesions.

I'm speechless. Pere has just pulled into the square and stopped
in front of a magnificent house. Could this be our new home? It
looks like a mini-palace, and it looks like we are expected, because
there are servants rushing about, unloading the carriage, and usher-
ing us in. I'm not disappointed with the interior either. The house
is lavishly furnished, and very bright. The colors are magnificent. I

wonder if it has anything to do with the fact that Lisbon is a harbor city, and a crossroad for many trade routes.

I'm shown to my room, which is more like an apartment on its own, with a bed fit for a king and large enough for a dozen people. Mere is in the doorway watching my reaction, and taking great pleasure in my glee. Her rooms are just opposite mine, larger and more palacial, much more. In my excitement, I've forgotten Pere, who is still outside seeing to everything.

I find him on the front drive, trying to coax Red to follow one of the men servants. She's having none of it, and is refusing to budge. I whisper in her ear, and in response, she swipes me with her tail and I almost lose my footing. In no uncertain terms, I grab her halter and lead her off to the back of the house and the stables. I reprimand her, I threaten her – I implore her to cooperate lest Pere sell her. I think she finally understands, as she licks my hand and the piece of sugar I'm bribing her with. I hardly leave the stables behind when I see a very impressive carriage pulling up to the house. I know it's carrying someone important, as there is a royal emblem on the door. My curiosity is getting the better of me, so I wait at the side to see who our visitor is. Pere is at attention as an elderly gentleman exits the carriage and mounts the few steps leading to the entrance doors. His cloak is shimmering in the sunshine, and I can't remember ever seeing this color on anyone. He is also wearing a cap in the same color, trimmed with fur. It not red, it's lighter, and brighter if that's at all possible. I'll have to see if Mere knows what it is. Pere is bowing to this man – and is receiving a bow in return – before showing him into the house and retiring to the library.

They've closed the door and there is no way I can hear what they are saying. I hover in the entrance and am rewarded a few minutes later when the door swings open; the man is ready to leave. Pere, seeing me, stops to introduce me: "Your highness, may I introduce my daughter, Freya." I curtsey, and it's at the tip of my tongue to inquire of the man what the color of his coat is, but I see Pere's raised eyebrow as he shows him out, and think better of it.

"That was His Highness, Marquis de Tordesillas, the prime minister. He's come on the bidding of the King to invite me to be Finance Minister for the Kingdom. Don Abarbanel told me he would do all he could for me, being so well connected to the Portuguese Throne, but being offered the post of Finance Minister is beyond my wildest dream. I'm to present myself at the Royal Palace tomorrow, when I'll be presented to the king."

Mere and I stand in stunned silence, both of us speechless, when hearing this overwhelming news. The silence doesn't last for more than a minute, and then we are jumping, laughing, and crying from excitement. We are making such a noise that even the servants come in to see what all the fuss is about.

Dare I be so happy? I think about Manu, and all those people that died on the road. I think about all our friends from Toledo, the ones that disappeared without a trace, and those that were sent across the seas to an unknown destiny. I'm frightened to be so happy, yet at the same time, so grateful, and I must remember to have special concentration and mindset when I say the Shema.

*

Pere is off to the Royal Palace, and Mere and I are going to explore the neighborhood. I'm very anxious to find Sofia's house, and we set off down the lanes heading for her address on Rua Jidiaria. Pere has made sure that we are accompanied by one of the male servants so that instructions aren't a problem and we can't get lost. We pass the Rua da Alfândega, where the Great Synagogue is located, and marvel at it's impressive architecture. I'm looking forward to exploring when I accompany Pere on Shabbat.

We arrive at Sofia's house, which is right behind the street of the Synagogue, and not ten minutes from our own home. She and her mother are both so excited to see us. We are invited in for a cup of hot chocolate and while the two mothers settle themselves into the salon, Sofia and I go upstairs to check out her room. It's very cozy, and the window opens out to the courtyard, which is ablaze with the most colorful and fragrant flowers imaginable. Her trunks have been unpacked and her wardrobe is stuffed to capacity with all her clothes. Being as her father is a textile merchant, everything is top quality. From the corner of my eye, I catch a chemise in that same color as what the Prime Minister had on yesterday.

"Sofia, this is amazing. I've only ever seen this color once before, and that was yesterday, on a visitor to our home. What is this color?"

"It's fuchsia, new from the Far East, and only available in the finest silk. My father had a small remnant, and made this chemise for me."

"Well, Sofia, you are in good company, as the other fortunate person to own a garment in that fuchsia is none other than the Prime Minister."

"Was he the visitor to your home? Oh my, I didn't realize that your father is such an important person. He seems so 'regular' and not self-aware."

Doña Selena is asking us to come down to the salon, as the chocolate is getting cold. The two mothers are already planning a sortie to the dressmaker's for tomorrow. Sofia's father, Don Simon Pinto, has all the necessary contacts, being that this is his specialty – supplying the upper classes and royalty with the finest fabrics – and the top tailors and seamstresses have already been knocking down their door.

I'm especially pleased that we'll be seeing a seamstress tomorrow, as Mere has been promising me special 'caps' to replace the scarves I'm wearing. I'm going to dream, and dream about a 'fuchsia' cap all night.

Chapter 11

ROSH HASHANAH, AND THE HOUSE IS A BEEHIVE OF activity. Mere has set the table with what she'd been able to salvage when we left Spain. She's anxious about letting the servants handle all of the very fragile items, and has been busy since early morning doing everything by herself. She's dressed the table with some of her finest linens and silver, and delicate hand-painted porcelain plates. I am given the job of folding the serviettes and putting them at every place. Below level, the cooks have been working hard in the kitchen preparing the most delicious foods – all the traditional goodies: the sweet carrots, the head of lamb, the fish in jelly sauce, and the different spices mingling in the air. I am looking forward to tonight's meal.

I have bittersweet memories of our Holydays in Toledo, shared with family and friends. Those were special days and no expense was spared. Mere set a table fit for a king, we were never less than twenty people, and every meal was more interesting than the next. Rabbinical scholars, men of science, musicians, and artists, Pere and Mere knew them all, and these people always seemed happy to share our table. It was a special time, one I always looked forward to.

It looks to me as though Pere, too, has been reminiscing, as he's invited some of the neighbors to come and enjoy our New Year with us. Just the three of us sitting around a feast table would have been very sad, indeed. Sofia's parents are sharing their meal with neighbors, so they have declined our invitation, but have promised to join us for a meal on Succot.

Mere has just finished lighting the candles when the first guests arrive. They are Doña Bella Azmira and her little girl, Ziva. I've fallen in love. Ziva is the most beautiful person I've ever seen. Doña

Bella tells us that she is four years old, with the happiest disposition, but extremely curious. She can't be left alone for a minute without getting into some kind of mischief. I am mesmerized; her skin is aglow and she has the largest violet eyes I have ever seen, framed by miles and miles of lashes. Her nose, a perfect length, and her teeth are shimmering pearls. Mere tells me to stop staring and take Ziva out into the garden as long as the daylight lasts.

Doña Bella cautions me to keep a watchful eye on her. We've hardly been outside for ten minutes, but Ziva is not very interested in remaining there, and is much more curious to see what's happening inside, so back we go. The next guests arrive together: Doña Graciella, with her daughter, and Doña Mona. I've met Doña Mona last week, when she came over to warm our house with a cake from her kitchen. She intimidates me. She has these very tight lips, and measures me from head to toe through squinting eyes. She also speaks in monosyllables, and hardly moves those lips. I was happy to escape her company last week after only a brief introduction and a few polite minutes serving Mere and her the hot, spiced mead, and I catch Mere's eye now, trying to make her understand that I do not wish to sit anywhere near Doña Mona.

Doña Graciella is accompanied by her daughter, Syma, who will be getting married in a few months. She's lovely, but very quiet and hasn't said more than a few words in greeting. Listening to Doña Graciella, I can understand why Syma is so reticent. So far, none of the other ladies has had the opportunity to get a word into the conversation; Doña Graciella has a monopoly when it comes to talking. I'm just about to tune out when I catch Doña Bella's eye and we both have to choke down our mirth; we silently agree that Doña Graciella is a chatterbox.

The menfolk arrive home from the Synagogue and there is a round of New Year's wishes. Pere is with Don Jose Azmira, Ziva's father, and right behind Don Samo Habib – Doña Mona's husband, with their son, Leon – and Don Isaac Aboab – Doña Graciella's husband, and father of Syma. Once all the introductions are made, we proceed to the dining salon.

Mere, I love you! You caught on and have seated me between Ziva and Syma. I can relax for the rest of the evening. That's what I thought; I didn't take into consideration that Doña Mona would be sitting directly opposite me and staring at every bite I take. I've lost my appetite and can hardly make conversation with Syma. Ziva is adorable and I think she is sensing my distress, as she keeps poking me and making funny faces. Syma whispers something to me and I bend over to catch the words. "I have been admiring your cap all evening. I'll be needing something to cover my hair once I'm married, and I was wondering if you could tell me where to get them."

"I'd be happy to go with you and show you where to order these caps. Exactly when is it that you are getting married?"

"The wedding is scheduled for the week before Passover, that's in close to six months. It is also a week before my fourteenth birthday." I'm so surprised to hear her age. She's thirteen, and already engaged to be married. I never imagined that Syma was just a year older than I am. She seems much, much older. I've got so many questions for her, but now is not the time, nor the place – especially with Doña Mona's beady eyes watching me like a hawk. I bet she's an expert at lip-reading, and I've seen her concentrating on my conversation with Syma. I invite Syma to come over after the Chag and we'll organize a shopping day.

Dessert is being passed around, and in spite of Doña Mona, I take a serious helping. Dessert is a candied fruit tower that Mere has prepared in honor of Rosh Hashanah. It's made of the new-harvest fruits, candied in a honey syrup, and assembled in a tower. I'm not the only one indulging myself, and I notice that even Doña Mona is enjoying her portion.

Pere leads the guests in the Bircat Hamozon, and at its conclusion, our guests rise to leave. I say a general goodbye to the assemblage, hug little Ziva, whisper to Syma that she stays in touch, and make a quick exit. There is something about Doña Mona that raises the hair at the back of my neck.

I'm up early the next morning and leave for Rua da Alfândegand and the Great Synagogue together with Pere and Mere. Pere has purchased seats, but it is advisable to come on time as to make sure to have the place. The inside is grandiose, with a double-tiered balcony for the women, and intricate stained-glass windows.

Mere tells me that the building was built with Moorish influence, and is unique in the world. I'm happy we've come this early, as the seats are rapidly being filled and I wouldn't want to have to stand the entire time. Sofia is also here with her mother; they are seated on the opposite side of the balcony, and I wave to her. The chazzan is on a mini-balcony at the front, and is surrounded by his choir. From the moment he starts until the moment he stops, three hours later, there is not a sound to be heard. The entire congregation is mesmerized by the delivery, and most certainly by the prayers themselves. Many of those present have had some trauma and loss, and it is the most precipitous moment to reflect on G-d's charity and His kindness.

Leaving the Synagogue becomes a hassle, as everyone is trying to exit at once. I get separated from Mere on the staircase, but I'm sure I'll find her and Pere outside. I'm almost down the stairs when I feel someone pulling my arm. I'm so sure it's Mere, I turn with a smile, to be confronted by Doña Mona. I try to keep my smile plastered on my face, but I'm not sure I'm succeeding. "Freya, dear, won't you be so kind as to help me outside." How can I refuse, so I crook my arm, let her hold on, and lead her outside. My worst fears are coming true; she's not leaving go of my arm and is steering me head-on toward her husband and son, Don Samo and Leon.

"Samo, Leon, look how Freya has rescued me from the stampede. Imagine surviving the 'running of the bulls,' just to be trampled coming out of the Synagogue." I think this is where Doña Mona wants me to laugh, and behave all giddy, but I am less than happy to have been manipulated into this situation. I am starting to think she wants me to be friends with Leon. I shudder at the thought. At the verge of panic, I search the crowd and see Mere and Pere bearing down on me. I've never been as happy to see them as I am now.

"Freya, we got separated, but I wasn't too worried, knowing you couldn't be that far behind me. Thank you Doña Mona for keeping an eye on our dear daughter until we caught up with her."

Mere, the heroine, who's saved me from the highwaymen, has now saved me from Doña Mona.

Chapter 12

FOR THE PAST FEW WEEKS, SYMA HAS BEEN A REGular visitor to our home, and we've become good friends. Last week we were out getting her some nice caps for her hair, and today, Sofia's father lets us browse through his wares. Syma has found a wonderful fabric for her wedding dress; it's a pale blue silk with tiny pearls and silver threads forming a cornflower pattern. Sofia cajoles Don Simon into giving Syma a bolt of fine gauze as a gift. It's the perfect material for a veil and Syma is ever so grateful. I've invited the girls back to the house for hot mead and some cinnamon cookies. We arrive home to lots of laughter coming from the salon.

Mere has formed her own attachments and has practically adopted Doña Bella as a younger sister, and with her, little Ziva, whom everyone adores.

"Ziva, come join us in the garden for chocolate and cookies." She zips past so quickly in her rush to get out, she's but a blur as we rush out after her.

"Why don't you take me out with you when you go with Syma and Sofia?" Very precocious, our little Ziva, and not a bit shy. We promise to take her with us on our next outing. Pere is home early today, and with the weather so mild, Mere is serving our meal out on the terrace overlooking the gardens. Pere is very happy at court, even though he is expected to be there long hours. He's explained to me how interesting his position is, advising King João II on his foreign trade and weapon-making.

This is an expertise that many Spanish Jews acquired, and Pere, as advisor to Queen Isabella and King Ferdinand, is very knowledgeable. He's helping the king set up a munitions-and-arms factory, and many of the Jewish craftsmen that arrived in Lisbon with us are employed there. I can tell that Pere has settled in well, as he reinstated his evening study sessions at home, with the Rabbi and a small group of men. Sometimes they come along with their wives, and that's nice for Mere, too.

While the men sequester themselves in the library, the women chat and have drinks in the salon. It's like old times.

*

Ziva's come crashing into my bedroom, jumped on the bed, and started shaking me awake. The sun is streaming in through the window, and I feel like toast under the down covers. Ziva is not letting up, pouncing up and down on me until I am fully awake and sitting.

"Freya, you have to come down and see what I have." That means leaving my warm bed – and here I fancied a lazy morning.

"Ziva, why don't you just bring whatever it is upstairs – and who brought you over anyway?" Ziva is giggling away, tugging at my hand and doesn't stop until I'm out of bed, wrapped in my morning robe, cap on my head, and being led downstairs by this very persistent young lady. "So what is it you want to show me?"

She leads me to the front door, which I open, and on the drive in front of our house is Ziva's father with a pony and a small sidecar attached. Ziva is jumping up and down, "What do you think Freya, isn't this the best Chanukah present? Now you see why I couldn't bring it upstairs for you to see." The child is absolutely ecstatic.

"Indeed, Ziva, you are one lucky young lady. And if you have just a little bit of patience, I'm going to quickly get dressed, and when I come down, I'll be happy to accompany you on a walk."

Since our first meeting on Rosh Hashana, my friendship with Syma has cemented. She's flowered from the once-shy girl into a bubbly bride-to-be, and together with Sofia, we do everything as a threesome. Pere is insisting that I continue my education, and it's worked out so well, as Sofia and Syma are both studying with me. The adults have hired a Talmudic student to give us lessons twice a week, and Doña Maria, a Portuguese teacher, to instruct us in language, music, and handwork. Sofia likes to imitate Doña Maria's walk; she glides into a room like a swan. I've seen Sofia's imitations before, but she has both Syma and me beside our selves laughing when she does her Doña Maria stroll.

Being that it's Chanukah, our neighborhood has come alive. The Great Synagogue has a fête every evening, and together with the candle-lighting ceremony, it attracts most of the Jewish families of Lisbon. I've helped the Rabbi's wife set up a children's table with sweets and other delights, and the adults are kept happy with warm wine and cakes. The week has flown by, and we are just leaving the Synagogue after the last candle-lighting when . . .

I still don't understand how this happened.

We were all milling around outside the Synagogue when we become aware of a great noise and tremble coming in our direction. Turning, we realize that a group of horsemen and wagons is racing down Rua da Alfândega, coming toward the Synagogue at high speed. We all clamor to press ourselves close to the buildings when I see Ziva walking straight into the path of the oncoming horses. I'm frozen in terror, I hear shrieks and screams, I see lots of flying dust, more screams, and then it's all over. The horses and wagons have disappeared down the lane, and in their wake, have left people in the street shouting and crying.

I can't see clearly, but I'm sure Ziva has been trampled to death. Someone is shouting for a doctor, and the circle that has formed around her is so tight, I can't see a thing. Luckily, Dr. Barzini was at the celebration, and as he steps forward, the crowd parts to let him through. I step in right behind him and make my way to where Ziva is lying in middle of the street. Lying in middle of the street, in a pool of blood . . . it's not Ziva, it's Mere. I start shrieking, and want to run to her, but I'm being held back by very strong hands. "Please, please let me go to Mere, please." After that everything is a blank.

*

When a family member dies, the custom is to stay at home and mourn for seven days. It is called the "shiva." We never did mourn Manu, and now we mourn both him and Mere. I don't know if I could have survived this week without Syma and Sofia. I still can't come to terms with this tragedy. Pere tells me that Mere saw the danger Ziva was in, and before anyone else could react, she stepped right into the path of the oncoming horses, plucked Ziva to safety, yet couldn't escape in time herself. The whole episode was but mere seconds, and Mere was the only one not frozen into inaction.

Doña Bella comes to see me every day and can't stop crying. Doña Mona comes every day with some cakes, and sits with me too.

She makes my skin crawl, the way she just sits around, stares at me with her little eyes and pinched mouth. If not for Syma and Sofia, I probably would have said something very nasty to her. Today is the last day of shiva, and as Doña Mona rises to leave, she tells me that Leon would like to console me. She brings him into the salon, where I'm sitting on a low stool, and prods him toward me. I am forced to look up into his face as he says the consolation blessing: *"May the Almighty console you, along with all mourners of Zion, and Jerusalem."*

I can't make out if he's looking at me, as his eyes cross and focus on different spots. His skin is pockmarked and oozing pus, and he is probably as short as he is wide. I shake my head in acknowledgment. There are more men who have come into the salon to console me and he is obliged to step aside and make place for the others. My heart is breaking as Pere beckons me out of the stool and leads me out of the house. "We must walk around the square in a circle and then return home, at which time you must remove your rent dress."

"Freya, you must believe me, Mere is at peace."

Chapter 13

*M*ERE IS AT PEACE. IF ONLY I CAN BELIEVE THAT. The nightmare of that Chanukah evening keeps haunting me; how everyone was having such a festive time, and in the blink of an eye, my dear Mere's life was extinguished. I pray that her selfless act has brought her merit in the celestial court. I pray that she is together with Manu in a very good place. I pray that Pere will smile again. I pray that tragedy like this will never happen to anyone, ever.

Pere is at the court for long hours every day, and I have taken over the responsibility of managing the household. Syma is at hand to help me with the staff and the shopping, while Sofia, ever the comedienne, lifts my spirits with her antics. I bless Pere every day for having had the foresight to organize lessons. Just the fact that Syma and Sofia come to the house every day cheers my spirit. Such loyal friends, how could I survive without the two of them.

What started out as a joke between the three of us isn't funny anymore. Doña Mona has taken to coming around on a daily basis with prepared food of one kind or another. On some days it will be soup, at other times a stew, and then it might be a dessert. She usually shows up just as our lesson is finished, and my friends have taken to raising their eyebrows and teasing me. Sofia does an excellent imitation of Doña Mona's 'sour expressions' and it takes all my willpower not to burst out laughing when I see her in person. However . . . it's starting to be obvious that Doña Mona has her eye on me, albeit, a little beady one. I've seen Leon again at the Synagogue and I am not interested. I'm not interested in him, and I am not interested in his mother.

Pere is back early from court today, and I am surprised to see him. "Are you feeling well, Pere?" He has a very troubled look on his face, the same kind of expression he wore when we fled Toledo.

"I'm fine, Freya, just a little tired, and I thought it would be nice to spend some time with you. Would you like to go for a drive with me?"

"Oh Pere! I'll be down in two minutes; I'd love to go for a drive with you." I'm tripping over myself running up the stairs trying to get ready in the "two minutes" as promised, so as not to keep Pere waiting. It's a real juggling act – the cape, the boots, the gloves, don't forget the cap . . .

Rushing downstairs, I practically run head-on into Doña Mona. The Greek bearing gifts, she has her arms extended toward me, holding a basket laden with the most exotic fruits.

"It's almost Tu B'Shvat, the new year's festival of the trees, and I thought you might enjoy some of these." She practically thrusts the basket into my hands, turns to Pere, and asks if she can have a few private words with him. Pere, ever the gentleman, shows Doña Mona into the study and closes the door, leaving it open a split. I am so tempted to tiptoe over and hear what the conversation is about, and it would be so easy to do so, as I don't have to worry that Luiza will drag me off.

Luiza . . . sometimes I wonder how she is faring in Toledo. I will have to control my "bad inclinations" and take this basket into the kitchen. I will also console myself with a cup of hot chocolate while I'm down here. I don't have too long to wait before Pere is down in the kitchen looking for me.

"Freya, I'm ready for that drive, how about you? And I'd like to take the break, so bring along a parasol." The break is the open carriage, which Pere rarely lets the women use. I am flattered that Pere is willing to take me out in it, and quickly get my parasol.

It's the perfect weather for a sortie in an open break: sunny, yet not windy. We drive in the direction of the port, through narrow, sloped streets. As we near the waterfront, the buildings are shabbier and more crowded, and the seasalt and fish smell is becoming over-whelming. Pere has been very quiet since we've started out and I'm sure it has something to do with Doña Mona. I try to distract Pere with my chatter, but I'm not very successful. Pere stops the break on a rise overlooking the harbor, pulling over to the side. What a wonderful sight – dozens of caravels, bobbing up and down in the water, their sails billowing in the wind. Dozens of men and donkeys hauling merchandise to and from the vessels, some leaving, some arriving. What a bustle.

Pere's attention is caught by some unusual activity. It looks like hundreds of children are being marched toward one of the caravels, and being herded on board. "Freya, I need a closer look. I want you to crouch down as far as you can in the seat, and cover as much as yourself as possible under your parasol." I've barely enough time to do as instructed when Pere whips the horses into action and guides them downward, toward the boats.

There's lots of noise on the waterfront, men shouting instructions back and forth, but there is a background noise of weeping children. We are almost at the spot where the children are being boarded onto the boats when our break is stopped by a soldier. "Halt, where do you think you are going?" Pere explains that he is expecting a shipment from the East and has come to see if the boat has docked.

The soldier informs him that this is an exceptional cargo and this section of the dock is off-limits. Pere is trying to inch his way closer, but the soldier blocks our way, lifts his sword, and tells us to go no further.

On the entire drive home, Pere is very silent, and very worried. I haven't seen him this unsettled since Mere's passing. On arriving home, Pere sets me down, escorts me to the front entrance, and tells me that he has to leave but hopes to be home in time for dinner. I assure him that I'll be fine, give him a peck on the cheek, which brings a smile to his lips, and wave goodbye. I ease the front door open and am confronted by Doña Mona, standing in the entrance hall. The maid is hovering and whispers that she told Doña that the master and Freya were out on a drive, but she insisted on waiting.

"So here you are, you little 'mestiço,' not good enough for my son, are you. My wonderful son, Leon, who is a descendent from the purest Jerusalemites. Who do you think you are, and where do you think you come from? And Ha! Who do you think will want you?"

The door is still vibrating on its hinges as she slams out of the house, but thank G-d, she's gone. What did she mean by 'mestico,' and what brought on this rage?

I'm still shaking from her onslaught, but I'm happy she's left and I think she's not contemplating coming back. As I head upstairs to change into something comfortable, it comes to me in a flash. Mestico is a half-breed. Why is she calling me a half-breed?

I've had dinner on my own, and Pere is still not back. I'm starting to get worried, but there is not much I can do. All thought of Doña Mona is forgotten as I pace in the entrance hall, waiting for the break that will bring Pere home. It's long past midnight when I finally hear the hooves and wheels against the cobblestones. I'm still holding my breath when Pere descends. In the few hours he's been out, he has aged years. He takes me by the hand, leads me into the house. "Freya, there is much to talk about, but it will have to wait for morning. Sleep tight, my dear."

Pere hasn't given me a chance to tell him about the episode this afternoon, nor to question him about where he was the entire evening. Without discussion, I've been sent to bed. I'm almost sure I've heard the rumblings of carriages and the voices of men the night through.

*

I'm not sure if I've slept more than an hour or two, and I must find Pere. Yesterday's contretemps with Doña Mona has left me shaken, as have all the goings-on last night. I'm sure something's up, and I won't be put off. I'm not a child anymore. There's certainly something going on, and just as I've arrived at the library doors, they fly open and out comes the Marquis de Tordesillas, the prime minister. He doesn't even stop to acknowledge me, just rushes out in a fury. Pere is one step behind him and he stops in his tracks when he sees me.

"Freya, how much of what was said did you overhear?"

In a small whisper, I admit, "Nothing, Pere."

"Freya, I want you to go upstairs and pack your trunks for a journey. We will not be returning, so pack everything you don't want to miss." I'm glued to the floor, and speechless. "Come on, young lady, I've seen how you can move; now is the moment for quick action."

Rushing upstairs, I don't know what to pack first. I throw open the wardrobes and am amazed at how many dresses and accessories I've amased in the past months.

How am I going to choose what to take and what to leave behind? I'm so engrossed in the job, I don't realize that Syma and Sofia are in the open doorway staring at me.

"What's happening Freya?" Syma, the older of the two has definitely bloomed since that first Rosh Hashanah dinner we celebrated together. "I'm not very sure, so I'm hesitant to speak, but I think we are leaving Portugal for good."

The shock is written on their faces as they race toward me and we all embrace.

How can it be that after the loss of Manu and Mere, I will have to leave my dearest friends behind? We stand there, the three of us clinging to each other and sobbing, when Pere arrives at the doorway, clears his throat, and softly says, "My dear girls, things will shortly be turning ugly for the Jews of Lisbon. I have notified the Rabbi and asked him to send messages around to all congregants 'leave Lisbon and Portugal as quickly as you can.' I witnessed something yesterday that has shaken me to the core. It has affected me more terribly than the auto-da-fé and the Inquisitor's tortures. The authorities have rounded up about 700 Jewish children and they are exiling them to the Island of São Tome. Little ones, not older than nursing children, pulled from their mother's arms. This is a cursed land; what will be . . . what will be?"

Chapter 14

*S*O THIS IS WHAT THEY CALL "SEA ILLNESSES." I haven't eaten for days, not since we left Lisbon Harbor for the open seas, and that, in such haste. Our departure was so rushed, I barely had the chance to say goodbye to all the friends I'd made. I did go out of my way to see Ziva and Doña Bella, who were as heartbroken as I over Pere's decision to leave.

I haven't left my cabin in four days, and Pere says with luck, it should be another six before we arrive at our destination. Pere has insisted that I stay in my cabin, and he's ready to serve me in any way needed. The only thing I want for the moment is my bunk, as even sitting upright has me lurching for a bucket. The smells coming out of the hold aren't helping. Pere tells me that the Portuguese are taking a cargo of pepper and cinnamon to Antwerp, and their strong smell has permeated the ship. Between being "sick" and sneezing, I am a total wreck.

There were some major problems on our first day out. The sailors were threatening the passengers with tossing them overboard if a huge ransom wasn't paid. It took the intervention of Pere, and his promise of gold and silver when, and if, we all reached our destination, to appease the sailors, and they haven't threatened the passengers again. Pere tells me there are sixty other Jewish families on board. Some will be put down in the Kingdom of Britannia, but most will continue on with us to Antwerp.

It's been a week now, and my innards are getting accustomed to the rolling motion of the vessel, if not yet to the spice smell. I'm able to sit up and walk around in the cabin without having the urge to empty my stomach. I've been thinking about the last few days leading up to our departure: Pere being visited at home – by officers of the court; by representatives of the Church; and, on that fateful day, by Minister Marquis de Tordesillas. All the signs were there, the persecution was about to begin.

Another thought is haunting me: my run-in with Doña Mona, her insulting me and her calling me a half-breed. I must speak to Pere; I wonder what she could have meant.

*

We've entered La Manche, that's the straight between France and Britannia, and we'll be arriving at our first stop, Dover, in a few hours. There is a lot of activity on deck, activity I'm unable see; I can only hear it through the open porthole. People sound excited and in a good mood. There is shouting and cheering as the sails are lowered and our vessel slowly enters the harbor. A fine mist of a rain hangs in the air, but that doesn't put a damper on the festive mood. Men, women, and children are rushing about, laden with trunks and carpetbags full of all their worldly possessions, happy to be leaving the ship. I have been saying my daily Psalms and I dedicate today's portions to all those weary travelers, asking for safety and success in their new home.

Pere is at the gangplank, helping the women with their bags, and making sure that all the children get off safely, and only then, once the caravel is again seabound, does he return to the cabin. "Freya, I'm so sorry, it's taken longer than I thought, and I've left you without even asking whether or not you want something to eat."

"Pere, I'm fine, but there is something that is bothering me. That day in Lisbon, when we went to the harbor, Doña Mona came to see me again, after your private conversation. She was livid, said some very nasty things, and called me a "mestico.""

"Oh, my dear, dear Freya; my beautiful, kind, sweet Freya. Don't ever let the words of 'small people' disturb you. Don't ever let their petty meanness make you doubt yourself. You are by no means a mestico; you have royal lineage. Your mother was a decendent of the rabbinic Kalonymus family of Worms, known as Chasdei Ashkenaz. The blond, golden hair was a family trait, and very misunderstood by Sephardic Jews who'd never seen Jewish people with light hair and blue eyes before. Mere, may she be at peace, had a similar situation as a young bride, when she came to Toledo before our marriage.

"Some 'small-minded people' tried to give *her* a hard time then,

· 125 ·

too. She took to covering her hair even before we were wed, and when you were born, she was always careful that your hair not be exposed, so as not to set ignorant tongues wagging. I've always taught you that pride is a bad trait; this, however, is not pride in yourself, but in your heritage. You should never feel less worthy because of your lineage or hair color."

"Oh, Pere, I'm so relieved. I started imagining all kinds of things, that I was a foundling, that my bloodline was a mystery. That someone left me on your doorstep and that . . ." . ."

"Freya, enough with your colorful imagination. You are decendant of Reb Yehudah haChasid, and not a foundling. You are your mother's child, you have the same golden-blond hair. Freya, put this nonsense out of your head; discussion closed."

*

Pere was right, the passage from Britannia to Antwerp isn't as rough as the first part of our journey, and although I'm not allowed out on deck, I do enjoy my view from the porthole. It hasn't taken more than two days and we are now on the River Scheldt.

Rivers are not as stormy as the sea and are easier to navigate. The cry goes up, "Land Ahoy," everyone cheering and all activity outside accelerates; we are coming into Antwerp harbor, end stop. I rush about the cabin making sure that nothing gets left behind, and that my journal is in a secure place. Pere enters the cabin and unlocks the trunk that houses his money coffer. I see him counting out a huge sum of gold and silver coins.

"Freya, you remember when we left Portugal and I'd promised the captain and his crew a certain sum when we arrive safely. They've kept their word, now it's up to me to keep my end of the bargain. Remember, dear child, always keep your word. A promise is a promise, never to be broken."

We are one of the last to leave the ship. Pere wants to make sure all the others are safely on their way before we head out. The bo's'ns are loading our trunks onto a carriage, Pere ushers me quickly inside, and we're off. The carriage heads down very narrow streets lined with houses. The houses are three and four stories tall, and they are topped with roofs in the form of steps. We travel through the streets, but I am hanging out the window. "Pere, do you see what I see? Look at all those people walking along the streets; I've never seen other people with blond, almost white, hair."

"Freya, sit down, you're tipping the carriage and we'll all fall out. Yes, indeed, I see lots of people with very fair hair and light-toned skin, they're extremely different from the Spanish or Portuguese. Your coloring fits right in, and you'll be able to dispense with covering your hair. That should make you happy."

I have mixed emotions. It saddens me that Mere's not here. How she would have marveled at this city, so different, with those narrow houses and strange step roofs. She would have rejoiced with me and shared my excitement at fitting right in, and being allowed the luxury of wearing my hair uncovered. Mere, I miss you so.

The carriage has stopped in front of number 43 Lombardenvest. It's a typically narrow street, and the houses are attached and very alike. Each house has shutters at the windows and an annexed carriage house. The driver has lowered the steps and laid out a wooden plank that extends up to the door, and it's not necessary for me to step into the dust and mud. I watch curiously as the driver is unloading our trunks and they're tied up with heavy rope, which has been looped through a metal ring on a plank that juts out from the highest step of the roof. The trunks are then lifted up until they reach the second story, where a servant is waiting to pull them in through the window. What an invention; someone clever has thought of a way to hoist heavy objects onto the higher floors of a house, and save men the backbreaking job. I am mesmerized until Pere gently prods me into the house.

The house is a smaller version of our homes in Toledo and Lisbon, but the furnishings are much more somber. The floors are made of dark wood shined to a patina, although rugs that are woven in dark colors cover most of the wood. The wall hangings – tapestries on brass rods, and depicting medieval scenes – dominate the two adjoining parlor rooms. They, too, are in muted tones. All the bronze kerosene lamps are burning and I'm quick to understand why. There isn't any sun coming in through the windows. Looking out, the city is grey. The buildings are grey, the sky is grey, the people are grey. I don't see anyone in a colorful frock or cloak. The men are all in black or dark grey, the women not much better, and the children, more of the same. I drop the heavy dark curtains back into place, and ask permission of Pere to explore the bedrooms.

I make my way up the stairs; an ornate banister and portraits line the staircase. Such somber looking people in the paintings: women in white starched hats and collars, always in dark dresses; men in

black cylinder hats with buckles; not one smile to be seen. Hmm
. . . very different from the paintings in Spain and Portugal. I get to
the top of the stairs, where there are two rooms. The more imposing
room, Pere's, is toward the back of the house and overlooks the
gardens. By some miracle, the hangings and floor coverings are in
a pale shade of blue and not depressing. I am relieved for Pere, and
even though he doesn't spend lots of time in his room, at least the
little that he does will not be in dreary surroundings.

Now for my room, and it's bad news. The room itself is large,
and facing the street, but everything is covered in a color I can only
describe as "mouse."

Mouse-colored walls, mouse-colored floors, mouse-colored bedclothes and draperies. This is not good and I can't imagine the person that decorated this room, certainly someone very sad or smitten
with colorblindness. I'll have to make this my first project, and it's
something I look forward to.

Pere is calling me to come down, and I arrive at the bottom of the
stairs to see Pere in conversation with the largest woman I've ever
seen. It takes all my power not to stare at her girth, so I force my
eyes to her face. That is when I really stare. She has the kindest eyes
I've ever seen, and the warmest smile. "This is Mevrouw Sneiders,
and she will be running our household," Pere informs me.

"Just call me Essi, my dear, and I am totally at your service. I will
need a list of your favorite foods, and instructions concerning any
special requirements."

I think I am going to be able to adjust very nicely to life in
Antwerp.

Chapter 15

SSI IS THE BEST THING THAT COULD HAVE HAPPENED to us. She is wise, and loving, and so jovial she has me wanting to spend all my time in the kitchen with her. We are lucky that she speaks Ladino, and she has taken to tossing some Dutch words into the conversation, so as to make learning this new language a game. We laugh over my pronunciation; Dutch sounds come from the back of the throat, and I haven't been able to master it yet. Essi assures me that my being proficient in German will help me understand Dutch and my fluency in Lashon HaKodesh helps in getting the sounds right. For the moment, I'm still struggling.

Pere is out most days trying to connect with some business people. Trading is prohibited to the Jews in Antwerp, and it is trading that is so flourishing here. Antwerp is the most prosperous city in Europe, and merchants from far and wide come to this city to do business. As Jews may not trade, they have gone into the business of lending money. This, too, is prospering, and Pere is trying to get a foothold into it. Most lending business is done out of a building on the Jodenstraat, which they have named for the Jews, and Pere spends a great part of his days there.

I have begun taking walks to the center of town with Essi. It's some experience, as people just turn to stare at her size, and are rude enough to laugh in her face. Essi takes it in stride and just laughs along. Today we are off to the Grote Markt, which is the main market square, crowded with vendors and buyers. I have very specific items in mind; I am looking for rugs and fabrics to redecorate my room.

We come across the perfect rug, an intricate pattern from the Ottoman Empire, birds and flowers in pastels and vivid blues. Essi, so amazing, haggles down the price by half. The rest is easy, and we find the right fabric for bedclothes, draperies, and wall hangings in no time. Essi makes sure that all the vendors will bring the goods home, at which time they will receive their payments. The excitement magnifies as Essi sends out for the carpenter and the seamstress, who will be responsible for transforming the room with the new materials. The carpenter agrees to come in tomorrow with his three apprentices and complete the work in one day. The bedclothes and draperies aren't a problem and can also be completed by tomorrow.

Once my room is done, I'm going to start in on the salons, then the stairwell; what with so many vendors at the market, their wonderful and exotic merchandise, I'm going to have my work cut out for me. This should keep me from getting bored, or getting into trouble.

My room is perfect. The walls have been covered with a pale blue silk, as have the bed and the draperies. The vivid blues and greens of the carpet are the finishing touch. The room has come alive, and it feels as though the sun is shining in. Pere, too, is happy with the transformation and has given me carte blanche to refurnish the salons. Essi and I have been to the market quite a few times; it is so accessible from the house, and an interesting way to pass the time. The market is huge, dwarfed by a towering gothic church just behind the square. Many of the buildings in the square have roofs decorated with golden ornaments in the shapes of fish and boats and other sea-related items. So many people come to the market, and from so many different places – I can tell by the way they are dressed, and I can almost always guess where they are from.

The people from the East wear colorful clothing, usually topped by some kind of pelt. Their hats are pointed and fur-trimmed. Of course I recognize the Spanish and Portuguese, and the Britains are recognizable in their dull black coats, but more so by the way they carry themselves. The Italians are short, colorfully dressed, and always laughing. Essi and I have perfected a game where we spot a group, guess from where they hail, slip in right behind them to hear what language they are speaking, to see if we had it right. It's hard not to get caught out at this, as Essi always attracts lots of attention, yet in spite of her being so visible, we manage to enjoy our outings.

The vendors have an exotic array of spices and wares and we've become acquainted with many of the stall owners. We flit from stall to stall and just when I think I've spotted some fine fabric, I dis-cover something even more beautiful at the next stall. Half the fun is going from vendor to vendor and letting them unroll their wares. We finally settle for a warm yellow silk damask. It is the first time ever that I have seen this kind of material; there is a design within the fabric, tone on tone, created by weaving the same thread into a motif in the silk. Essi again sees to it that the merchant gives us the best price, and that the fabrics are sent to the house. The workmen are summoned and the renovation gets underway.

The transformations are a great success. In just a few short the house has taken on new character. The walls have come alive, and the rooms are warm and welcoming; so much so that for the past few weeks, we've had numerous visitors joining us for meals. Pere has made many new friends, and he has always enjoyed sharing his table with people. With Essi in the kitchen, people are clamoring for an invitation. Most evenings Pere entertains twelve to fifteen guests and the universal language at the meals is Ladino, as the Jews from all over speak it.

I am picking up expressions and words in at least five different languages, and sometimes I find myself starting a sentence in one language and ending it in a different one, with still different foreign words thrown in.

Pere always has the most interesting people joining us. This eve-ning, one of our guests will be a portrait painter who has worked for the prince, and for many of the other Habsburgs. Also invited are Mijnheer DeBruin, his wife, and their daughter, Hela.

Mijnheer DeBruin is the leading figure at the money exchange, and probably the most important Jew in Antwerp. I've met Hela when I've gone to the Synagogue, but haven't had the opportunity to get to know her. I'm hoping that this evening will change that, and although I love Essi, I'm in need of some company my own age.

I watch from my bedroom window as the family DeBruin arrive in their carriage. The footmen are in purple velvet livery, and the family, as they exit the carriage, are magnificent in their finery. I put the last touches to my hair and rush down the stairs just in time to be there as they enter our home. I'm thinking how lucky I am that so many people in Antwerp have this light color hair, and I am able to abandon wearing caps. The entire family DeBruin is fair-haired, and Mijnheer DeBruin has an enormous mustache that is almost red in color, as opposed to his blond hair. Hela's hair color is about

the same as mine, but is missing the shine that my hair has. I wonder if it has anything to do with the fact that I grew up in countries
where the sun always shined. Pere has to nudge me, as he's asked me
something and I have been in my own little world thinking about
hair color. "Freya, I asked if you would like to show Hela the house
and the gardens, while we wait for our other guests, and before we
sit down to dinner."

I am more than happy to get Hela on her own; and I guide her
up toward my bedroom. I see relief on her face as I steer her in and
close the door.

"Thanks Freya. I'm nervous about this evening, because your
father has also invited a marriage broker to dinner. Freya, your
mouth is open . . . Freya, please say something."

"I'm stunned. Pere hasn't said anything about a marriage broker
to me. I hope he isn't thinking that I want to get married."

Hela, who I learn is two months older than me, is very excited
about the prospect, albeit a bit nervous. She tells me that it is the
done thing to introduce one's daughter to the brokers when they
become of age. I am surprised that she feels sixteen is "of age," but
Hela assures me that there are fourteen-year-old girls getting betrothed, and sixteen is "very old." Hela just hopes that whoever is
presented to her will not be too old, nor too fat, and will be happy
to stay in Antwerp. I've never even thought about my future in that
way, and am paralyzed into immobility until Hela gives me a shake
and says we should be going down.

All the guests have arrived and Pere is making the introductions.
There are the DeBruins, of course, the artist Albrecht Dürer and
his wife – they are from a place called Nuremburg – then Mijneer
Hagel and his wife – he is a money lender – and finally, Mijnheer
Stooms. It must be Mijnheer Stooms who is the marriage broker, as
I see he homes in on Mijneer DeBruin, and like a dog with a bone,
he isn't letting go of him.

He is a comic-looking man, his graying hair is standing in every
which direction, and he has huge eyebrows that can almost compete
with Mijnheer DeBruin's mustache. He is missing a tooth in front,
and this gives his mouth a lopsided look, almost as though he has
a constant smile. I am relieved to see that when Pere seats us, I am
entirely out of the view of Mijnheer Stooms. This pleases me to no
end, as it proves Pere has no intention on marrying me off right
now, and Mijnher Stooms is here solely to meet Hela.

I've been seated between Mevrouw DeBruin and Frau Dürer. My German has improved over the last year and I am able to hold a decent conversation with Frau Dürer. She tells me how popular her husband's works are in Germany, and how the Royal Family in Antwerp have commissioned his work, thus making it necessary for them to be in Antwerp for the next few years.

Pere is deep in conversation with Herr Dürer, and Mijnheer Stooms still hasn't allowed Mijnheer DeBruin the chance to converse with anyone else at the table. Hela is trying to lip-read what Mijnheer Stooms is saying to her father, and Mijneer Hagel and his wife are innocently enjoying Mevrouw DeBruin's company while relishing the food that Essi is piling on everyone's plate. All in all, it's been a very enjoyable evening for me, watching all the interaction, and having some stimulating conversation with our guests. Hela, on her way out, promises to be in touch, and perhaps we can visit together again soon.

As the last guests leave, Pere asks me to step into the salon again, he has something of importance to tell me. I can't believe that he has plotted to marry me off, even though I did see him speaking with Mijheer Stooms. I bite my lip, and enter the salon; Don't jump to conclusions, I tell myself; let Pere speak first.

"Freya, I have a surprise for you" – Oh no, Pere, please don't say it . . . – "Freya, tomorrow morning you will dress in your finest dress . . ."

"Oh Pere, please don't say that you have gone into a contract with the marriage broker, Please . . ."

Pere begins to laugh uncontrollably, and I don't think this is a laughing matter.

"Freya, my silly, impulsive daughter, tomorrow you are having your portrait painted by non other than Albrecht Dürer."

Chapter 16

A DILEMMA, WHAT AM I GOING TO WEAR FOR THIS portrait? I have probably tried on every dress in my wardrobe, and that at least twice. I've finally whittled it down to either the dress in honey colored silk embroidered with pearls in a lace motif all over the bodice or the deep green silk with the silver thread embroidery all through the skirt in the pattern of vines and grapes. I've never been so undecided and I'm going to have to rely on Essi to help with the final choice.

"Essi, quick, it's an emergency! I'll be posing for Herr Dürer in less than an hour and I can't decide on a dress. I need your opinion right now."

I try on both choices and Essi is pretty sure that the honey colored silk with the pearls is the right one, considering my coloring. She says it does wonders for my hair, and compliments my complexion. Decision made, I am going to have to rush and get dressed if I'm to be on time and not keep the artist waiting. I've decided on small pearl earrings with a matching necklace that were my mother's, and dainty golden slippers. I quickly brush my hair and go downstairs, and am told that the artist has arrived and is in the salon setting up his equipment.

I'm not sure exactly what is expected of me as I enter the salons, but Pere is on hand, and the artist puts me at ease by telling me exactly where to sit, how to pose, and to just relax and think pleasant thoughts. My mind goes back to the party yesterday evening and Hela's restlessness in the presence of matchmaker Mijnheer Stooms. I'm hoping for her sake that whatever suggestion he presents will be someone that is young and handsome. It brings a smile to my lips when I remember how she was trying to read her father's lips.

"Perfect, my dear young lady, just keep smiling like that." I've been so engrossed in my thoughts I hadn't remembered I'm sitting in front of the artist.

Before I know it, it's noontime, and Pere says we'll be stopping for an hour. I'm thankful for that, excuse myself, and go to my room; I need to slip out of my dress and lie down for a bit. This is even more tiring than going to the market.

Essi has brought up a tray with food; I am hungrier than I thought, and I dig in with gusto.

Pere and the artist are studying the canvas, and as they move aside I get to see the work in progress. I can't believe what I see in front of me: I'm looking at myself staring back at me. The artist has only managed to outline the room, the background, and my figure. However, my entire face is completed and it's come alive on the canvas. I'm standing, as in a trance. I can't pull myself away from myself in the portrait. It's really me, and Herr Dürer is a real artist.

He'd like me to sit for another hour, and then he'll return tomorrow and the next, and the next, until he's completed the piece. I'm happy to sit, and it's not too long before the artist dismisses me and starts rinsing off his brushes.

"Fraulein, it's been a pleasure painting you, and within the week, your portrait will be ready."

"And thank you, Herr Dürer; I enjoyed sitting for you very much, and I can't wait to see the finished product."

Back in my room, I'm happy to remove my dress and hang it in the airing wardrobe. It's been a tiring, yet wonderful day, and Pere has made me feel very special. As I prepare for bed, I again thank the Almighty for all these wonderful things that are being bestowed on me. I promise to try and be worthy of it all.

The De Bruin carriage has just pulled up in front of the door and it's Hela, on her own; being shown in. As I head down the stairs, I wonder why she's here. "Freya, I have the most wonderful news, and I just had to share it with someone. You were so sympathetic the other night that I just knew I could come here to speak with you. Papa and Mijnheer Stooms will be traveling to Venice, where there is a large Jewish community. Papa hopes to expand his business and Mijnheer Stooms is hoping to meet some eligible men. Naturally, he will be keeping his eyes open for someone special for me. They won't be gone for more than four weeks, and are both very optimistic at the prospects."

"That's wonderful, Hela. At the very least it gives you a bit of breathing space, and being at the source, your father will have his pick of the best eligible men for you."

"Exactly what I thought. Freya, I'm so excited, will you come out with me? On my way over, I noticed that there are troupes of jugglers this morning at the Grote Markt, and we can also visit the stalls with lace. I'd like to browse because I think that I might need something fine for the near future. Please say you'll come, please, please."

"Hela, your mood is infectious. I'd be happy to join you, but Essi will have to come too. Pere never lets me go out to the Markt on my own."

So here we are, Hela, Essi, and I, having a great time at the Markt. Indeed, the jugglers have attracted lots of attention and there are more people than usual in the square. It's amazing to see so many different peoples, in so many different national costumes. Hela and I start a contest to see who can spot the most unusual person.

Hela wins. She has spotted a man with very yellow skin, his eyes are barely visible through their slits, and his hair is tied in a braid down to his waist. He is wearing a red silk robe with sleeves so wide they almost touch the ground. To compensate for being short, he is wearing shoes on very funny platforms. We are not the only ones to notice this little yellow man, and as he proceeds past the stalls, all business is suspended as everyone watches his progress. One of the stall owners is saying that this little man has come all the way from Peking in the East, and is here to trade some kind of leaves called 'tea.' The stall owner finds this absurd, and begins laughing, "Bringing leaves to Antwerp, and for some kind of strange drink – who's going to buy that?"

We are not really concerned with these 'leaves' and start our search for the lace stalls. Essi has stopped at a stall with the most unusual fabric. The merchant assures us that he has superior lace, and proceeds to unwrap a parcel wherein lies the most delicate piece of lace. As we "oh" and "ah" over how intricate the pattern is, the merchant tells us that this lace is produced in Brugge by a group of nuns in a cloister.

I can't imagine a human hand being able to make something so fine. It is really the work of angels. Hela promises the merchant to return with her mother tomorrow, and we slowly make our way back home. Hela's coachman is still waiting for her, and before she leaves, we set a date for next week.

Pere is waiting for us in the foyer when we enter. "Essi, we will be having unexpected guests this evening, some scholars from Prague. Freya, see if you can give Essi a hand with the cooking. There will be eight of us in total."

I feel so grown up. This is the first time Pere has asked me to do things in the kitchen, and it's a wonderful feeling of his trust and confidence that I am capable of an adult job. Essi, already busy in the kitchen, has all the ingredients out, and I help peel and wash, dice and slice, everything that goes into creating this four-course meal. Once everything is bubbling and simmering, I head upstairs to get ready for our guests. I settle on a lavender silk dress, with matching slippers. It's not one of my finest, but I didn't get any signals from Pere that that would be required of me.

I'm downstairs putting the finishing touches on the table setting when the guests arrive. Six men in total enter the foyer, and Pere extends his hand in the traditional Shalom Alechem. From my place in the salon, I can see that the men are all in very traditional clothing, dark coats and beaver hats, but I can't determine any detail from this distance. Pere enters the room and makes a general introduction to the men that I am his daughter, Freya. He then signals to me to be seated at his right, and the men assume places around the table. This is the first time I'm at a meal where I am the only girl/woman and I feel uncomfortable, until the man opposite me looks me in the eye, and tells me that he has a daughter, Yachet, sixteen years old, back in Prague.

He, Reb Zalman Ganz, continues to tell me that they have been sent here by the great philanthropist Mordechai Maisel to raise funds for the refugees pouring into Prague from Germany, France, and Spain. Antwerp, being the heart of Europe, and its most flourishing city, must surely have Jews wishing to help their brethren. His attention is diverted to one of the men sitting further down on my side; he is regaling Pere with stories of Mordechai Maisel's generosity. My eyes wander down the table and I can only see the men on the opposite side, unless I'm ready to stick my head out and see who is sitting two and three seats away from me on my side. It doesn't seem important enough for me to be so obvious, the men probably all look more or less like Reb Zalman Ganz, and the two

men next to him. From what I'm able to understand – and that is
no mean feat, as the conversation is conducted in a language called
Yiddish, a mixture of German and Hebrew with some Spanish and a
language called Polish all mixed in – the group have found a willing
contributor in Pere, and he has promised them an introduction to
all Jewish homes in Antwerp. The meal ends, and none too soon, I
am the first one to bid everyone good night in the general direction
of the table and make a hasty escape to my room.

*

I've been summoned down to the salon. Essi says that Pere and Herr
Dürer are in the salon, and would like to see me. Could it be that
my portrait is done? I fly into the room, only to be confronted by a
very worried Herr Dürer. He is pacing the floor at such a speed he's
going to wear a hole in the rug. He is so agitated he sputters some
words at me, but he's not to be understood. Pere who's already heard
what he has to say turns to me. "It seems that the Prince Charles
wants to have your portrait. He's seen it at Herr Dürer's studio and
will not settle for another." Pere seems more worried than annoyed,
and has begun pacing in the opposite direction of Herr Dürer. I'm
not so sure what has agitated Pere, but just as I'm about to ask, there
is knocking at the door. Pere seems not to have heard the knocking
and as I'm near the foyer, I open the door.

I don't know what to make of this person standing on the stoop.
He is tall and slim, and must be just a few years older than I am,
and not much darker in coloring. He has a neatly trimmed beard,
and is wearing an exquisite suit of clothing and very fine accessories.
His eyes are sharp, yet gentle, and his lips seem to try to keep from
smiling. I vaguely hear Pere asking from the salon as to who is at
the door.

"Oh, I beg your pardon, I was lost in thought, and didn't mean
to keep you standing outside. Whom, uh, who is it you wish to
see?"

"I'm here to speak with Don Salamon HaLevi. I was here a few
evenings ago with Reb Zalman Ganz, and didn't have the chance to
thank you for being such a gracious hostess. I'm in Antwerp with
Reb Zalman, as my father is one of the bankers working alongside
Mordechai Maisels, and I'm very knowledgeable when it comes to
currency transactions."

Oh yes, now I remember. This young man kept Pere and the rest of the assembled men fascinated with his Talmudic knowledge.

Pere has seen David in the doorway. "Hello, David, nice to see you again. Freya, please show David into the study and I'll be with you shortly." Pere returns to Herr Dürer and I'm left to show David into the study. I ask if he would like some refreshment, and, as he declines, I excuse myself and make a hasty retreat.

Chapter 17

I'M DOWN IN THE STUDY ALONE WITH PERE, WHO, while pacing the room, addresses me: "I was trying to understand what David was telling me about the details of his father's network, but he was in a trance. When he finally did manage to answer my questions, he stammered and sputtered and his words were just gibberish. I think there is something else on his mind, so I've sent him on his way and asked him to return tomorrow, as it's important for me to evaluate the information he has regarding the workings of the Bohemian financial circuit. As for the portrait, Herr Dürer is going to try to stall the prince, and perhaps offer him some other of his fine paintings."

*

David has been in and out of our home these last few days and has made a very good impression on Pere. He is learned in the Talmud, and is very astute in the field of finance. He comes from a fine family, his father is a respected scholar and philanthropist, and his mother keeps busy with charitable works.

David has again appeared, and I am summoned by Pere to the salons. As I enter, David rises to his feet and approaches.

"Freya, I have your father's permission to address you. Will you grant me the honor of courting you?"

I'm incapable of more than nodding my head in agreement. David is interested in me, and I'm speechless. I think I've heard David asking me if I would like to take a drive with him, but I'm not sure I've heard right, and I'm afraid to answer, just in case I've misunderstood. I think I'm having an out-of-body experience, and David is looking at me in a very strange way. Finally, Essi appears holding a tray laden with drinks and desserts. I am happy to have something liquid and a distraction to recoup. I'm less nervous and I coyly tell David, "I'm so sorry, what is it you were saying?"

David turns to Pere, "I thought it might be nice if Freya would accompany me for a drive. It's such a nice and sunny day; we could drive through the park, or along the Scheldt."

*

This has been the best afternoon of my life. David is so kind and humorous, and very intelligent. He is also extremely learned and regales me with stories and parables of our great sages. He tells me all about the history of Antwerp. The city goes back to the third century and was part of the Holy Roman Empire before it became the Duchy of Brabant that it is today. Antwerp is one of the greatest cities in the world, certainly for commerce and art. David has taken me down streets I've never seen and told me facts I've never heard. Not only does he know so much about Antwerp, his knowledge of Bohemia is by far greater.

I've learned that Prince Charles of the Luxembourg dynasty, born in Prague, 1316, became the King of Bohemia. I've learned that Prague is an important commercial center, one of the first stops on the land route to the Far East. I've learned that Prague has a very large Jewish community, and growing daily, as immigrants arrive from many Western countries that have expelled them. David plies me with facts and stories and humorous anecdotes. I'm so disappointed when the carriage finally turns into our street, that a huge sigh escapes my lips.

"Freya, I'm so sorry. I've been going on and on, and I'm afraid I've bored you. Please say I may come again, and I promise not to fill your head with nonsense."

"David, please come again, I've had a wonderful time."

*

David has been coming for the past two weeks, and I haven't been bored for one minute. We've seen most of the sites in Antwerp; we've even had a tour of Herr Dürer's studio. My portrait was sold to the prince, but Herr Dürer has promised to let me sit for another one.

This morning David arrived earlier than usual, and he and Pere are in the study with the door closed. It's unusual that I haven't been summoned, and all sorts of ideas are popping into my head. But if I've learned anything from Pere, it's to face problems head-on, so I'm going to knock on the study door and see what's up.

Pere answers my knock, and beckons me in.

David steps forward, clears his throat. "Freya, I've come here this morning to ask for your hand in marriage. I offer you my heart, and all my worldly possessions. I promise to honor, support, and protect you with my entire being. Marrying me would mean that you'd be leaving everything familiar to you and coming with me to Prague, where I have a position in my father's business.

"I've also come to implore your father to come with us. Men such as he are what we need in our growing Jewish community. His integrity and intelligence will stand him in good stead, and I'm sure his business would flourish there, too.

I turn to Pere, hope in my eyes.

"David is being generous in the extreme by including me in this proposal and, Freya, after the shock and upon reflection, I am happy to accept. I will be most happy to move with both of you to Prague."

I turn toward David, who stands pale and anxious, waiting for a verdict. The smile on my face and the shine in my eyes is enough to transform him.

"Yes, David! Yes, yes, yes, I will be most happy to become your wife, and I'm so happy that Pere is to join us in Prague."

*

My trousseau is complete and Essi has been a magician. I would never have been able to assemble everything in two months without her, let alone find the most beautiful items in all of Antwerp. Hela, too, is engaged to be married. Her betrothed is an Italian, and we've had some wonderful times, she, Essi, and I, doing the rounds of the market stalls and the specialty shops. Pere is very busy concluding all his business, selling our house, and seeing to all the packing.

My wedding dress is draped over a bust in my room. In just a few days, David will be arriving with his family for the wedding and I will be wearing this beautiful dress. Just looking at it takes me back to Lisbon, to a time when Mere was busy seeing to all my clothing. How she would have loved to accompany me under the wedding canopy. I know she will . . . she will be at my side, and in my heart forever.

To my dear best friend, my dear journal.

Tomorrow I wed, and leave for lands unknown with David. Tomorrow is the beginning of a new chapter, but one I will not be writing. You have been my best friend, affording me the luxury of imparting all my deepest thoughts to you. Tomorrow, I become a half to a whole, and David, my husband, will be my confidant. You, dear friend, you have seen me through some very hard times, but the moment has come for me to take on the role of wife. I will always treasure you, I'll keep you safe, but this book is closed. Farewell, dear friend.

· BOOK III ·

Tonya's Story

Chapter 1

*S*OME PEOPLE ARE BORN WITH A SILVER SPOON IN their mouth; some of us are less fortunate.

I was born on the first day of Cheshvan 5393, the twenty-third of October 1634. I was born to tragedy. My mother died giving birth to me, and with her dying breath, she asked to cradle me in her arms. Looking down at me with love shining bright in her eyes, her final words were, "Call her Tonya."

Papa brought the Oma, his mother, and his only remaining family, to live with us and care for me. I was showered with love, and not knowing any better, Oma was my mother.

I was a happy child and lacked for nothing. I remember our little house in Krakow: flowers in the front garden, chickens running loose in the back. Papa was out of the house for most of the day, studying with the other men, and thanks to Oma, the house ran smoothly and I was well taken care of. I still remember the smell of baking bread, which intermingled with other delicious cooking smells, and Oma made sure there was always a treat for me, "Something sweet, for my sweet Tonya's sweet tooth." I wondered why my 'mother' was so much older than everyone else's, but I never questioned her or Papa.

When I was thirteen, Oma passed away in her sleep, and during the shiva, the seven-day mourning period, Papa told me all about how I lost my mother and how Oma took over my care when I was born. He gave me a book, pages of parchment bound in leather and wrapped in a velvet cloth, and said that the Oma specifically left me this legacy; it was something she greatly treasured. I was careful to place the book in a safe place – with my clothing in the wardrobe – to be read at a more opportune moment.

Months passed, and one evening Papa came in, cleared his throat, and said we had to talk. I knew immediately, watching his facial expressions, that he was about to broach a difficult subject.

"My Rebbe has recommended that I remarry. There is a scholar in my group, Reb Nussen, and he has suggested a match with a widow in Nemirov who has a daughter about your age. Letters have been sent, and if this woman is in agreement, we will be moving to Nemirov."

I was thirteen, almost a woman, but the idea shook me. "Papa, I promise I'll try harder to do everything Oma did. I'll be a better cook and bake many more delicacies. I'll mend and clean harder; I'll do anything you tell me." My entreaties didn't sway Papa, who had strict orders from his Rebbe that it wasn't appropriate for such a young man to remain without a wife. Within a short few weeks, the dreaded reply arrived. We were moving to Nemirov.

*

Nemirov, southeast of Lublin, and a much more primitive city. We arrived just before the first snows and stayed in a tavern for the first three days until the wedding took place. The ceremony was on Friday morning, and as I was not allowed to be in attendance at the ceremony, I stayed in the tavern in the care of two of the townswomen. Just before Shabbes, the same two women escorted me to father's new home.

The house was larger than any house I'd ever seen, and Papa was at the door to greet me, alongside him a beaming woman and girl. The woman welcomed me in, kissed me on both cheeks, and introduced me to the girl standing right alongside her. "Tonya, this is your sister, Gina, and from now on, I want you to call me 'Mamusha.'"

Gina is eyeing me, as I her, each of us taking the other's measure. She's a bit taller that me, and much heavier, and where I have thick braids, the color of ripe corn, she has very dull, straggly hair. I learn that she's sixteen, and "Mamusha's" only child.

"Gina, take Tonya to the room she will be occupying, and hurry, there's not so much time left before I have to light the candles." Gina escorts me to the kitchen, and just behind the cooking area, there's a space with a bed and a small chest. "You sleep here, and don't even think about sharing my room." I quickly put my clothes in the drawers, taking special care to put Oma's journal under some of my linen. I return to the rooms at the front, just as "Mamusha" is finishing lighting the candles. Papa wishes us all "gutten Shabbes," puts on his greatcoat, and leaves to Shul.

Mamusha spent the next hour grilling me on Krakow, on Papa's habits, his likes and dislikes, and then telling me exactly what was expected of me. During the week, Panie Dora, a Jewish house-keeper, comes in to help out from seven in the morning until eight in the evening. I'm to be her assistant, and help her with the house-work and cooking. On Shabbes, as Panie Dora isn't working, I'll be responsible for serving the meals and washing the dishes – not this week, of course, but starting on Sunday. Mamusha turns to Gina and says some words in what sounds like a dialect. I soon learn that they are proficient in Ukrainian, and will be using this "code language" whenever they want to say something without my understanding.

*

The weeks, the months fly by, and the only thing that is keeping me sane is Panie Dora. She reminds me so much of Oma – a younger version, of course – and she has become my protector. Gina is be-hind every corner, trying to catch me out at any mistake. Panie Dora has saved me on more than one occasion from Mamusha's wrath by taking the blame for any mishap. I spend most of my days in her company and hardly see Papa. He is out from before dawn with the Chevra Tehillim and returns at night from his learning just in time to wish me a good night.

Something happened today; something terrible, yet wonderful. I went back to my room after my morning tea and found Gina rummaging in my linen. She was holding the wrapped book that Oma bequeathed me, and which had lain hidden and forgotten these past months. "So, Tonya, what's in this secret package, some forbidden treasure?" I tried retrieving the parcel, but Gina, much stronger than I, wouldn't release it. A tug-of-war ensued, and we both managed to pull the velvet apart and drop the book. Gina quickly grabbed it off the floor and opened it up.

Turning the pages, she asked me what was written on them. I told Gina the book was given to me by my grandmother and written in German, a language I can't read nor understand. Losing interest, she dropped the book at my feet and left the room. Dora – she's told me to drop the formality – standing just outside my 'space' in the kitchen, has heard all the commotion. She takes the book from my trembling fingers, and asks if she may look inside. I hand her the book, nod my head in agreement, and try to collect my composure.

"Tonya, this is very interesting. It's a journal written by a young girl in England, a girl called Dina, and continues on with entries written by a girl in Spain called Freya. I speak and read German, and both parts are written in what seems to be 'old German,' so it will take me longer to decipher than the German I'm fluent in. I'll be happy to try, and read it to you, bit by bit every day."

The book is only a quarter full, and with so many empty pages, I've decided to do just as Freya did. I'm going to add my story.

*

Gina is up to her nasty tricks again. While I was serving her lunch today, she deliberately knocked my hand, and the soup spilt all over her dress. Mamusha, having ears for Gina's version only, has sent me to the cellar and I have to remain here until Papa comes home. I'm terrified of dark places, so I stand on the highest step next to the locked door, staring down at little glass eyes darting back and forth. They must be rats, for sure, and I don't know what I'll do if they come up the stairs towards me. Mamusha, allows me out just in time to join the evening meal, but I only receive bread. Gina is sitting opposite me, slurping her soup and smirking. I've been sent to my room before Papa returns.

Mamusha manages it so that I only get to see Papa on Shabbes, and never alone. Papa has suggested more than once that he would like to go out for a stroll sometimes, but Mamusha always manipulates it so that either she or Gina come along. I guess she fears what I would tell Papa, but I wouldn't complain to him; I wouldn't want to cause him any pain.

True to her word, Dora has been reading me Dina's story bit by bit, and translating it. What an adventure, what a sad time for Jews in England, what courage this girl must have had. I look forward to the sessions with Dora, and can't wait to hear about Freya, too. These sessions have become the highlight of my existence.

As time goes by, I've learned to keep out of both Gina and Mamusha's way, suffering their torment in silence. I do it for Papa. He seems content and is blind to what is really going on in the house. It's because Mamusha never disciplines me in Papa's presence and Gina is as sweet as honey when Papa is around.

Papa is in very high spirits. At the Shabbes table, we learn that he has been chosen to accompany his Rebbe to Lublin for the semi-annual gathering of the Council of Four Lands. He patiently explains that this council convenes twice a year to deal with legislative, administrative, judicial, and spiritual matters concerning the Jews of Poland, Russia, Lithuania, and the Ukraine. Rabbinic authorities from far and wide make an effort to attend this conference and share their thoughts, perhaps get some new vision. I smile to Papa, excited for him, less excited for myself. He will be away for three whole weeks and only return a month before Rosh Hashanah. Can I last that long in this house without his protection?

Chapter 2

"*S*TOP YOUR WHINING, IT'S NOT GOING TO HELP; your braids have to come off!"

Mamusha has taken it into her head that the braids are getting in the way of my work, causing me to spill and knock over things, and will just have to be cut off. Intervention by Dora falls on deaf ears, and Mamusha, wielding scissors, commences to chop off my braids. Much as it feels as though she is tearing out my heart, I do not shed a tear. I refuse to give Gina the satisfaction that Mamusha is inflicting terrible pain on me. Closing my eyes, I tell myself that the hair will grow back, thicker and more beautiful.

*

Papa has sent a messenger with a letter that Mamusha reads aloud:

"My dear wife and daughters, Lublin is indescribable; more commerce and many more Rabbinical students, more than I could ever have imagined. The autumn trade fairs bring merchants from far and wide, as does the Council of the Four Lands bring Rabbis and scholars. I feel privileged to be a part of this. We are lucky to have very decent lodgings in the inn run by one of the local Jews. I am sharing the room with only another three students, and the innkeeper's wife has offered to cook our meals for only three zloty. I miss you all very much; however, the Rebbe has decided to extend our stay, and we will only be returning a few days before Rosh Hashanah.

"I am hoping that you are all faring well, and still enjoying the fine weather. Winter will be upon us quickly enough once the Yomim Tovim are over, so make the most of the sunshine.

"My greetings to all of you, Yisroel."

Mamusha is in a rage. It's fortunate that she is venting in the Ukrainian dialect, and Gina, for once, is trying to calm her, rather than incite her, in her usual manner. I am assuming that she is annoyed at Papa for staying away so long. His extending his trip saddens me, too, but I try to hide my feelings. I will not give them the satisfaction to know how disappointed I am.

It's been a week, and I finally get the chance to see my reflection in Mamusha's looking glass. I'm horrified at how I look, but then burst out laughing. Can this funny creature be me? I resemble a plucked chicken, wisps of hair standing in every which direction. Quickly, I leave Mamusha's room, which is off-limits to me; I don't want to be discovered and unleash her wrath. Back in the kitchen, Dora, who is busy at the stove, raises an eyebrow as I plant a kiss on the nape of her neck. "And to what do I owe the pleasure, being given a kiss on a regular Wednesday morning?"

"Dora, I love you for not telling me how comical I look since my haircut; I love you for not laughing at me, and for always standing by my side. I just love you, all those reasons, and no reason at all."

*

I'm busy peeling potatoes in the kitchen in preparation for Rosh Hashanah, when I hear a commotion – Papa is home. Wiping my hands in my apron, I rush into the hall. It is Papa; he's returned, and is laden down with bulging coffers. Seeing me, he drops everything to pick me up in his arms and swing me 'round.

"Papa, I'm too old to be lifted and swung around like that, I'm almost sixteen." Papa quickly sets me down on my feet and stares me in the face. "Where have the days gone? The months, the years? Look at you, you're a young lady. Oh my, what have you done to your hair?"

Before I can utter a word, Mamusha intervenes, rushing Papa to the main room, so that he can be given a warm drink and some sweet delights. I'm left out in the hall, all alone, with so much to say, and nobody to tell it to. It dawns on me; Papa is a victim as much as I am. Saddened by this revelation, I return to the kitchen, and help Dora with the rest of the potatoes.

I've begun taking a break every day while Mamusha and Gina are having their afternoon 'siesta.' Dora has encouraged me to go out a bit for some fresh air, and I have discovered an old apple tree on the rise not far from the back of the house. I can see most of Nemirov from that spot, and it's become my own little oasis. There, the old, gnarled tree affords me shade and also yields delicious apples for an afternoon snack. That's just where I head to now, with my journal in tow. I have to record my feelings before I explode. Of course Mamusha doesn't want me telling Papa my version of why she's cut off my braids. I overheard her saying that I had contacted lice and she was forced to cut my hair before everyone was infested. Papa is sympathetic, hoping that it wasn't too traumatic for her to have to deal with a head full of lice. I am happy to record this, in the hope that one day Papa will read my journal and laugh, together with me, over some of the tragic/comedy situations.

*

Again, Mamusha has struck me where it hurts most. During the Rosh Hashanah meal, Papa has been telling us that this year, 5408, is to be a wonderful year for Jews. We should all be preparing for the Messiah, for, according to the Kabbalists, this is the year he will be coming. Papa suggests keeping some stocks of food, as according to the Zohar, the coming of the Messiah will be preceded by a war, and wartime means hunger. Hearing Papa's rendition of what it will be like for us in the days leading up to the Messiah's arrival, Mamusha had declared she will make her own sacrifice and cut down on the house staff. Before she even utters the name, I know she is referring to Dora. Dora is too expensive, Dora is receiving a large salary, and even though this will bring hardship on Mamusha, she is going to let Dora go.

She has told Dora that her help is no longer needed, and that I am old enough and capable enough to take over Dora's duties. I know this has nothing to do with Papa's announcement, but I am helpless in finding a way to keep Dora on. I'm sure that she is being sent away mainly due to the fact that she is my guardian angel, and Mamusha and Gina are jealous.

Dora leaves just after the Succot holiday, and I am given a list by Mamusha of exactly what my duties are. The cleaning, the washing, the cooking, and then the mending, and Mamausha says that Gina will assist me. Seeing is believing; and so far Gina hasn't lifted a finger to do any of the chores. The only time she gets busy is when Papa is at the Shabbes meal, and she helps serve and clear the table.

Losing the camaraderie of Dora was painful, but I have adjusted to this, too.

*

My hair is looking better, not as chopped off, and I quite like the way the soft curls frame my face. I catch Gina staring at me sometimes, and I try to think of a way to ward off the 'evil eye,' as I'm sure that is what she is giving me. The winter is bitter cold and seems longer than the last. One of my chores is to bring in the water from the well, and this is the job I hate the most. Cracking open the ice and bringing in the freezing water, which inevitably sloshes over my shoes, is really a job for someone stronger. Mamusha insists that I bring the water in early in the morning so that the water has time to be heated and she and Gina can bathe. Papa is delayed one morning on his way to the Chevra Tehillim, and sees me carrying the heavy bucket of water. He's livid, and I don't know exactly what transpires between him and Mamusha, but I do not have to bring the water in any more.

*

Pesach 5408 – 1648 on the Gregorian calendar. Tales have been circulating in Nemirov about Bogdan Chmeilnicki. A cunning Ukrainian, the son of a nobleman, he has organized a band of Cossacks and peasants from the Ukraine and Russia. With Chmeilnicki at their lead, the band has crossed the Dniester, moving westward, death and destruction in their wake.

The Jewish populace is the main target of the Cossack invasion, and stories are being repeated around town too gruesome to imagine: Jews being captured, their flesh being torn from them as they scream for mercy, and their limbs being thrown to the dogs. Be it man, woman, or child, no one was being spared. Jews were treated as just so much 'meat.' It took months, but the barbarians were finally haulted in Lvov, and a truce was signed between Chmeilnicki and the Poles. He was given a noble title, and in return, he had to commit to halting the carnage.

By some miracle, we in Nemirov were spared, and our townsfolk were more than happy to receive the Jews fleeing the marauding hoards.

*

Pesach 1649, and the weather is wonderful. Yom Tov was a treat, as it always is when Papa is home for so many days in a row. The work doesn't disturb me when I know Papa is on hand to say a kind word to me, and Mamusha and Gina are careful not to display their true colors when he's around. A few days after Pesach, and Papa is off again with the Rebbe for Lublin. The Rebbe assured him that it will be safe to travel, as Chmeilnicki is now at peace with Poland.

Papa has hardly been gone for a day, and the trouble has started. I'm at the end of my tether. Gina has accused me of stealing the necklace she received from her mother for Pesach. I try to explain that I haven't seen Gina's necklace and I certainly haven't taken it. Mamusha insists on conducting a search, barging into my little room and upending my belongings. The necklace is found, hidden amongst my linen, and no amount of denying on my part helps. I am sent to the cellar, and all the while, Gina is purring like the kitten that's swallowed the bird.

I've just enough time and wherewithal to grab my journal and pen before heading to the cellar, Gina just two steps behind me. She doesn't close the door, she slams it, almost knocking me off my feet. What they are unaware of . . . I have, with time, discovered an escape route, a trapdoor at the very end of the cellar, that opens up into the overgrown part of the garden, and although I hate being sent to the cellar, I can control my fear until I am out the trapdoor and into the fresh air. Fortunately, I haven't been caught yet, but I don't know for how long they will remain "in the dark."

I've settled myself under my favorite apple tree, and use my shawl as a blanket to lie on; the journal becomes my pillow. Staring up at the sky, so blue with not a cloud to be seen, I start to dream of faraway places . . . and sleep overtakes me.

*

I awaken to a very strange feeling. The earth is vibrating – no, trembling under me. Could this be what they call an earthquake? The rumbling increases, getting stronger and louder, and as I sit rooted to the spot, I hear shouts. I'm about to get up from my comfortable 'bed' when I see hundreds of riders descending on Nemirov. A war cry goes up; they are beating down on the city, and they are torching some of the houses. I see people, my neighbors, fleeing and being caught on the tips of the swords and thrown into the air. I am paralyzed at first, but a voice in my head is telling me to get up and hide. I blank, I can't think where, where can I run, until I turn to "my tree" and shimmy up the gnarled trunk, then hide in the foliage. I can't see what's happening, I can only hear terrible shrieking, and smell the fires burning. The rampage goes on for hours, and although I am shaken by the sounds of the horror, I am exhausted. To keep me from falling asleep in this exhausted state and tumbling out of the tree, I tie myself onto a branch with my shawl.

I must have dozed, and I wake to an eerie silence. I smell charred flesh and burning wood. It is very dark and I don't know if it's the beginning or the end of the night; I can't imagine for how long I've been sleeping. I think it's best if I remain where I am until full light.

Chapter 3

I SHOULD NEVER HAVE CLIMBED OUT OF MY TREE TO see what was happening. Morning has come; I untie my shawl and slip down out of the tree. I slowly make my way back down the foothill to where our house was. Indeed it was, and it is no more. There is just a pile of smouldering bricks in an outline where the house once stood. I pick my way slowly past the house and nearly faint at what I see next. Decapitated skeletons piled on what looks like a pyre. I want to look away, but my eyes keep returning to what I perceive to be little hands and little feet.

This past year we've been hearing stories of the Cossack brutality, but nothing has prepared me for what I am now seeing. I pick my way through Nemirov and it becomes very evident that no one has survived this massacre. The carnage is everywhere I look. The stagnant river waters are red with blood, and body parts float around like miniature sailboats. I remember Papa's words . . . is this what the coming of the Messiah looks like?

It feels like I'm being watched. The hair on the back of my neck is tingling; I feel someone is staring at me. It's very unsafe to be standing out here in the open, and I should try to find a hiding place as quickly as possible. I return to the apple tree, as that is on high ground, looking to see if I've been followed. I see no one, but I can't remain here either, I'm not sure that any place in town is safe. I keep thinking of Mamusha, Gina, and dear, dear Dora. What pain and torment did they go through before they were killed? The devils are loose, who can stop them.

I've decided: I'm going to try and make my way to Lublin, and Papa. I have no idea where the city is, only that it is a long distance away, and in the west. I'm not even sure that Lublin hasn't been devoured by these madmen, and the same slaughter that has befallen Nemirov has befallen them in Lublin as well. I'm going to have to put those thoughts out of my mind if I'm to stay sane through all of this. What's worrying me most about trying to reach Lublin is having to pass through unknown towns and villages, not knowing if the inhabitants are friend or foe. One thing is sure: the quicker I leave here, the better.

*

I've been wandering for days, and have been living off the land. Berries, mushrooms, and if I'm lucky, I come across a fruit tree with either pears or apples. I've become an expert at sleeping in the trees. It's not only the Cossacks I fear; the forests and woods are full of foxes and other hungry animals. I have no intention of having survived Chmeilnicki just to be eaten for animal dinner. I've learned to secure myself so well to the larger branches of the trees that releasing myself in the morning becomes an art.

I've lost track of the days, and the weeks are starting to run into each other. I have no idea when it's Shabbes, and I am sure I've missed Shavuos. Perhaps somewhere, somehow, I'll get back on track. For the moment, I'm working on keeping myself alive and I try to make sure that everything is recorded in my journal. It's important that someone record the atrocities visited on the Jews of Nemirov.

Bells, I hear bells, so it must be Sunday. I can see people milling about in the city square dressed in their finery. Last night, I stole into a barn and climbed up into the hay loft. There is a window up here and it affords me an excellent view of the town. I don't know what city I'm in, but perhaps with a bit of ingenuity, I'll be able to figure it out.

Dubno, that's the name of this city. And I've missed more than Shavuos. I've missed all the Yomim Tovim. I can't imagine that I've been on the run this long, and that I'm still not anywhere near my destination. Yesterday I got up the courage to climb out of the loft, mainly because I needed something to eat and drink, but I also had to find out where I am. Dubno once had a Jewish community, but Chmeilnicki saw to its 'elimination' last year. Those who weren't butchered by the Cossacks fled for their lives. I was able to glean this information from a young girl I met at the city well. She mistook me for a Polish peasant, and I didn't offer to re-educate her.

She told me that the weather will be turning in a few days, and that will be the end of the autumn.

My body has developed a protective layer, and so far, the elements haven't affected me. I am, however, skeptical that I'll be able to withstand the harsh winters out in the open. I manage to find some abandoned corn and drink some water before returning to my hiding place in the loft. I'm hoping to stay on for another few days, sleeping peacefully in the hay, and then getting on my way northwest, the direction for Lublin.

*

I didn't count on falling victim to "scarlet." At first I thought I was stiff from lying on the hard wooden floor of the loft, but as the day progressed and my body temperature rose, I knew that my illness was serious.

I'm not sure where I am, but Oma is standing over me, soothing my burning forehead with her chilled fingers, and Dora is massaging my legs. Papa is pleading with me to try and sit up. I can't answer anyone because my throat is so swollen, I can't even get the saliva down. All I want to do is keep my eyes closed and sleep. I'm going to sleep forever.

I'm shivering, shivering and screaming. I hear voices, but they aren't familiar. Someone has wrapped me in a blanket and is carrying me down a ladder. Warm milk is being spooned down my throat. I'm sleeping again, this time in a bed. I'm dreaming that there is an angel standing over me and smiling. The sun is coming through a window. I can slowly get my eyes open and it takes a moment for them to focus. There is an angel looking at me. She has the clearest skin I've ever seen, raven black hair, and enormous black eyes. She's smiling down at me, telling me to rest, and she'll be returning when I am fully awake.

I've been here a week now, and Marishka has been very kind. She cooked up a chicken broth especially for me, but when I tell her that just the smell nauseates me, she replaces it with cooked oats and milk. I feel my strength returning, and would like to leave as soon as possible, but the snow has come, and I'm aware that there is no way I can survive out in the open, alone, in this weather, with no shelter and improper clothing.

Marishka, I learn, is the medicine woman of Dubno. She knows all the classic remedies and some secret ones as well. She tells me

I was a victim of 'scarlet fever' and I was very lucky that the boy in charge of the stable heard me cry out when I did. That was the point that my fever broke, and it was crucial to have me warm and hydrated if I was going to survive. She had him carry me down from the loft and into her house, put me in a warm bed, and spooned milk into me until the danger passed. I owe my life to her.

I've been here for weeks, at Marishka's insistence, and she and I have bonded. She has stopped asking me to eat things that "nauseate" me, and lets me be "lazy" from sundown Friday until night fall on Saturday. She has never questioned me, and calls me her mystery girl. I feel badly sometimes in that I am accepting her hospitality without revealing myself to her in return, but I know that that information might put her as well as me in danger. Harboring a Jew might just bring down the wrath of the townspeople on both our heads. Soon, with the melting of the snow and the first blooms of spring, I will be leaving, heading toward Lublin, hoping to find my father.

Chapter 4

I'M ON MY WAY. I'VE BID MARISHKA FAREWELL, AND I'm on my way out of Dubno, with a small detour. I have to stop off at the stables and retrieve my journal from the hay loft. I hid it in a crevice just before I became ill, sure that it would be impossible to find unless one was specifically looking for it. The ladder is just where I remember it being and I gingerly climb back up into the loft. Moving the straw to the side, I recall just where the crevice is, but the space is empty. This can't be happening; I know I left the journal here, and the straw looks undisturbed. And this is the crevice, there are no others. I scramble around, tossing the straw about, looking again and again in the same spot . . . no journal.

Heartbroken, I descend the ladder and bump straight into Marishka. She is holding out my wrapped journal. "Are you looking for this, Tonya?" I can only nod, as my mouth has become even dryer than when I was down with the 'scarlet.' "I also wanted you to have some more provisions and things for the journey, so I've packed you a small bag. G-d speed!" She hands me the bag of provisions, hugs me, and waves me off.

I make haste to leave town, as I've lost good time looking for the journal and I should be kilometers from here before sundown. I've again chosen not to travel on the roads, as being a girl alone, it can be very dangerous. Instead, I walk through the woods and hills parallel to the road, trying not to lose my direction.

With the sun high overhead, I know it is noontime, and my growling intestines are confirming the fact. Stopping on a patch of green, I unpack the bag Marishka has given me. There are apples and pears, carrots, and an entire loaf of bread. There is also something wrapped in cloth at the bottom. I unwrap the small parcel carefully; it's a very small leather-bound Siddur. I sit and ponder this entire interlude. The months I spent with Marishka, without really knowing her. It's not me that's the mystery girl, it's her. Who are you, Marishka?

*

Lutsk – I've set my goal on arriving within a week. I now realize that I'm not as strong as I thought, and my illness has seriously weakened me. The week turns into ten days, but I rejoice and gain at least some moral strength when I see the city in the distance. My experience in Dubno has given me the courage to openly walk into the town. I now realize that people are mistaking me for a Polish peasant, due to my hair and eye color. One doesn't often see Jewish girls with golden hair and blue eyes, and my non-Jewish appearance is now standing me in good stead.

There is lots of traffic in the streets, and although Lutsk is a smaller town than Dubno, it seems much busier. I am careful to walk in the shadow of the buildings, trying to attract as little attention as possible. I'm also trying to decide where to look for a hiding place to spend the night, when I come face to face with a bearded Jew. He can't be anything but, in his traditional caftan, with his tzitzit peaking out from under. This is 'heaven sent' – and now all I have to do is follow him home and present myself. I daren't stop him on the street; I'm trying to attract as little attention as possible, and getting into a conversation with a Jewish man in middle of a busy thoroughfare is not the way to remain invisible. I do an about-face, and follow this 'Yid' at a discrete distance.

He's gone inside a building that must surely be the Shul. I can't follow him in – I might cause a scene if they don't have a women's section – and I can't remain standing outside, as it's getting dark. There's a carriage parked a short distance away, and on closer inspection, I see a blanket on the bench. I consider climbing into the carriage and hiding under the blanket until I hear the men leaving the Shul. Then all I'll have to do is climb out and follow the old Yid. The plan is perfect, and I get into the carriage and under the blanket. What I didn't take into consideration was how tired I was feeling and that I might just fall asleep, which is exactly what happened.

I wake up to the rocking movement of the carriage and I panic.

Throwing off the blanket, I come face to face with a man, staring at me in silent amusement.

"My dear young lady, haven't your parents taught you never to drive off in carriages with strange men?"

I open my mouth but the words don't come. Terror grips me as I see we are not in the city anymore but on an isolated road, heading for who knows where. There is a driver at the top of the carriage, but he pays no attention to me. He is certainly in the employ of this man, and obeys commands from him.

"Come, come, and don't be worried. I'm sorry if I've been amusing myself at your expense. I'm not going to harm you. Just tell me why you are in my carriage, and who you are."

"I'm, I'm . . . my name is Marishka. I'm, I'm . . . on my way to the fair in Lublin."

Why is he studying me like that? I think he can tell that I'm lying.

"Very well, Marishka, but now I'm going to kill you." He has removed a sabre from its sheath, and is holding it so that it catches the moonlight. I have never thought that I would draw my last breath in a place and situation like this, but here I am, about to be slaughtered. I raise my eyes heavenward and utter the "Shema."

"Good, excellent, that is just what I was hoping to hear." I open my eyes and see the man replacing his sabre and chuckling gleefully. "Marishka, indeed; where did you pick up such a name?"

Again I'm speechless. I've been expecting a beheading, and I've had a reprieve.

"I'm Yehudah Shumacher, at your service. And you are?"

I've finally gotten my voice back, weak, but at least a sound is coming out. "I'm Tonya Shnaider, and I really am on my way to Lublin."

"Very well, young lady, but you can't spend the night out in the town, unprotected; besides which, the temperature drops when it's dark and you might just freeze to death. I'll bring you home to my wife and you can spend the night with us, and if you wish, you can be on your merry way again tomorrow."

The Almighty is truly watching over me. Sometimes I think about not being born with a silver spoon in my mouth. I had a rough beginning, but He has sent angels to watch over me ever since. They helped me cheat Chmeilnicki in Nemerov, I cheated the angel of death in Dubno, and found a guardian angel in Marishka.

Now, I have been rescued by the Schumachers. For all of this and more, I thank the Almighty.

*

What should have been an overnight 'visit' has turned into an extended stay. Miriam Shumacher, as she insists I call her, is a very lovely young lady. She and Yehudah have been married for ten years, but have been unable to have children. From the moment I walked through the door, they have both been showering me with attention. Their home, on the outskirts of town, is even larger and more lavish than Mamusha's. Yehudah has a very flourishing business in shoes, and the moment I stepped through the door, he immediately set about finding a pair in the right size for me. Miriam, catching sight of me, instructed the maid to prepare a room, and she, herself, got busy setting another place at the table, already set for two. I tried recalling the last time I had eaten chicken broth.

I've been here with the Shumachers over Pesach, and it is the first time I've been at a Yom Tov table since last Pesach with Papa. I'm having flashbacks, of those times in Nemirov. Papa, resplendent at the head of the Seder table in his snow-white 'kittel.' There's Gina, in her new outfit and her new necklace. Mamusha, who's sitting on Papa's right, preening in her role as mistress. I'm not even aware of the tears streaming down my cheeks until Miriam hands me a handkerchief.

*

Achron shel Pesach – the days have passed so quickly, and I'll be on my way in a day or two. Miriam has prepared a dish called 'kneidlach,' which is made from crumbed matzoh and eaten in the chicken soup. It's a heavenly dish, and I'll have to learn how to make it. At the close of Yom Tov, after the Havdalah, Yehudah asks me to remain seated. He and Miriam would like to have a few words with me.

"We'd like to adopt you. You know that we are unable to have children, and you are searching for a father that might not be alive. You could search for years and never find him. We, on the other hand, have so much to offer you, our home, our friendship, but mainly our love and security."

I'm overwhelmed, and at a loss for words. They both mean so much to me, but how can I just forget Papa, and become Tonya

Shumacher? How can I word my refusal so as not to hurt them?

"There is a man, his name is Yisroel Shnaider, and he is in Lublin. He hasn't slept this past year because he feels that I, his daughter, am alive, he just knows not where. I, on the other hand, feel Papa's presence; I lay awake at night and I hear him calling me from a distance. I do know where to find him, and I must expend all my resources to do so."

"If that's your final decision, then I and Miriam will do everything in our power to help you locate your father. You say your father is in Lublin, then it is off to Lublin for us on the morrow."

Chapter 5

W E DIDN'T LEAVE THE NEXT DAY. YEHUDAH FELL ill, and it took weeks before he regained his strength. It was the week after Shavuos before we finally got underway. We left at the crack of dawn, as Yehudah said it was good to get a head start on other travellers and be the first out on the roads before they got too congested. Miriam has made sure that there is a basket filled to the brim with food that will last at least a week. Yehudah informs us that the distance from Lutsk to Lublin is about two hundred kilometers, but the roads are still unsafe – with Cossacks, Poles, Ukrainians, and Tartars, all thirsty for the blood of Jews – and our trip might take longer than it should. Yehudah explains that there is safety in numbers, and we are going to try to travel only in daylight, and in close proximity to other travellers.

So far, we've been very fortunate. There are many carriages on the road all headed for Lublin and the semi-annual mercantile fairs. Many are laden with merchandise, while others are carrying only passengers. We travel caravan-style for protection, and try to stop at wayside inns before dark. As yet, we haven't been refused rooms in any of the inns because of our Jewishness. Miriam thinks that the closer we get to Lublin, the more accustomed the peasants are to Jews.

Chelm, we've arrived in Chelm. I smile just remembering the stories Papa told about the Chelmer 'fools.' One story in particular has stuck in my mind. It's the tale of a group of men trying to move a house to the next village by pushing it. The men are working hard and begin sweating under the mid-day sun, so they removed their coats and leave them in a pile behind them. Still pushing, they don't notice when a thief comes and carries off all the coats. After a while, they stop for a breather, and low and behold, the coats aren't there. How excited they all are, that they've pushed the house so far, they can't see their coats anymore.

Papa was also careful to make sure that I understood that the fun poked at Chelm was created to ward off the 'evil eye.' In fact, it was known that the people of Chelm were very clever.

Chelm happens to be a fascinating place. Chmeilnicki and his marauding bands have somehow overlooked Chelm, and the Jews here haven't suffered too badly from their own home-grown villains. Jewish shops and businesses are prospering and Yiddish is heard more often than not on the tongues of the townspeople. As we've arrived here on Thursday evening, Yehudah is more than happy to accept an invitation from one of the men in Shul to be his guests over Shabbes. Miriam and I are more than happy to explore the town on Friday. Miriam wants to know how Chelm compares with Nemirov. I'm not very helpful in my reply. I hardly went further than the house and the apple tree; I certainly never visited any shops in Nemirov.

*

Back on the road on Sunday, and my heartbeat speeds up. Yehudah thinks we're not more than a day or two from our destination.

We arrive in Lublin after crossing the tributary, Bystrzyca, without problems. There was a flatbed ferry that Yehudah hired; we drove the carriage straight on the ferry, and in less than half an hour, we were on the left bank of the river, and in Lublin. There is a festive air to the city, stalls and banners literally lining every street. What seems out of sync is that the Jews are not visible. As the carriage carefully picks its way through the crowds, Yehudah calls to the driver to halt the carriage. He's seen a Shul and gingerly steps down to see if he can find anyone and get information. He's only gone a few minutes and returns with the following announcement:

"Today, the twentieth of Sivan, is a fast day, as proclaimed by The Council of the Four Lands. It's to commemorate the 6000 massacred Jews of Nemirov. I think it only fitting that we, too, should join in the fast."

I'm having trouble with the number 6000. I can only see a handful of faces, and if I can't see all the others, who will? Who will remember the rest of the dead? Who will cry over their spilt blood, their chopped limbs, and their charred bodies? Who will retrieve their remains from the jowls of the dogs, and the waters of the river? Will these souls collectively bang on the gates of heaven and beg for mercy for their brethren? Will they in their unity be able to save us and our children from future massacres? How many more Jews to be sacrificed before the final Redemption?

Finding a guest house was no simple feat at this time of year when rooms were at a premium. Somehow, Yehudah manages to procure two rooms at a reasonable price.

We settle in quickly and I am anxious for Yehudah to start making inquiries into Papa's whereabouts. I think he senses my tension, because he is already waiting for me in the common room, and tells me his plan.

"The best place to begin is at the 'council' house. I'm sure that all visiting scholars and rabbis register when they arrive, and I'm sure they still have the registrations from last Pesach. It shouldn't take me long to get some kind of lead on your father and I promise to be back in time to break the fast with you and Miriam."

Miriam and I spend the next few hours sitting in the common room, waiting for Yehudah to return. Just as night is falling Yehudah is back with downcast eyes.

"The news is not very positive. Shortly after your father arrived, the Rebbe was forced to disband the Yeshiva and flee with his students to Krakow. There, he has re-established, and it has become the greatest Torah center in all of Poland. Your father, hearing of the Nemirov massacre and learning that there were no survivors, chose to go to Krakow with the Rebbe. I spoke with one person at the council center who remembers Yisroel Schnaider well. He tells me that although he learned of the death of his family, Yisroel couldn't mourn. He kept seeing a vision of his daughter swaddled in hay with angels dancing around her. The vision kept repeating, 'I am lost, but alive.'"

Papa back in Krakow; it's like the other end of the world from here. I'm thinking that it must be at least double the kilometers that we've already travelled from Dubno. How will I ever manage to cover that distance alone?

"Tonya, I can read you like a book. Put all the worry out of your mind. We've come this far and we're going to see this to the end. Miriam and I are going to take you to Krakow and help track down your father."

Chapter 6

𝒲E MAKE PLANS TO LEAVE THE FOLLOWING MORN-
ing, but our plans are thwarted. The carriage driver refuses to go further west, and certainly not to such a great
distance as Krakow. He leaves from one moment to the next, and
we are unable to find another driver. Yehudah isn't as perturbed as
Miriam and me, and he proposes to undertake driving the wagon
himself. I don't know too much about the skills required, but
Miriam seems to be fine with this idea, and with only a few hours'
delay, we are on the road to Krakow. We meet fewer and fewer carriages travelling west; most people are going in the other direction,
to Lublin and the fair. Yehudah seems to be managing nicely; the
carriage is travelling at a smooth, even pace.

Yehudah has stopped the carriage at a shabby inn, but it's the
only one we've seen on this road and it is getting dark. We have to
be extra careful to find lodgings before nightfall, as we are almost
always alone on the roads. Yehudah negotiates with the innkeeper,
but later whispers to us that he doesn't trust the man. Yehudah suggests that Miriam sleep in my room so that I won't be alone and in
danger. "We should be on the road as early as possible, Radom is
not too far off, and there is a large Jewish community there where
we can find food and lodging."

*

Miriam is shrieking. Having risen early and dressed quickly, she's
gone into the next room to see what's keeping Yehudah, and has
found him murdered. The innkeeper is on hand and swears he
hasn't heard a disturbance during the night, and all of his other
guests are present and accounted for. He's speaking to Miriam, but

she is dazed and not reacting. I try to concentrate on what he's saying.

"Murder is commonplace here, and a murdered Jew is a daily occurance. No use notifying the constable; he's drunk most of the time and a big anti-Semite. Why don't I just pop him in a coffin and drive you to Radom. It's the only place in the area that will give him a Jewish burial. It'll cost you 100 zloty, for me to drive your carriage and get a ride home. Otherwise, we can just bury him out back."

I'm happy that Miriam is in shock, and hasn't heard the callous manner in which this peasant spoke. I'm not convinced that he is innocent of Yehudah's death and I'm not sure it's a good idea to let him drive us to Radom. The decision has fallen on me as I can't seem to rouse Miriam from her trance, and I have to think quickly.

"The gentleman has left us without money. If you can get us to Radom, I have an uncle there that will pay you 200 zloty for bringing us safely to him."

The innkeeper is quick to jump on my offer. He must have thought I was going to haggle the price down from 100 zloty, and here I am offering him double. It's our insurance policy to get away, and the only means of assuring that Yehudah gets a Jewish burial.

*

Radom, not a full day's ride from the inn, is another world. I'm not sure if it was the situation with Yehudah, or that the community is always this hospitable, but Yehudah had an honorable funeral and was accompanied to his final resting place by many Jews of the town. This was my first ever attendance at a funeral and my first visit to a cemetery. I was terrified to hear screeching and crying as we made our way to the plot, only to be told by a woman at my elbow, "Don't be nervous, child; it's only the 'klugerins' and they are harmless." They kept up their wailing all through the burial, and only once the coffin was covered and the grave completely closed did they approach Miriam with outstretched palms for a sou. If this wouldn't be such a solemn, sad moment, I think I'd be crying tears of laughter. Was this how this rag-tag bunch of women made a living? Is this custom particular to Radom, or is this typical of all Jewish funerals? It's something to remember and investigate.

The shiva week is drawing to an end. We have been warmly welcomed in the home of the community head, Reb Zekel, who also collected enough money to pay the innkeeper. Miriam has been left a financially secure widow, but all her assets are in Dubno, and it will be a while before she can repay the Radom community's generous loan. Miriam has assured me again and again that only my quick wit got us out of a very dangerous situation and enabled Yehudah to have a decent burial.

We are at an impasse. I want to return to Dubno with Miriam, and she wants to continue with me to Krakow. In the end, Miriam wins out and we make plans for getting to Krakow. We are probably 100 kilometers from the city, but we have been warned that it is a dangerous stretch of road. People are accosted daily, robbed and murdered, or just murdered for the sport. I again try to persuade Miriam that we should return to Dubno, but she is adamant about continuing.

We are going to have to hire a driver and perhaps some men for protection. I think a Jewish driver would be safer, and then this brilliant idea comes to me. I whisper it to Miriam, afraid for even the walls to hear what I'm saying. She listens and as I lay out my plan, her excitement is visible. Tonya, you are an ingenious young lady, and the best person to be with in a tight spot. Let's see if we can't put your plan to action.

Chapter 7

*K*RAKOW, JUST OVER THE NEXT RISE — BUT WE daren't show ourselves now. We've come this far and it would be a pity to ruin this plan in its final hour.

We are travelling in a hearse. There are signs on the sides of the wagon declaring the transportation to be contaminated and on its way to the cemetery. Our driver, Menek the '*bal'ahguleh*,' is in on our little charade, and was very happy to play along. We've only been travelling for a day and a half, but have been stopped twice on the road. When Menek declared his cargo to be contaminated and contagious, the robbers fled even before Menek finished his sentence. I confess to Miriam that I read a similar situation in the journal that I inherited, where a mother rescues her daughter and an entire travelling caravan by proclaiming that there is 'plague' about. The idea must have stayed with me, and made an impact, as it was the first thing I thought about when faced with the dilemma of getting to Krakow.

Menek shouts down through the slats that we are entering the city gates, and there seems to be a Jewish welcoming party waiting. Miriam tells Menek not to reveal our presence yet, as there could be other individuals standing by.

I hear conversation going back and forth between the welcoming party and Menek, and then the wagon starts moving again. Menek somehow lets us know that we are being escorted to the cemetery by a quorum of men and some rabbis so that the dead will have their Jewish burial according to the laws.

Miriam tells me that we'll have to put a stop to this before it gets out of hand. The rabbis will be furious if they think we've deceived them for the sport. She knocks on the underside of Menek's bench, to attract his attention and tell him to stop the hearse just outside the cemetery. Miriam is sure that the peasants haven't followed us here; there is no money nor sport to be had from corpses.

We hear Menek climbing down from the seat, and we hear him speaking to the group. The hatch is pulled open and Miriam and I shield our eyes from the daylight. The rabbis are milling around, not quite sure of what to do, when on of them steps forward, bids us welcome, and offers us the hospitality of his home. We are both happy to accept; we are both ready for some food and, if we are lucky, a comfortable bed.

Reb Anshel and his wife hear our story in fascination; I tell it from the beginning, from everything leading up to the horrors of Nemirov, until my meeting with Yehudah, may his soul rest in peace. Miriam picks up the story in Dubno and recounts all that has happened to us until just a few short hours ago.

"This is incredible, this is incredible, this is incredible." I'm sure Reb Anshel can say more than just those three words, but so far, that's all he's been muttering, from beginning to end. As Miriam concludes the story, he asks his wife, Rebbitzen Baila, to make us comfortable, as he has business to attend to, but should be back within an hour or two.

Both Miriam and I have taken a short nap and it has worked wonders. We've been revitalized, and having washed and put on fresh clothing, we are both starting to feel human again. The Rebbitzen is serving us tea and cinnamon cakes when we hear Reb Anshel's key in the door. He enters all flushed and right behind him I see . . . "Oh my, it's Papa." I throw myself at him, I'll never let him go, never, and the tears just flow. Rivers of tears, oceans of tears. Papa is overwhelmed, too, and he has to clear his voice a few times, I think in order not to cry.

I again begin the story from the day he left Nemirov, and again, Miriam, in a much shyer tone, recounts the story from Dubno onward. Her voice breaks when she recounts how Yehudah was murdered, and how I came to her rescue in her hour of need. We sit for hours, the three of us telling and retelling the day-to-day happenings of the last year.

It's Rosh Hashanah 5410 (1651), just three years since the barbarian Chmeilnicki began his slaughter of Polish Jewery. Papa has offered that he and I would accompany Miriam back to Dubno after the Yomim Tovim so she could get back to her life, and back to her business. For the moment, we are all healing, but I am hoping that as the days pass, something more than just a friendship will develop between Papa and Miriam and then we can all be together in Krakow.

Tonya, Krakow 1651

· BOOK IV ·

Necha's Story

Chapter 1

EXPLOSIONS. BURSTS OF COLOR. BRIGHT YELLOW sunflowers heaving in the fields for miles and miles, swaying in the wind to their own music, their silent dance. How I love this season. I could happily spend hours watching this ballet, but I am anxious to get to The Babeh Reizel's house.

I've always been a frequent visitor to the Babeh's, my dear grandmother's, although since my marriage to Yankel a few months ago, the visits don't last quite as long as they did when I was single. I love spending time with the Babeh, who lives clear on the other side of town, not far from her youngest daughter, my aunt, Ruchel Langer. My Babeh's a very independent lady, not wanting to be a burden to her children, and the only concession she's agreed to make to her family is living in close proximity to one of the children, refusing to actually live with any of them. Thank G-d, she's capable of doing everything for herself. I'm a frequent visitor at the Babeh's house; I love spending time with her, as she has wonderful stories to tell about the Maggid, her father. I've heard some of the tales from the townspeople, but she's such an excellent raconteur, it doesn't matter if I hear stories from her again and again.

I knock, and enter, not waiting to be shown in, as I don't want to drag her from something important. I find her in the great room, davening. The great room isn't such a great room, but that's what it's called. It's the bedroom, and the visiting room, and the eating room all in one. The cooking is done on a semi-terrace, half-covered by a roof, but mostly unenclosed, so that the smells don't accumulate in the "great" room and in the summer, it doesn't get too hot. Water is brought in from the well outside, and heated as needed.

*

I try not to disturb the Babeh during her davening, and sit quietly on a chair, fidgeting, anxious to share my news. The Babeh is well aware of me, but doesn't let anything distract her from her concentration during davening. I always marvel at what a beautiful woman she is. In spite of always wearing a *"sterntechel,"* she is very well dressed, walks without a cane, has the complexion of a woman half her age, and the only tell-tale sign of her true age, eighty-four, is her failing eyesight.

She has been finding it difficult to read the fine print in the newspaper, even with her spectacles. I am more than happy to accommodate her, and once a week, I read her the serialized story of Emperor Franz Josef in the German language paper. She doesn't hesitate to remind me before every reading that my mother, her daughter Fraida Pesel, was the only child chosen from public school, at the age of six, to present the Emperor with a bouquet of flowers on his visit to Sambor. She, in return, received a leather-bound book of poems, with the Emperor's seal and signature.

*

After what seems like hours, but is probably only a fraction of that, the Babeh has finally completed her tefillos. "Child, why are you squirming in your seat like that? What are you bursting to tell me?"

"I have the most fabulous news, Babeh. Yankel and I have found an apartment and will be moving at the end of September. I can't believe our good fortune; I can't believe that it's so close to der Tateh and de Mameh's house. I'll be able to continue my jobs at home and in the shop, I'll still be able to help Sarah Ratze and Toby manage their babies, and best of all, I'll still be able to visit with you as often as I like, and read to you."

"Calm down, Necha, calm down. This is wonderful news. By the way, what ever happened to the job offer you had at the Bais Yakov?"

Babeh has touched on an extremely sore subject. I'm thinking back to my "basic" Hebrew classes. When I was growing up, there was no Bais Yakov in Sambor. Der Tateh hired a memlamed to

· 180 ·

come after school and teach the three of us, Sarah Ratze, Toby, and me, how to read and daven, and some Parsha.

The *melamed* would arrive, make himself comfortable at the table, and almost immediately fall asleep in our warm, cozy great room. We didn't have the chutzpah to wake him, and we didn't dare tell der Tateh. As a result, my Hebrew skills are practically non-existent. How was I going to hold down a job in the new Bais Yakov school, where everyone was so learned, even though my job would be to teach handwork?

"Babeh, I'm not sure I'll be accepting the job, as I feel a bit incompetent."

"Nonsense, Necha; such a clever girl like you, you have so much to offer the children, and they'd be lucky to have you."

There are lots of reasons why I adore the Babeh, and her confidence in me is one of them.

"Come, I've baked your favorite honey cake. We'll make some tea, and then you can read me the next installment of the Emperor's story."

My German is excellent. Our part of Galicia has been part of the Austro-Hungarian Empire and we were required to learn German in school, as well as Russian. Knowing languages has its advantages; I'm just sorry that my Hebrew is very poor.

I spend the greater part of the afternoon with the Babeh, yet it seems like minutes.

I'm ready to leave, and the Babeh has prepared a parcel for me to take home. Honey cake, cheese deltalach, and potato pirogen. She's an amazing balaboste even at her age, and she never allows me to leave empty-handed.

I've decided to take the long way home, enjoying the fine late-summer weather, and walk via the Blich. The Blich is the older part of town, the neighborhood where most of the shops are to be found. Narrow streets and even narrower alleyways, it's a real maze. Many of my friends live on that side of town, and I'm hoping to see some of them so I can share my news.

The first person I run into is Yitta, Reb Shloime Zalman Orlander the shochet's daughter, and my sister Toby's friend. She's pushing her infant in a perambulator, and I'm a bit surprised to see her, knowing she moved to Berlin about two years ago. What a beautiful young woman she is. I've always admired her poise and carriage; there is definitely something regal about her.

"Hello, Yitta. I see you're home for a visit."

"No, actually it's not a visit, I'm here to stay. Life has become very difficult for us in Berlin; since Kristallnacht, the government has begun expelling her non-citizens, rounding up Poles and dumping them at the border. Since the end of October, and the forced expulsions, things have turned very ugly for the Jews in Germany. My husband's business was confiscated, and my in-laws were forcibly put out of their house. I'll be staying with my parents until we find other accommodation, so when you see Toby, please let her know I'm back and would be happy to have her visit."

Yitta continues on her way, and has left me with dozens of unanswered questions.

I slowly walk home trying to assess how this situation is going to affect us here in Poland, and specifically in Sambor. Sambor has always been considered an important commercial, as well as strategic, crossroad. Rich in gas and oil, situated between two parallel rivers, the Dniester and the Strwionz, I fear that our city is going to play an important role should a war actually break out.

I know that de Mameh has been stockpiling staples such as flour, rice, and kasha, ever since there's been talk about a war, yet no one really thinks that Germany is looking for another war after the Great War of 1914–18. Some of our friends and neighbors think that de Mameh is overreacting because of her previous war experience. De Mameh was left to care for five young children when der Tateh was conscripted into the Polish army. For four long years, between 1914 and 1918, she had to fend for her whole family, while helping her widowed brother-in-law, Yosef Maier, with six small children, as his wife had succumbed to typhus. Those years have left their mark on her and she is never without ample foodstuffs in the storage cellar.

I arrive home with my parcel from the Babeh at the exact moment that de Mameh is returning from work. My parents own a fabrics store in the new part of Sambor, and they make a nice living from the proceeds. Their customers are not only the townsfolk, but my parents also sell fabric to the gentiles of the surrounding villages for their market stalls. Der Tateh has an excellent reputation and is known far and wide as "the honest Motye."

"Ah, Necha, you're back. Tell me how the Babeh is. I see she's been busy again preparing her delicious specialties for Shavuos. I'm hoping she'll agree to spend at least one meal with us this Yom Tov."

De Mameh doesn't expect an answer and is already busy getting dinner ready for der Tateh and Yankel. Out come the pots, and before you know it, there is a soup on the boil, the meat is in the oven, and potatoes are being peeled. I gently remove the knife from de Mameh's hand and continue the peeling. I have always had pity on my dear mother. She lost the top of her index finger on her right hand to gangrene. This, during the Great War, when she was on her own, and taking in mending to make ends meet. One evening, she pricked herself with a sewing needle and her finger became septic. The only solution for saving her life was amputating that part of her finger. I am constantly trying to do all the menial jobs so that she won't have to do them herself, although I've never once heard her complain.

"Mameh, I met Yitta, the shochet's daughter, on my way home. She told me that the situation is very bad in Germany. Do you honestly think that we are on the brink of a war?"

This is really not a good subject to broach with de Mameh. I hear her at night sometimes, screaming out in her sleep. She had such a hard time during the war; how can I confront her with this question? I try to change the subject, but de Mameh is having none of it.

"Necha, there is a madman loose, and all of Europe has fallen under his spell. It's just a matter of time before he'll swallow Poland. I fear for the next generation, for my children and grandchildren. I feel terrible times are coming."

Mameh's monologue has given me the chills and raised the hair on my arms. Something deep inside tells me that this is not just a panicked memory, but a holy prophecy.

Der Tateh and Yankel arrive and I quickly forget what's happening outside my front door. The atmosphere in our home has always been one of calm and caring, an oasis in the desert. People have constantly been drawn to my parents and, needless to say, our home has been an anchor for all the family, as well as friends and the needy. Tateh always has some story to recount about his day in the shop, and on most occasions, he tells it in such a humorous way that we are all holding our sides from the laughing stitch.

"Jadwiga Shultz was in the store today, Necha, and her daughter Stanislawa is very happy that you are teaching her those intricate embroidery stitches. Jadwiga says that if Stanislawa will be able to embroider half as well as you, they'll manage to sell her handworks and have enough money to purchase some more chickens for their farm. I assured her that you were more than happy to do it, and that Stanislawa could stop by any time for more instruction."

Der Tateh, whom I love and admire, truly amazes me. He's such an enigma, my father. Steadfast in his religion, yet so in tune to the needs of all those around him, male or female, always concerned with the well being of others. No wonder the gentiles, as certainly his Jewish customers and friends, adore him.

My new husband, Yankel, is one of Tateh's greatest admirers. They get along so well it makes my heart swell. It also makes living under one roof with my parents that much easier. We were very fortunate to be the first on the list for the apartment on Drohubitcha. The young Dornbush couple is leaving for Palestine, and the apartment will only be free at the end of September, but it is definitely worth the wait. Imagine: running water in the cooking room. I won't have to go out to the well to bring the water upstairs. What a luxury.

I help clear the supper dishes, and head out to the courtyard. Although it's evening, there's still light outside, and enough to allow me to read.

Babeh Reizel gave me this journal when I got engaged. It's a worn, leather-bound book, and the Babeh has wrapped it in a soft linen bag. It's a journal: Dina in England, Freya, a young girl at the time of the Spanish Inquisition, and the story of Tonya, a girl surviving the Tach V'tat. The Babeh received it from her mother on her wedding day, and she felt that now was the right time to pass it on. Dina and Freya's stories are written in German, and as I'm proficient in German, Russian, and Polish, having studied those subjects in the gymnasium, it's easy to follow. I've been reading and rereading the journal these past few weeks, and I've questioned the Babeh about the writers. She doesn't have any detail other than that she, too, received it from her mother, who knew nothing about its provenance either. I'm not sure why she's given it to me and not Sarah Ratze nor Toby, who are both older, but I'm happy she has. Babeh, I promise to be the keeper of the journal.

Chapter 2

OU'LL HAVE TO FORGIVE ME, DINA, AND FREYA, and you too, Tonya. How can I even think of writing on these pages, next to the stories of such heroines? But I have no choice. For I, too, am a witness, and testimony has to be recorded of the ensuing events. I am now a "link," as you all have been, to crimes perpetrated against our Jewish brethren.

Today, the first of September, Germany attacked Poland without warning, and today, we are burying four Jews in our city of Sambor.

This 'madman,' as de Mameh refers to Hitler, has told his commanders that he plans to send SS units to Poland "to kill without pity or mercy all men, women, and children of Polish race or language." That was an exaggeration, and a lie. He doesn't mean all Poles, he means all Jews, and indeed, four innocent people were killed today as the Luftwaffe strafed the city with total disregard to human life.

De Mameh's anxiety is contagious, and justified. As Jews start pouring into our city from places further west, Sambor's citizens are nodding their heads, Reb Mordechai's wife was right, and the "madman" does mean war. People are arriving from Krakow and Lublin, from Radom and Turka, from Lemberg. My brother Mayer, the youngest, has come back from the Yeshiva in Lublin, which has been evacuated.

My parents are happy and relieved to see him, and welcome him, along with some homeless bochurim he's brought to stay with us. We are an amazing people, we Jews. Homes that were occupied to their capacity just days ago have opened their doors to these refugees; all of a sudden, there is room for everyone.

My older brother Yitzchok, we call him Itche, and his wife Sara, living on the Rynek with their two little boys, Yisroel Isser and Tanchum, have two entire families – a total of twelve people – staying with them. Theirs is what is called a "city apartment" – more luxurious and larger than most, and therefore the perfect place for hosting guests, although I don't think it was meant for that many people.

De Mameh has sent me down to the cellar to bring up flour and kasha and she's ready to cook up a storm.

"Mameh, I thought you were stockpiling for a time of need," I ask, as surely things will get worse; this is just the beginning of war.

"Kind, leben, dear child," she answers. "How can I hoard supplies in the cellar when these people are in need now?" The activity in the kitchen accelerates; Sarah Ratze and Toby have joined us, and they've rolled up their sleeves and manage to lighten the atmosphere with their kibitzing. We are now four women in the cooking area and at least ten men in the great room. Der Tateh is organizing everyone into jobs for the coming days. Mayer and Yankel are to go out to the suburbs and see if there are any eggs, potatoes, onions, or carrots to be found on the farms. Mayer's two friends have been sent to find wood on the edge of town. With Rosh Hashanah in two days, and so many more people to feed, we are in a frenzy to find all the staples necessary to tide us over.

We aren't the only ones with the same idea, and half the townspeople are out in the suburbs looking to buy food. Our gentile neighbors, sensing the urgency of their Jewish counterparts to find food and fuel, have started charging exorbitant amounts of money for their products. Our neighbors and friends, anticipating shortages, are outbidding one another for foodstuffs. Where is this going to end?

Mayer and Yankel brought home some flour and potatoes, as well as two chickens, which we'll have to take to the shochet. The students, Mechel and Yosek, found enough wood to keep the fires burning for a week. Der Tateh was able to find butter and milk, which is vital for the children.

I've been dispatched to see if the Babeh has everything she needs. She has people staying with her as well, and it's not easy for her to assemble the items she needs to prepare her Yom Tov meal. We've been trying to get the Babeh to move in with us, but she refuses to daven anywhere but at her father's Shul, the Bais Hamedrash of the

Maggid, where she has been davening for the past eighty-some years and is warmly welcomed by all.

*

The Germans have entered the city with great fanfare. In trucks and tanks, they have parked themselves along the Dniester, the river running alongside the town, and pitched their tents in full view of the city. The soldiers have taken over all government buildings, hoisted the German flag, and imposed a curfew.

In town, we are doing our best to ensure that the great day, Rosh Hashanah, not be sullied by worries or thoughts other than those of how to serve the Almighty. This is not an easy assignment. With the food shortage and the overcrowding, it is taking a huge effort by the townspeople to usher in the New Year in the same spirit as previous years.

News has reached Sambor of refugees being herded into a ghetto in nearby Lemberg. The refugees have come from many of the towns in Western Galicia, forcibly pushed east by the Germans, east into Lemberg, and are being cramped into inhuman living space. Soldiers are attacking Jews and rounding up able-bodied men for work forces. I have many friends in the Lemberg district and my heart goes out to them.

Rosh Hashanah 5700: there is an eerie stillness in Sambor as Yidden usher in the Yom Tov. Der Tateh has gone through the courtyard to the neighbor's house, where a minyan of men have assembled to daven. The curfew siren sounded a while back and the streets are deserted; the citizens know better than to anger the Germans. De Mameh has done her best with the supplies on hand, and her finest linens and dishes. I can almost make myself believe that this is a festival just like any we've ever had. What is missing are the non-stop visits from family and friends dropping by to wish "a git gebencht yor" and "kesiva vechasima tova, le'alta le'chaim tovim u leshulem," all the traditional greetings.

Sunrise, the first morning of Rosh Hashanah, and it is a glorious day. The trees have started to change color, and the sun is shining bright. I'm up early, and I prepare the table so that it is ready for the meal when we return from Shul. We are davening in the Begleiter Shul, which is just minutes from the house at the end of our street, Lelova. The men have been in Shul since before dawn, and I am somewhat relieved about that. There are so many people living in our cramped little apartment that I crave a bit of privacy, and with the men already out, I go about my preparations in a more relaxed fashion.

All set, and walking alongside de Mameh, we make our way down the street to the Shul. Der Tateh has bought seats for us, and these are clearly marked with our name. We barely have the chance to take our seats when we hear the stomping of boots and the purr of the tanks' engines. The marchers are coming closer, and the davening has stopped, replaced by an eerie silence. German soldiers burst into the men's section of our Shul, grab a handful of men, pulling some by their beards and pointing their bayonets, rush them outside.

They force the Yidden, still in their Talleisim to bend down and polish the boots of the officers, kicking them for not working quickly enough. They've taken the *shamesh*, Gimple Freilich, still in his Tallis, and are forcing him to collect the horse droppings with his bare hands. All the while they are joking and taking photographs, even posing with the bewildered Jews. Terrified, the rest of us watch, not knowing what sport comes next.

The Germans, having had their fun, give it up and return to their campsite. In their wake, they've left humiliated men, those that were forced into the street, and especially those not taken, who were too terrified to put up resistance and defend their friends. We are nervous as we all resume our places and the chazzan continues where he left off with the Rosh Hashanah tefillos. Most of the women and many of the men are sobbing. De Mameh, in her usual caring way, is trying to console some of the women. It takes a while for things to calm down, but everyone remains very subdued. At the end of the tefillos, we leave in small groups so as not to attract attention.

I'm relieved when we're all safely reassembled back in the house for the Yom Tov meal. Poor Tateh, I feel so sorry for him; he is feeling so remorseful. He was standing right next to Gimpel Freilich when the soldiers pulled him out of Shul. The little *shamesh* that's never harmed anyone. We all tell der Tateh that it wouldn't have made a difference had he gotten involved; the soldiers would just have dragged him out too, and perhaps inflicted worse abuse on Pan Freilich. I'm not sure we've convinced him, and I hear the lump in his throat as he makes Kiddush.

Itche's come running from the Rynek; someone's told him that der Tateh's Shul was attacked, and he's come to see that we're all alright. He tells der Tateh that the Germans have also "visited" the Blich, smashed windows, and plundered merchandise from the Jewish stores. Some of the shopkeepers live above or behind their businesses, but the cunning Germans are well aware that today is a holy day and the Jews are at Shul, therefore they'll find unoccupied stores and no resistance. Itche doesn't stay long; he's anxious to get home and make sure his family are alright and that all his guests have returned safely. The rest of the day passes uneventfully, as does the second day of Yom Tov.

This whole week, we've been hearing about other towns and villages in our part of Galicia. Our brothers in Stari-Sambor, the old city, have not fared as 'well' as we have. On Rosh Hashanah, the Gestapo drove all the people out of the Shul, and forced them to the marketplace where, in their Talleisim, they were compelled to clean the streets. They then dragged Pavel Lerman and Mendel Dornbush away; no one knows where. The Gestapo proceeded to round up 1200 people and march them in rows of four to Strzelbice, a distance of six kilometers. They were forced to dig a huge pit, and the Gestapo told them there were to be shot, and buried there. By some miracle, news came that the Russians were about to enter the city and the Jews were released.

There have been lootings and beatings and murders, here and up and down the countryside these past weeks, but today, 7 Tishrei, the Germans are retreating. The Jews of Sambor heave a collective sigh of relief, as the Soviets move in and fill the vacuum.

The Soviets are a different element, but I doubt if it's going to be paradise under their occupation. The first thing they've done is taken over all the municipal buildings and agencies. They've nationalized all the shops and put everyone on ration cards. All of this has befallen the community on erev Yom Kippur. How will we cope? Surely there won't be a repeat of the attack on Rosh Hashanah that the Germans carried out. Hopefully the Soviets will be more tolerant, and respect our religious practices.

The Soviets are setting up an infrastructure, and to help run the government, they've recruited Jews to replace the Ukrainians. This can't be good for promoting good will between Jews and Ukrainians, but the Soviets are the last people to worry about popularity. These recruitments have all of us worried. The Ukrainians never had much love for their Jewish neighbors, and losing their jobs to Jews might just provoke them to attack us.

Chapter 3

*S*AMBOR IS BEING OVERRUN BY PEOPLE FLEEING THE L'vov area, which is closer to the fighting front and the raging Germans. Food is getting even scarcer, and the lines in front of the shops are getting longer and longer. On one of my trips to the baker's, I meet Yitta waiting on line. She has been here for more than an hour and she is still a long ways from the front. She tells me that their apartment in the Blich was one of the only ones spared when the Germans went on the rampage the second day of Rosh Hashanah. She also tells me that Reb Pinchas of Ostilla, son-in-law of Reb Yissochar Dov of Belz, and his Gabbai are lodging with them on the Blich, while the rest of Reb Pinchas's family are staying with families all over the newer part of Sambor. What he would really like is to find an apartment that would accommodate himself, his Rebbitzen, and perhaps some of the children.

Yitta also tells me she is concerned about her little boy, Berish. With the food shortages, it is difficult to find the fresh vegetables and fruits that are necessary for his development. As we inch our way forward, Yitta offers to do any sewing that our family might need for a minimum wage. I thank her, and tell her I'll keep it in mind. I don't want to disappoint Yitta, but although she is an excellent seamstress, I don't think she'll find many customers who can afford, or have the inclination to sew new dresses.

It took me a total of four and a half hours to finally get the bread I set out for, and I was one of the lucky ones. Many of the people that arrived after me went home empty-handed. On the way home, I stop off at der Tateh's fabric store to leave some of the bread with him. He hears me out when I tell him about my encounter with

Yitta, and how the Ostilla Rov is looking for lodgings. Before the entire sentence is out of my mouth, der Tateh hangs out a "closed" sign in the shop window, and tells me to warn de Mameh that he might be home later than usual and not to worry. He's going to the Blich to see the Ostilla Rov.

We are getting new neighbors. Der Tateh has arranged for the Ostilla Rov and his family to take over the empty rooms at the other side of our courtyard, and today is moving day. The Rov and his Gabbai are coming from the shochet's house in the Blich, and the Rebbitzen and some of the children are arriving from different homes all over Sambor. The layout is such that the Rov will be able to set aside a room for a Bais Medrash. I don't want to sound frivolous, but with the Rov in our midst, there is a spirit of festivity in our neighborhood.

The weather has turned bitter, and I fear we are going to have a long, hard winter. Heating is going to be a problem, as all the different types of fuels are being rationed. The Poles and Ukrainians are already chopping down the trees and hoarding much of the firewood. It looks like it's going to be an especially difficult winter for me, personally. The Russians have conscripted Yankel into a work battalion and have taken him away from the Sambor area with dozens of other young men. People are saying that the men will not be returning for a few weeks and perhaps not for months.

I'm wallowing in self-pity; I haven't had anything that even resembles a "newly-wed year." Since the beginning of September, and the overflow of refugees, living space is at a premium; we've been living in my parents' home, men in one room, and women in the other. That hasn't afforded Yankel and me any privacy, and it's anyone's guess when he'll be returning, or when things will improve. At least I know where he is, and that he is under some kind of protection from the Russians. There is still no news of the missing Pavel Lerman and Mendel Dornbush. We all fear for their lives. I'm going to have to learn to curb my selfishness; it's a dead-end street and won't get me anywhere.

It's amazing how when something becomes a habit, even hardships seem normal. The lack of food and fuel have become so common that subsisting on one meagre meal a day, and heating the house for one hour, have become the routine in most households, and are even considered a luxury. The greatest worry for most of us is the regular beatings that the Ukrainians and Poles are inflicting on the Jews. Their anger at being denied jobs, or being replaced by their Jewish neighbors, has so infuriated them that they take every opportunity to soothe their anger by beating us. Life is grim, and the general mood is one of depression. Der Tateh chides me one evening, "Necha, my nightingale. I haven't heard you singing in so many months."

"Tateh, we are never just the family anymore, so many strange men around, and besides, there isn't much good reason to sing."

The minute the words are out of my mouth, I'm sorry I even said them. Der Tateh's face has fallen; I know my words sadden him, and I also know none of it is in his control. I'm sure he's remembering better times, as are we all.

Stanislawa Schultz has been coming on a regular basis for embroidery lessons. I've asked her to see if they have some extra scraps from their vegetable garden that they can spare for my nieces. Sarah Ratze's children, Goldie, little Necha, and Moishe, as well as Toby's daughter, Chana, are starting to look a bit undernourished. It would be so welcome to receive anything the Schultzes were discarding. On her next visit a few days later, Stanislawa arrives late in the evening wearing a heavy, oversized coat. She looks very comical until she unbuttons the garment and potatoes, onions, and carrots fall out from the inside pockets.

I am so excited I whip her around and do the jig; I kiss her on both cheeks and thank her over and over again, and tell her please to thank her mother, Jadwiga and her father, Stanislaw. I tell her what a great deed she has done in helping feed the children. I recommend that she make haste, and get home before the curfew. She is tall for her eleven years, and mature, and I warn her to be careful of the Ukrainians when she goes home. The Shultzes, "volksdeutsche," have suffered from the Poles and Ukrainians since the end of the Great War. As Germans living in the East, they have never integrated, and have always been "outsiders" here in Sambor. Stanislawa assures me that she has been defending herself against the Ukrainian bullies that have peppered the town for the last few years, and has brought her brother, Bronislaw, along for safety. Although he is two years her junior, he is huge for his age, and anyone would think twice about attacking her.

For the next few months, Stanislawa's weekly visits are always done in the oversized coat and always filled with some kind of vegetable, and on the rare occasion, an egg. Jadwiga Schultz also comes on a weekly basis to get materials from der Tateh, and she brings barley and kasha. Der Tateh pays royally for all the staples, we are just so happy to have such a good source.

An idea has been forming in der Tateh's head, and on Jadwiga's visit yesterday, der Tateh broached the subject. How would she feel about keeping our massive inventory of fabrics at their farm? Without more than a moment's hesitation Jadwiga agrees, and arrangements are made to transfer the stock without alerting the Soviets, who would surely confiscate the load in its entirety. Der Tateh is relieved; hopefully in a few months when the war is over, and life returns to normal, he will still have his business.

Spring is in the air, and with it comes Pesach. The Ostilla Rov has set up a facility for baking matzos; although there is a shortage of flour, the Pesach Seder is kept according to its ancient tradition, to the best of everyone's ability. Der Tateh even managed to find a bottle of wine in the cellar.

"*This is the bread of affliction* that our fathers ate in the land of Egypt. Whoever is hungry, let him come and eat; whoever is in need, let him come and conduct the Seder of Passover. This year we are here; next year, in the land of Israel. This year we are slaves; next year, we will be free people."

Indeed, our home is open to many people, and the table, over-crowded. De Mameh has seen to it that all possible food is prepared, so that we can share it with the needy. The curfew has posed a great problem, so after the Seder, all the guests just find a spot on the floors and that is where they spend the night.

Is it the hunger, or the excitement of the day that keeps me awake? As I lay quietly on the straw mat, the line from the Haggadah has me thinking. "This year we are slaves; next year, free people." The Jews were enslaved in Egypt for more than two hundred years. Please, Heavenly Father, please, don't make us suffer that long . . . please bring us the Redeemer.

*

Almost spring, and the days are getting longer, the temperature warmer. I like to head down toward the Dniester, the river that flows past our town, and just look out past the churning water, across toward the hills and the Carpathian Mountains. It almost makes me feel as though things are back to their normal pre-war status. I arrived back from my jaunt this afternoon to see crowds assembled near the Rynek, the central market square. I wonder what the fuss is about. I stop the person closest to me, "What's happening?"

"The men from the work battalion have finally returned home, after six months," he replies.

Oh my, oh my, that means my Yankel is back, but I don't see him here among this group. I turn and run down the streets until I'm at the house. I peer through the window, and sure enough, sitting at the table with my father, a skeleton of himself, his hair white as virgin snow, is Yankel.

Chapter 4

*I*T'S TAKEN WEEKS, BUT YANKEL HAS FINALLY RE-gained some of his strength, and most of his spirit. The Soviets were hard taskmasters, but at least, job done, the forced laborers were sent back home. Pavil Lerman and Mendel Dornbush, taken by the Gestapo at approximately the same time, have yet to return. We fear the worst.

The Soviets have started to "crack down" on foreign elements in the cities. They've given an ultimatum to all of the non-residents. By the end of June, any refugee refusing Soviet citizenship will be deported to the interior of the Soviet Union. Rich Jews were not being given any choice and were being immediately transferred. Tragically, Rela Zelinger, our pharmacist, together with her husband and young daughter, has committed suicide for fear of being deported. Sambor is in a state of shock, there is an air of dread, and the mood is one of depression.

Trainloads of Jews, being evicted to Siberia, are passing through Sambor. It is Shabbes, and the Soviets are not allowing the people off the train. The Ostilla Rov has implored the citizens of Sambor to take all available food and supplies to the poor souls on their way to exile even though it is the Holy Shabbes. We are given the permission to carry, as it's "pikuach nefesh." This is just the first of many trainloads of refugees. Entire families, the displaced, from Galician cities behind the front, are being shipped eastward by the Soviets. No one spared. Those that will not accept Soviet citizenship, or are deemed too anti-Soviet, are being exiled to the hinter regions of Siberia. I wonder if we will all eventually end up in that barren icebox.

It's been months now, and the exodus to Siberia hasn't let up. Siberia must be full to overflowing with Polish Jews. The Yomim Tovim have passed; we've celebrated the year 5701 in subdued spirits, remembering last year, and praying for an end to this war. We were happy to have the Rov's Shul in our courtyard, where the davening was done in a discreet and safe atmosphere. De Mameh worries about the coming winter. She is insisting that the Babeh, who has been with us over all the Yomim Tovim, move in permanently, so that she can share our food and fuel. After a lot of resistance, the Babeh agrees. I've given her my mattress – she wasn't easy to convince – and we all settle in, in anticipation of a very cold Polish winter.

Cold is not the word – frigid. The icicles are hanging from the windows and the well has frozen over. The old and infirm are dying without proper food, heat, and medicine. The "chevra" pass by our house with their wagon daily on the way to the cemetery, their job doubly difficult considering the frozen ground. Every street has at least one family sitting shiva.

The Schultzes, who have kept their end of the bargain, and allow der Tateh to carry out what little business there is from their barn, arrive weekly with something for the pot. It is either Stanislawa, or Jadwiga Schultz herself; on rare occasions Stanislaw. But they do come, and at least what they bring is not rotten, even though it is very expensive. We divide up the parcel, giving some of the items to Itche, Sarah Ratze, and Toby and their families, and do our best to make the most of what's left. My brother Mayer has always been a picky eater and very little of what is available agrees with his taste buds. This also worries de Mameh. How will "Mayorchale" have the strength to survive the winter?

I try to explain to my "baby brother" that now is not the time for acting "ferpieshtchit," which is just another word for "spoiled." I tell him that he can fall victim to so many illnesses, or die of malnutrition, as so many people in the Great War. I'm hoping that if he gets hungry enough, he will be ready to eat what is put on his plate. It is the Babeh that finally convinces Mayer to eat the soup/ stew that de Mameh has prepared. From her frail stature comes a powerful message: EAT. There are no ifs, or buts, and this little lady cows Mayer. Babchu, I do love you so, for reasons innumerable, but especially for your backbone. I think it, but daren't say it, for fear of being disrespectful.

Der Tateh has been in the Ostilla Shul the entire morning. He and three other mispallelim were asked to stay on after davening, and they haven't come out yet. When he finally does come into the house, we all listen attentively to what he has to say.

"The Rov is very worried about Pesach. There is a shortage of flour, and how will we be able to feed all the Yidden in Sambor? No Matzos, hardly any vegetables, some preserved fruits, and no fish or fowl. If the Yidden aren't allowed to eat the little bit of bread they receive for their ration coupons, what will they eat?"

The Rov, as once before, declares that "pikuach nefesh" is the first consideration, and that people not try to be heroes.

"Ha lachma anya" – I try to remember what I was thinking about last year as I said these words. I know that we had more people at the table. We had Mayer's Yeshiva friends and some refugees that der Tateh brought home from Shul. This Pesach, it's just the family. My brother Itche and his family, my sister Sarah Ratze and her family, and my sister Toby with her family. Mayer has somehow procured a bottle of wine and I haven't seen der Tateh as excited as this since the outbreak of the war. He keeps repeating how happy he is to have real wine for the "arba kosos."

*

The warmer weather is a blessing. People are again venturing out of their homes and the fields and trees are starting to bloom. That means soon there will be fruits on the trees and vegetables will be growing. If we're lucky the Ukrainians and Poles will not overcharge for the products.

Something is happening in Sambor; the Soviet soldiers are out in force, searching houses and rounding up people. They are arresting Ukrainians, leaders and followers of the Ukrainian Nationalist Movement. I've seen them march groups of men past our house and toward the Rynek, past which lies the prison. There has never been any love lost between the Jews and Ukrainians of Sambor, but I do have compassion as they are led by. I assume they will be interrogated and shipped off to Siberia. But days pass, and I hear nothing more, nor do I see any more people being led to the prison.

The rumbling wakes me up. Babeh Raizel is already looking out the window, dressed only in her morning robe and tichel. I take a place next to her and see columns of Soviet tanks, and hundreds of troupes on the march. They are headed east, away from Sambor and back to the Soviet Union. They are leaving town, and I don't know if I should rejoice or cry. I'm not left long to wonder. It is June, the month of sunshine and flowers, and the month when the Nazi skull and bones return to our midst.

Chapter 5

JUNE 1941, IT'S THE BEGINNING OF THE END. THE Nazis have returned with a vengeance, and have given free reign to the Ukrainians to express their own hatred of the Jews. In gangs, with clubs and knives, they sweep through the streets attacking Jews wherever they see them. They snatch up people from their homes, from the courtyards, and force them toward the city prison. Unknown to most of us, the Ukrainians that were incarcerated in prison by the Soviets were all murdered and their bodies left to rot. The Jews are now forced to remove and bury all the bodies, after which they are beaten and many are murdered. On this July 1, 1941, over 200 Jews were murdered in the Ukrainian pogrom, among them my uncle, my mother's brother, Duvid Elyah. When the news reaches his mother, the Babeh, all she says is, "Hashem nosan, Hashem lukach," over and over.

Instead of some humane reaction from the Germans, who are considered by most of the world as the supreme "civilized race," they organize their own "discipline" against the Jews. They begin with a decree that all Jews must wear a white ribbon with a print of the Star of David on the right sleeve. No one is to be exempt; the law is for man, woman, and child. It tears at my heart, as I sew the ribbons on my nieces' and nephews' clothing. Goldie, Sarah Ratze's daughter, asks if I could put some embroidery on hers. She wants something just a bit more special so that the children in school will not laugh at her. Little do we all know, all Jewish children will be denied entrance to the schools, and we are subjected to stricter curfews, house searches, and are denied access to trains and all public transportation.

It is Erev Rosh Hashanah again, 5702. There will be no gathering in the Shuls. It is much too dangerous; we all remember what happened the last time the Nazis were present during the Yomim Tovim. Most people will remain in their homes, and although we are fortunate enough to have the Shul in our courtyard, we must be careful to daven very discreetly. The Nazis have a free run of the city, breaking into homes at all hours, and the slightest thing ticks them off. We tiptoe around them as one would around a sleeping rabid dog.

Again, the winter has begun early. The temperatures have dropped to below freezing and people have started breaking down their furniture in order to fuel their stoves. There are still a few remaining Jewish merchants conducting dwindling businesses, but they have had their shops ransacked, their goods confiscated, and their windows boarded up. There are no rations, and no shops to dispense the little bit of bread and goods available.

The Nazis have signs posted at every corner. All Jews are to hand over their furs, radio sets, gold, and silver, all to go to the occupying forces. Anyone caught refusing, or withholding anything, will be shot. De Mameh has been busy looking for a good hiding place for her few pieces of jewellery, and the life savings in dollars that she and der Tateh have been squirrelling away for a rainy day. Once she settles on a place, she shares the secret with me. I have to beg the Babeh to give up her silver cane, it's an inheritance and she's had it forever. It's hard for her to part with it, but in the end, I convince her that it is just too large to hide, and too dangerous to keep.

The Nazis have established a Judenrat. It's a council of Jewish elders, a liaison between us and "them." I wonder who's the mastermind to have thought up this cruel institution . . . Jews aiding Nazis in carrying out their anti-Semitic policies. It is certainly someone with a twisted mind. They've appointed poor Dr. Schneidscher as chairman, and they have conscripted my Yankel into the committee. My poor gentle Yankel.

Der Tateh has decided to risk going to see Stanislaw Schultz. He tells de Mameh that he has some important business to attend to, and will be back before curfew. I've seen him leave, and I wait in the window until I see him returning. With a sigh of relief, I open the door and wait anxiously to hear what he has to say. We all gather round the table and der Tateh tells us that he has negotiated, yet again with Jadwiga and Stanislaw Schultz, to build us a hiding place somewhere in their home. It has cost der Tateh a considerable sum of money, but we all feel it is well worth the expenditure.

This arrangement with the Schultzes hasn't come about soon enough, as this morning, on every corner, there is a Nazi edict proclaiming certain streets in the city center off-limits to Jews. All those residing on the listed streets must find different lodgings. The Nazis have chosen the worst possible time, as if any time could be good. The snows are knee-high, and getting possessions out of the homes is an impossible feat.

Der Tateh and de Mameh are leaving to hide in the home of the Schultzes. The Babeh refuses to go with them, but has asked that they take Tante Ruchel and her husband, Avrumche Langer. The Babeh and I, along with Itche, Toby, and their families, and of course, Yankel, move to the Blich, which has the only apartments available that are not restricted to the Jews. Sarah Ratze and her family have chosen to return to Dobromil, where her husband Zishe's family have 'connections.' The Ostille Rov has moved back into the home of Reb Shloime Zalman the shochet, together with his Gabbai; his Rebbitzen and children have found lodgings in the same building with us, on the Blich.

Yankel is very distressed. The Nazis have levied an enormous tax on the Judenrat, and are requesting 100 young men for a work battalion. Yankel is expected to submit a list with names by tomorrow. He and Itche whisper and argue quietly till all hours of the early morning, neither of them getting any sleep. I don't know when I finally dozed off, but I awoke just as Yankel was putting on his tattered coat, Itche at the door with him. He turns, gives me a weak smile, waves, and closes the door. I don't have a good feeling about this; what can Yankel do to prevent young men from being dragged off to forced labor? If anyone, he can understand how terrible it is to be part of such a work battalion. I feel so alone. Der Tateh and de Mameh aren't on hand to pick up my spirit, yet I am happy that they are out of town and safe.

Sambor is swarming with SS. Announcements have gone up at every corner that unless the workforce of 100 men is assembled within the next 24 hours, and unless two million zloty are paid, action will be taken. I've heard stories about this terrible Obersturmführer Rokita, head of the SS division, who's now in charge of Sambor. They say he has been responsible for the massacre of thousands of Jews in Lvov, and is now here to "clean up" Sambor.

He has a local girlfriend, Yanka, who was with me in school. A beautiful girl this Yanka is, and I've heard he is totally smitten, and that's one of the reasons he agreed to come to such a backwater as Sambor. I hope Yanka will distract him, for, where Rokita goes, death follows.

I don't know how I have the strength to record this, but as I have taken it upon myself from the beginning to bear witness, write I must.

They have hung Yankel, my dear, gentle Yankel, along with six other Judenrat colleagues; they have strung them from the balcony of the Judenrat building. Runek Holzman has come running from the Rynek, and asks to speak with Itche privately. He recounts how he was about to enter the Judenrat building when the SS arrived in the city square in a caravan of black Mercedes. He pulled back into the shadow of a building, and saw everything firsthand. They hung seven men, including Yurek Finer, our dentist.

Itche returns, carefully drops hints to me about the situation at the Judenrat, little bits of information until I understand exactly what has happened. Yankel, oy, my Yankel, such a pure, gentle soul, couldn't supply the SS with a work force . . . Couldn't, or more accurately, 'wouldn't.' Itche tells me that they were up the whole night, he and Yankel, trying to think of a way to avoid submitting a list. Yankel was well aware of how dangerous it was, refusing to submit names, but said he'd never comply even at the risk of his own life. I'm numb, not really processing what has happened. Itche and Mayer leave me with the Babeh while they try and recover the body.

"Stop your pacing, child; it's not helping you or anyone else." The Babeh's words pull me up short. Indeed, everyone is frightened, and my anxiety is just increasing the level. But, what is taking so long? Why haven't Itche and Mayer returned? They do return, after some hours, and sadly recount how they helped bury all seven of the Judenrat officers. Mayer tries to diminish my pain by saying that at least Yankel has had a Jewish burial, but for the moment, I remain inconsolable. After some days, it is the Babeh's soothing and wise words that bring me back to the living.

*

Pesach, in the ghetto – for that is what the Blich has become, a ghetto. People are starving and dying. I try to keep my nieces and nephews occupied and calm, but hunger has become a problem for us, too. There will be no matzos or wine this year; we are surviving on potatoes and onions, and that in small quantities. I haven't heard anything from my parents since before Yankel was killed. It has to be better and safer where they are. At least the Schultz family will see to it that there is enough to eat.

They're back. My parents have decided to return to the city and abandon their hiding place. Der Tateh couldn't take the isolation, and worrying about the rest of the family gave him no peace. He is determined to wait out this war with the rest of us.

Berel Achtel was caught this morning trying to board a train. He was shot on the spot. The SS are everywhere, with dogs, and armed to the teeth, just looking for sport. I haven't been out for weeks; the safest place is still at home. Der Tateh is not worried about leaving the apartment, and has been visiting with the Ostilla Rov and some of his friends. He brings back the news that most people are preparing hiding places, in event of a raid. We have been hearing that in Rzeszow, in Zolkiew, in Stry, in L'vov, in most of Galicia, Jews are being rounded up and deported to work camps, and resettlement facilities. What der Tateh has also heard is that the destinations are in fact extermination camps. Der Tateh begins working on a plan for hiding places for the entire family.

Itche, who has been out scavenging for food, is the first one to come home with the news. They've arrested Jadwiga Schultz. Someone from the village has accused her of hiding Jews and the Nazis were there yesterday at the crack of dawn to drag her from her bed. What they discovered was an extra bedroom, equipped with beds, bedding, and even electricity, and although the room was clean and empty, it gave the impression that it was available for occupancy. Der Tateh is beside himself with worry. Coming forward will not help in her release, it will only make things worse for her, and get them and us shot. We are all overcome by fear for the fate of Jadwiga Schultz, and Stanislaw, and the children, Stanislawa, and Bronislaw.

She's out; Jadwiga has been released, and our family heave a collective sigh of relief. The Nazis have freed Jadwiga, but have informed her that she remains under suspicion.

If I thought that the winter was bitter, I didn't take into consideration what the heat would do to us in such crowded quarters. The children are extremely irritable and constantly begging for water, which we are also rationing. Disease is everywhere. We are all infested with lice; sanitary conditions are non-existent. I've been leaving the apartment more often; staying in such a cramped space is getting to me. I'm not the only one. More and more people are out in the heat, looking for relief in open spaces. The gutters are littered with the dead and the dying. Young and old, corpses are everywhere. I try to look straight ahead, so as not to see, or at least pretend I haven't seen, for I am helpless. So on my jaunts around the block, I become deaf and blind, and I tell myself I am not here in Sambor, I am somewhere else, perhaps in Krenitze or in the Carpathians, anywhere but not in the ghetto on the Blich. Foolish me, who am I kidding; I can forget the misery for perhaps a millisecond, but even in our own apartment, the tragedy is visible. Toby looks ill, and not just malnourished. If it's typhus, we are all done for.

*

Something bad is happening. I feel it in my bones. This morning the Nazis have herded in thousands of Jews from many of the neighboring towns, as well as Stari-Sambor, and compressed them into the former stables of the Polish Army, just a short way from here. The SS surround the stables and there are dogs, two and three abreast, guarding the perimeter, making sure that no one escapes. There are rumors circulating that soon the SS will begin rounding up the Jews of Sambor. News comes with the deportees that yesterday there was an *Aktzie* in Dobromil. Sarah Ratze and her children have been caught; Zishe has been carted off to a labor camp. My parents are at their wits' end. Such innocents, what will happen to them? Where are they now?

Terrible pictures are running through my head. As much as I try to ignore the deteriorating conditions and all the rumors, I shudder; I've heard the stories of the death camps. Der Tateh, trying to distract us all, makes sure that each of us memorizes the fastest and safest route to our individual hiding places.

Kriger, a name as dreaded as Hitler, head of the Gestapo of Stanislava, has arrived this evening with hundreds more troupes. The sound of the transport trucks, a constant drone in the background.

*

Dawn, August 4, 1942, 21 Av 5702 – the beginning of the first mass *Aktzie* in the city of Sambor. I hear trucks screeching to a halt at the corner. I'm the first at the window, and just in time to see old Yoel Genuth from across the street being tossed out of the window, silently falling to his death. "Quickly, everyone to the bunkers." The alarm has been raised. As the screams intensify outside, de Mameh quickly guides half of the family to a bunker that is very well hidden, behind the cellar of the building. The bunker can accommodate some forty people, and many of the Ostilla family have been assigned this hiding place, too.

The Babeh has a safe place behind the kitchen stove, very well camouflaged. Der Tateh is on the roof with some of the men from the building. There is a trapdoor from the attic to a crawlspace just under the eves of the roof. Itche's family and I have a place under the outhouse. We all settle down and hold our breath. The shooting and the screaming from down the street intensify; the barking of the dogs sends shivers down my spine. A few days ago, I saw Gestapo dogs unleashed at an old man, unable to outrun them. They ripped apart his limbs, until he was unrecognizable as a human corpse. Sometimes I think it's the dogs I fear most, but then I witness a different atrocity that seems far worse, and being mauled by the dogs doesn't seem such a bad end.

I can hear them getting closer. They're in the building next to ours; I hear shouts, I hear children crying, I hear screams of hysteria. I bite my knuckles, afraid that I will join in the screaming and inadvertently give up our hiding place. Itche's boys are so good, not a peep; they just lay on the ground, fear in their eyes, not saying a word, not uttering a sound. I hear the Gestapo running from floor to floor in our building, I hear furniture being moved, there is shouting, a baby is crying. There seems to be a commotion on the stairs, more shouting, "Raus, raus," as the Gestapo are hustling the captives out of the building.

I've bitten through the skin of my knuckles, and the blood is running down my arm. I can't control the shivering, Itche's wife, Sara, has started to whimper, and Itche himself is in a catatonic state. I smack Sara, and she immediately stops. I bring my finger to my lips, hoping it's enough to keep her calm until the Gestapo leave. I'm sure they've discovered someone in our building, and I have a strong premonition it's a member of our family.

The Gestapo have gone on to the next building, and slowly, the sounds diminish as they move further and further away. There is an unnaturally eerie silence. Itche has regained his composure and we decide it must be safe to leave our hiding place. He is the first to leave, and returns a minute later; the Gestapo is gone and we can all come out. While he is helping Sara and the children out of the hiding place, I run as quickly as I can upstairs and into our apartment. The little bit of furniture we had, only a table and chairs, has been smashed to bits. The stove has been pried away from the wall, and the hiding place is just an open, empty gap. The Babeh has been taken. I'm staring at the hole when Mayer burst into the apartment shouting, "De Mameh, oy, de Mameh, she's been captured!"

Chapter 6

MAYER WAS DOWNSTAIRS IN THE BUNKER WITH de Mameh and most of the other neighbors in the building. That included the Ostilla Rov's son Reb Duvid, his wife and infant, Toby and her family, and some other neighbors. In total there were thirty-nine souls in the hiding space. The baby started to cry and some of the people hiding began shouting at the young mother to leave, she was putting them all at risk. The young woman too began to cry, "I can't leave, and I'm scared." De Mameh, assessing the risk, told the young, frightened mother that she would go with her, and remain at her side. De Mameh calmly left the bunker with mother and child and they returned to the young woman's apartment.

I now realize that the cries I heard coming from our building were those of de Mameh, the young mother, and her baby. At the same time, the Nazis discovered Babeh Reizel in her hiding place. Satisfied with their "catch," and convinced that they had "cleaned out the house," the Nazis looked no further and the people in the bunker, as well as our group behind the outhouse, were spared. Der Tateh and the group he was with are safe, too. I have a hard time looking at der Tateh. The pain of loss has put furrows on his brow, has further whitened his hair, but worst of all, has taken the light from his eyes.

Tuesday, the twenty-first of Av, the fourth of August 1942 – a black day for Sambor. It's a black day for many cities all over Galicia. In fact, the *Aktzie* here lasts until the sixth, due to the lack of train space for all those captured. We hear crying, screaming, and gunshots coming from the area surrounding the train station. For two days, not a soul ventures out, the terror hanging in the air.

During these two days, the Nazis have rounded up 3000 Jews from Sambor, "their quota." Among those captured are my Aunt Rochel Langer and her husband Avrumche. All those captured have been taken away, we know not where. The Judenrat is telling people to please be calm. Those captured are being either resettled or taken to work camps. Stahl, head of the Jewish 'police force,' comes looking for Mayer; he has a message from de Mameh.

"I was on duty at the station just as your mother, together with a young woman and child, were being loaded onto the trains. Your mother recognized me, and beckoned me. "Please tell my family, I have not a moment's regret. What I did, I did with the full knowledge of the consequences and the hope I was saving many other lives.""

I can just hear de Mameh uttering those words; I can picture her standing erect and proud and not losing her dignity. I thought I'm strong, but I crack; I can marvel at de Mameh's fortitude, yet I disintegrate. I start to cry so uncontrollably that only being shaken violently by Itche pulls me out of my hysteria. Everyone is eyeing me, especially the children, eyes huge as saucers, trying to follow the adult conversation. In the meantime, Mayer is trying to pump Stahl for more information. Has de Mameh's train left Sambor? Yes. Do you know the destination? No. Do you know how far the train is travelling? No. Do you know if there are provisions of food and water on the train? In this heat, they must have water. No.

In a fog, I hear Mayer's questions and I want to laugh; he's gone crazy, he can't be sane. I can't imagine that Mayer hasn't heard of the death camps. Does he think that the Nazis are taking all these people to a work camp, or on vacation? What kind of work can old women and men or babies do? Mayer, are you so naïve, or are you putting up a front for everyone else's sake?

Sara, my sister-in-law, has decided to return to her parents, who are on the other side of the ghetto. She has been told that that part of the Blich hasn't been affected by the *Aktzie*, and she has a feeling they will be safer there. As the bunker her parents have created is very small, Itche will be remaining with us. Tanchem and Yisroel Isser hug me with such force as they leave, and I again have to bite my knuckles to keep from screaming and crying.

A letter is circulating in Sambor. Reb Nachmen from Rawa Ruske has somehow gotten this missive through:

The transports of captured Jews from Sambor, Old Sambor, and

Turka that have passed through here, Rawa Ruske, on Wednesday 22 of Av, all those souls have been gassed on Thursday 23 of Av in a 'camp' called Belzec.

*

Shabbes 22 Elul, 5702, 4 September, 1942 – another *Aktzie*. Everyone, again, is running to the bunkers and hiding, but this time, the Nazis only want the elderly. In total they have captured more than one hundred old people, among them, Rav Chaim Yitzchok Yeruchem, the elderly Rov of Stari-Sambor. One of the prominent senior members of the community, Reb Yekele Turkel, has sent for Mayer and his good friend Abish Fensterbush. Something must be done to get Rav Chaim out of the clutches of the Gestapo. Mayer and Abish, with great trepidation, make their way to the Judenrat, and plead on behalf of the old Rov. Because it was the will of the Almighty, the Judenrat somehow procured his release, and Mayer and Abish bring the old, frail Rov to the home of Reb Yekele, where he passes away quietly a few days later. The remaining captives have all been sent to Belzec.

Der Tateh has regrouped the family, and reissued hiding places. The Ostilla Rov has moved in with his family, thus the hiding arrangements have to be reorganized. I am again allotted the outhouse bunker, together with my father's brother, the Fetter Avrumche, Toby and her husband, Yehoshua Feldman, with their daughter, Chana. Der Tateh will be hiding in the bunker in the cellar with most of Reb Pinchas's family, Mayer and Itche have taken the space under the roof with some other men. Der Tateh makes everyone do a 'trial run' so that we can practice getting to the bunkers as quickly as possible.

I have made two resolutions. I will not surrender without a fight, and let them cart me off to Belzec. I would rather get a bullet in my back, than end up being gassed; that is what they are doing to the people being transported to the camps from all over Poland. The charade is up; too many horror stories have been trickling back to us from people working the gas chambers and the burial teams. My second resolution is to sew a pouch for my journal. I've found some scraps of material and I get to work putting together a type of knapsack to wear on my back, under my dress.

I scavenge around and find treasure, some more 'bleishtift' pencils in many of the abandoned apartments. I imagine they have no trading value; can't even be used for fuel, otherwise they would have been long gone. To this treasure, I add de Mameh's jewellery, which I've removed from its hiding place. Funny how, armed with the journal, and de Mameh's life savings, I feel as though I can conquer anything.

The decision has been made; we are all going to the bunkers. Staying in the apartments is too dangerous. The Nazis have posted signs in all public places that a litre of vodka and five kilos of sugar will be given to anyone turning in or catching a Jew. We live from day to day, expecting the worst, yet hoping for the best. The Poles and Ukrainians are excellent executers of the German will, and assist the Gestapo happily.

*

Shabbes, always Shabbes; 17 October 1942, 6 Mar-Cheshvan 5703 – they are out again in force, the murderers are on the hunt again. The shouts, the shooting, the dogs, the screams, and more screams. I hear it all from my place in the bunker behind the outhouse. I am amazed at Chanaleh. Not a word, nothing, and although Toby has terror written all over her face, Chana is expressionless. They are in our building, I can hear them clomping up and down the stairs, and then the shouts, lots of shouting, then shooting, and then all is silent. I am tempted to have a look, but my brother-in-law Shia warns me of the danger. They might be coming back. It takes a few hours before we hear the last of the trucks, and the Blich falls silent.

I crawl out and make my way slowly toward the building, but Mayer is blocking my way. "What's happened?" Mayer is at a loss for words, but finally squeezes out a sentence. "Don't go in. One of the neighbors has been slashed to death on the stairs. Der Tateh's bunker was discovered. They've taken everyone, The Rebbitzen, their sons and daughters, and all the grandchildren. The only one of their sons not in the bunker was Reb Itchele."

I must have fainted. How I've come to be back in the bunker, I don't know, but Toby is hovering over me. Mayer is also down here for the moment, and he tells me that there are those who are trying to rescue Reb Pinchas and his entourage. It will probably take enormous sums of money, but the group is hopeful of success. This is such good news that I am again restored and all faintness has gone. Indeed, Reb Pinchas returns with the Rebbitzen. The Gestapo has refused to release the rest. The Rebbitzen refuses to return to her apartment, as does her son Yizchok. Reb Pinchas climbs the stairs wearily and with a broken heart. "They have taken my whole family. Everyone. Don't they realize that my family are not cut out to be laborers."

On this day, the 17–18 of October 1942, 6 Mar-Cheshvan, they have captured and sent to their deaths 2000 Jews from the city of Sambor. Among those taken are Reb Shloime Zalman Orlander, the shochet; his wife, Taube; and their youngest daughter, Chaya. I haven't heard about Yitta, her husband, or her child, Berish. I do not know if they are still alive.

*

We are scrambling for our lives again. Everyone runs, back into his or her holes like rabbits. It is now 11 Mar Cheshvan, 22 of October. The Nazis have increased the pace. An *Aktzie* right after the last, they've caught us off guard. Back I rush into the bunker. Toby and family are already there and Shia is urging me to close the hatch. I'm barely in before I again hear the yelping of the dogs, and the shouting of the soldiers. One of the dogs is barking right outside the outhouse, and I can hear the door being pulled open. The Nazi looks in, and in an aggravated voice, pulling at the chain of the dog, says, "Dumb animal, no one here, stupid beast . . ." . ." and the door slams shut. I'm sure that if he waits one moment longer, he'll hear the loud banging that my heart is making against my ribs. With bated breath, we hear the soldier retreating from the outhouse and going back into the building. Shia insists that we remain silent and hidden even though we haven't heard any noise for the last hour.

The knocking at the trapdoor spooks everyone. "Efents auf siz Shiku" – Open, it's me, Shiku. I am the closest to the latch, so I'm the one to rush forward, but Shia stops me, and signals not to open. The knocking and entreaty continue until I finally can't refuse and open up. Shiku Holzman is looking in, white as a ghost. "They've caught Itche and Mayer and have brought them to the horse pens near the station."

Chapter 7

*M*Y KNEES BUCKLE UNDER ME. I CAN'T LET THIS
happen. Besides for Toby, Itche and Mayer are all I
have left. In minutes a plan has formed in my head. I
know exactly what I'm going to do. I am going to find Yanka, for
surely she wields clout with Rokita, and she can't have forgotten
how kind my parents were to her family. I'll offer her anything, just
so that they'll release my brothers. I can't tell anyone where I'm going; I know my family will try and stop me. I slip past Shiku, and
head toward the city center. In sync with my footsteps, a voice is
chanting to me, "Necha, may the Eibishter watch your every foot-
step, and keep you from talking too much. Be matzliach, come
home safely." It's the Babeh, I'm sure. I can hear her as though she
were standing right next to me. I can almost feel her accompanying
me. Babaleh, what do you mean by, "keep me from talking too
much"?

I can't find Yanka. She is not at her place of work, and I'm not
sure where she lives or if I'm even allowed in that neighborhood. I
do recall that she likes to frequent one of the only coffee houses still
in business. It's on the Rynek, restricted to Jews, and crawling with
SS. I pull my scarf over my head, and try to inconspicuously make
my way there. Sure enough, I find Yanka over a cup of coffee, and
to say the least, she is very surprised to see me.

"Necha, how come you're here? I'm not sure you should be in
this area of town."

"Yanka, please, I need your help and am willing to pay nicely
for it. My brothers have been taken to the station, and I know only
Obersturmführer Rokita can get them out. I have a golden Jaeger
watch for him and a two-carat diamond ring that he can give you,

if he will only release them. Please help me, for old times' sake." I know Yanka is remembering how my father helped her father establish a stall of fabrics at the market, and how he gave him goods on long-term credit.

I am about to tell Yanka that I also have American dollars, and other diamonds, I am willing to give up everything, my parents' entire "fortune," when she nods in agreement and says she will try to intervene. There's that mysterious voice whispering in my ear again: "Good, you've been the boss over your words." I kiss Yanka's hand, and she promises to meet me in the morning near the corner of the corral, to make the exchange.

I return to the bunker, and no one is questioning me. I am thankful for this. I think that all of us, as I am too, are holding our breath and waiting for the hammer to drop. I hope I've not put myself into the lion's den and entered a trap, but it's too late now to back down.

As arranged, I am at the corner near the corral at seven in the morning. From afar I see what looks like hundreds of men milling around. It doesn't take long before Yanka arrives and guides me to the passageway between two houses. "Let's see what you have."

I remove first the watch, and then the ring from my pocket. She looks over both items very carefully, tells me to wait, and makes her way toward the corral. She has no fear of walking past the dozens of SS standing at attention with their rifles; they all seem to recognize her. I see her at the entrance of the corral standing right next to Obersturmführer Rokita. I imagine it's him because Yanka is greeted very warmly, and I see them flirting with each other. After some moments, I can see her whispering into his ear, and she points toward the men in the corral. Ten minutes pass, probably the longest ten minutes of my life, before Yanka is back at my side. "The deal is done. Your brothers will be released, and I suggest you get out of here and head back to your house." She turns on her heal with an air of superiority, and leaves me standing. I have to do something to let them know they'll be safe, but what?

I run to the Judenrat building, forgetting that they have hung Yankel from the balcony. Memory floods back as I see the façade, but I steel myself, I must focus on Itche and Mayer's plight. Nothing can stand in the way of getting them released, and certainly not my feelings. I ask to be shown into Dr. Schneidscher's office.

The good doctor is surprised to see me and is quick to console me for the loss of Yankel. Accepting his kind words, we speak for a few moments about my dear Yankel, but knowing the seconds are ticking away and the danger Itche and Mayer are in, I ask for permission to be the girl carrying out the enormous soup kettle to the captured men. How strange that the Nazis permit this compassionate act on the part of the Judenrat, letting the men be fed before being shipped off. I wonder if it is just a means of not panicking the entire populace, food for the "work force." Dr. Schneiderscher agrees to let me be the person on the second handle of the soup kettle. I run down to the kitchen and find two people just about to head out. I replace one of the girls, grab onto the handle, and we slowly make our way across the Rynek toward the train station and the horse corral.

There stands Rokita, the tiger watching the little pigeons. How arrogant he stands, his head raising above all the rest, feet apart, surveying the prey. The captives have been told to undress and pile their clothing at the left side of the corral, shoes on the right side. It's March, and still bitterly cold; the men are hesitant to do as they are told. Rokita raises his gun and shoots the man closest to him. That gets everyone moving and undressing quickly. I am trying to catch Itche's eye, or Mayer, but they are both too far away, and don't notice me.

Rokita again raises his gun and shoots into the air, "Izak Lamet, Mayer Lamet, forward, now!" I see the fear in their eyes as they step forward, half-clad, and I shout, "Hots nisht moiré," don't be afraid. Rokita turns in anger toward me, "Verdammte Jude," one more word and I throw you in there, too.

I lock eyes with this cold beast, Rokita, the angel of death. It was just seconds that we stood there staring at each other, but the memory of the moment will stay with me forever, frozen till eternity.

Itche and Mayer have made their way over to Rokita, who points them in the direction of a smaller group, able-bodied men and boys to be leaving shortly for Janov. He has assembled them outside of the pen and the Jewish police are watching them. Itche and Mayer shuffle quickly across to where he has sent them, and I make my way to a dark ally from where I can watch. After a time, the group is released and they all disburse immediately. Having observed all of this from the sidelines, I quickly signal Itche, and he and Mayer follow me away from the pens. How can I thank the Almighty for this gift? The sword has been lifted from my brothers' heads in the eleventh hour.

*

December 1, 1942/22 Kislev 5703 – the Sambor ghetto has been cordoned off with barbed wire. The fear has magnified a thousand-fold. The winters are getting colder and colder and we are starving. Typhus is everyone's bedfellow. There isn't a home that is not affected. The bodies of the dead are left in the streets. We have no access to the cemetery and no equipment to get the bodies there and buried. During the last days of Kislev, the Ostilla Rov falls ill with the dreaded illness. Mayer has taken it upon himself to care for the Rov, as he is immunized against the disease. Day by day, the Rov gets weaker, and Mayer refuses to leave his side. He nurses the Rov and slowly brings him back to health so that the Rov is soon able to attend his own minyan and lead the assembled.

January 6, 1943, 6 Shvat 5703, and Sambor is eerily quiet. Snow has been falling for the past week, and the cold is unbearable. I've volunteered to go out and forage for food, and despite Mayer and Itche's protests, I bundle up as best I can and make my way outside. There are other bundled people – it's difficult to know whether they are male or female – slowly moving down the street, fighting the wind. A blast of Arctic wind nearly knocks me off my feet, and probably would have if I wasn't rooted ankle-deep in the snow. I decide to make my way in the direction of the Judenrat, and the more central part of town.

Walking is slow, the snowdrifts hindering my progress. As I pick my way carefully, I see that the streets are littered with frozen corpses. I make out the outlines of adult as well as tiny bodies, mostly naked, and frozen into the most grotesque of positions. They've been "picked naked"; I'm sure their clothing is now keeping other people's bodies warm. I pass through this 'field of death' just as the other pedestrians do, observing, yet not breaking step. Turning away from the scene, I try not to let the image distract me from my goal.

I finally arrive at the Judenrat, but realize that coming here was not a very good idea. The street is ghostly empty, and the building boarded up, the door locked. Staring up toward the balcony from which Yankel was hung, I vow to his memory that I've come this far, and I'm not going back with empty hands. I'm sure that if I can get a board off the window, I'll be able to crawl in and find something. Looking around, there isn't a scrap of wood or metal to be seen. Even if there might be something lying around, it is covered by many centimeters of snow. There is nothing out here that will help me pry the boards away from the window. I am left with only my bare, half-frozen fingers to try to get the wood off.

Feeling a real sense of defeat, I approach the window, when an idea occurs to me. I remove the shawl that's been wound a few times around my neck, and pass it through the opening in the boards, careful to thread it downwards and pull the ends out again. I've now created a loop, which I pull with all my might. The board is nailed on the four corners, but two of those nails look very rusty. I hope this will work in my favor. On the third try, I feel something giving way, and with the fourth hard tug, the board comes away. Heartened by my success, I use the same system to pull two more boards loose, creating just enough space to allow me to crawl into the building.

The Judenrat feels recently inhabited. Although there is hardly any furniture left – a small, pitted writing desk and rickety chair in the center of the large ground-floor room, and an enormous metal bookcase leaning against the left-hand wall – the room feels cozy, almost warm. There must have been people in here just a few hours ago. I make my way cautiously toward the back, and what I suppose to be the kitchen area. Sure enough, the back room is the kitchen, with a battery of pots strewn over the counter surfaces. The doors to all the cupboards are hanging open revealing empty shelves. With my heart beating in my throat, I go from cupboard to cupboard, running my hands over each shelf, delving into each corner, and not believing that they are all bare. I have failed my family. I'm returning with empty hands.

I slip out of the Judenrat the same way I came in, through the window. I'm just about to take my first step toward home when I remember to take the three boards I've pulled from the window. At least we will have a bit of firewood. I make my way back the same way I came, passing again the macabre collage of frozen bodies. I, too, am a half-frozen snowman by the time I present myself back to my family.

Toby is waiting just inside the doorway and I fall into her arms, exhausted. I didn't realize the effort it took to be out in such freezing weather. Toby is unwrapping the shawl, coats, my various sweaters, and me, bit by bit by bit by bit, and then she starts on my feet.

These are beginning to thaw and are very painful. All the while, Itche and Mayer stand in the background and as I start to groan and cry with Toby's ministrations, they slowly creep away. What is it about a woman's pain that a man can't support. I continue whimpering long after Toby is done drying my feet, and long after they have returned to "normal." Toby again takes me in her arms, rocking me back and forth . . .

"Toby, I think all is lost. I know I am. I walked past dead babies, women, and men, their bodies exposed to the skies, and all I could think about was reaching my destination. I walked past, as others did, not stopping to even say a tefillah over the dead. When did I lose my humanity, my feelings for my fellow man? This apathy is worse than the atrocities the Germans and Ukrainians are subjecting us to."

"Shh . . . Necha. If we're to survive, we have to stop feeling, and we have to stop thinking."

*

Shabbes 5 Nissan, 10 April 1943 – hundreds of German soldiers on their way to the Russian front are temporarily in Sambor. The Gestapo, with not much resistance, convinces the soldiers to help murder and destroy – some good practice for those going to the front. Hundreds upon hundreds of soldiers surround the ghetto and while two or three stand guard at every doorway, the rest break into the buildings and houses, smash every cupboard, every cellar door, every chimney, dragging people out of their hiding places, until they are convinced the house is "clean." Thirteen hundred people are captured in the Nazi nets and led to the prison.

Again, we have been lucky in our hiding place behind the outhouse, but for how long? We are eight in the bunker, and the air is crackling with fear: Toby; Chana; Shia; Uncle Avrumche; Itche; Mayer; Yachet, a young girl completely on her own; and myself. This time it's Mayer who is the first up to check if the coast is clear. Mayer returns a few minutes later to say we can all come up. The area is deserted. Deserted, indeed. The Nazis have again taken Reb Pinchas and the Rebbitzen captive. Everything is done to gain their release, and on the seventh of Nissan, the Rov is set free.

The Rebbitzen, Chana Ruchel bas Reb Yissochor Dov, is

marched – with a total of twelve hundred men, women, and children – through the city, past the Blich, in broad daylight, to the Jewish cemetery. The Polish and Ukrainian collaborators have prepared an open grave and stand by watching as the Nazis begin the slaughter. Layer upon layer, indiscriminate, wholesale slaughter; the shooting doesn't stop until after sunset. The rumbling of German trucks, filled with the clothing and possessions of the murdered, being shipped back to Germany, resounds through all of Sambor until the dawn.

Itche has gone to the other side of the Blich to see how his young family and in-laws fared during this *Aktzie*. He returns a short while later, walking in a trance. The bunker is empty – Sara, Tanchem, and Yisroel Isser, the entire family, gone, taken with the thirteen hundred Jews to the cemetery. Much as we all try, we can't get Itche to react. He's fallen into a depression, and I fear for him.

Day 32 of the Omer, 22 May 1943, and the Germans finally succeed in deporting the Ostilla Rov and his young son Yitzchok to Belzec. One hundred Jews have been taken to the outskirts of Sambor and shot, among them Yitta's brother Hertz. I've still had no word of Yitta, and am assuming she and her child, Berish, have been killed.

June 8, 1943: Today, deputy Dr. Zausner of the Judenrat has announced there will be a public speech made to the Jewish community. I have every intention of going, but Mayer says he will attend, and I am to stay put. At the last minute, Itche joins him. They are gone for about three quarters of an hour and on their return, they tell us the following:

"The Germans want to work with the remaining Jews, not only hand-to-hand, but heart-to-heart. What is needed now is cooperation, all they ask of us, the Jews, is to bring around all our jewels, furs, and leather goods and in exchange, the ghetto will be revalidated and the people given work and food."

Itche is reanimated, and fuming, "Do they take us for idiots; they want to make their jobs easier and are trying to catch us with honey." Mayer is of the same mind, as are we all. The Nazis are not to be trusted. We will stay hidden.

Chapter 8

*M*AYER HAS GONE LOOKING FOR SOME WATER. The heat and the hunger are unbearable. He returns and hastily signals all of us to stillness. We hear them, the Gestapo, and we retreat to the back of the hole. Mayer, while looking for water, saw the Gestapo coming our way, and in his rush to warn us, he hadn't had the time to close the hatch; the bunker entrance is wide open. We hear the soldiers enter the house and they make their way into the courtyard and toward the outhouse.

"Fritz, I tell you, I saw someone running past a window."

"Oh yeah, so where is he?"

"He has to be here somewhere; look, perhaps he went down this hatch, give me a match, it's too dark to see."

The soldier strikes the match, which immediately fizzles out. "Give me another match, Fritz." Again, the match flickers and dies.

"Come on, this is a waste of good matches. I have a better idea, I'm going to shoot inside."

"That's a waste of a good bullet. Save it for when you really have someone to shoot. Can't you see there's no one in there? If someone would still be down there, we would have heard him or her by now. What you saw must have been a cat." The soldiers leave, but we daren't move, or even breathe.

*

It's been decided. To stay means certain death. We are sure that the Germans are preparing to liquidate the ghetto, and somehow, we have to get out. We've worked it out; we've agreed to split up into two groups. Itche, Mayer, and myself, will comprise the first group. We'll crawl under the barbed wire and wade through the river until we are in the open fields. We'll wait until the second group arrives and then proceed. The second group is Toby, Shia, Chana, and the young Yachet. Uncle Avrumche has said he is too old and weak, and will just be the cause of our all getting caught. He will remain behind, and look for a different hiding place.

We leave in the middle of the night, Erev Shavuos 5 Sivan 5703, June 8 1943, and make our way through the stream and under the barbed wire, until we come to the open fields of wheat. In exhaustion, we fall into the sheaves and remain there waiting for the second group. It doesn't take long before Toby's group arrives and from exhaustion, we all fall asleep.

Smoke and shooting awake me, and I nudge Mayer to get up. It's not even dawn, but the noise and the smoke is coming from the Blich. We can hear the shouts and cries all the way across the water. In the stillness of the night, every sound carries. The Nazis are burning down the ghetto, or smoking out the Jews from their hiding places. They are determined to make Sambor "Judenrein." I stand and watch until Mayer pulls me into the rushes. Day is breaking, and someone might see us. We're going to have to hide here until nightfall and then look for a better place.

*

It's dark, and Itche, Mayer, and I head in the direction of the farmhouse belonging to the Schultz family. Stanislav Schultz opens the door to find the three Lamet siblings on his doorstep. "You are crazy to come here; my Ukrainian neighbors will report both you and us, and we will all be shot."

Somehow, we convince him to give us some bread and a bucket so that we can draw water in the river. He is terrified to even talk with us, but agrees to get us bread and a receptacle for water, and also promises not to cut down the wheat in the section of the field where we are hiding.

Toby, Shia, Chana, and Yachet have gone to a different farm. The farmer welcomes them into the barn and gives them food and shelter. Two days later, Stanislav Schultz comes out to the fields to tell us that his neighbor called in the Gestapo and they have carted away the four Jews. I marvel at myself. I have no tears left, I have lost almost everyone, and I can't cry. Have they made me inhuman? Have the Germans turned us into automatons that have no feelings?

He also comes with the news that on the ninth of June, the first day of Shavuos, the day after we escaped, the Nazis cleaned out the ghetto, and declared it "Judenrein." They then piled all the captives into trucks and took them to Radlowice, a village six kilometers from Sambor. There, in the forest, they murdered 1500 men, women and children.

Stanislav has brought more bread, but will not contact us again. The Nazis are all over the place looking for hidden Jews and he can't risk coming in this direction. He tells us he'll leave two loaves of bread at a designated place in the fields every Monday, and we'll have to come and collect it. The place indicated is about a kilometer from his home, and at least double that distance from where we are hiding. He draws us a small map on the ground with a twig. Once he's sure we've memorized the map, he stamps out the design with his shoes. He will allow us to stay here until the end of August, at which time he must cut down the wheat, and we will have to find another place.

I lay here in the open fields, under a blue sky, the earth my pillow, and thank the Almighty again and again for keeping us alive. I've made some new friends, lying here on the ground, staring up in the sky. I have discovered at least five different specimens of birds. My favorite is the little fellow with his grey mantle, and yellow and blue vest. I am entirely ignorant as to the different names, so I allocate my own. This one, I call Charlie Chaplin. I remember seeing a silent moving picture in which he was featured, and these little birds remind me of him. Then there are the crows, coming down to nibble on Stanislav's crop. Those, I call Rokita. Humans do not intimidate the black birds, and they have the nerve to land not an arm's length away, and stare me down.

Then there is a bird I'm sure is a stork. I remember, as a little girl, the peasants coming to der Tateh's shop and telling me their good news . . . a stork has arrived at their house with a baby. I've never seen one before, but by the description, this must be it. I've started calling them Pinocchio, after the little wooden puppet. Then there are the geese. I've seen so many different color geese, it's hard to keep track. What I do know is my mouth waters every time one flies by.

It's Monday, and tonight Mayer will go to retrieve the breads that Stanislav has left for us. It gets dark very late during the summer months and it must be about midnight before Mayer sets out for the place that Stanislav drew on the "map." I start to worry when I think he is gone for too long a time, but I dare not panic Itche. Just when I'm about to voice my concern, I hear movement in the fields and Mayer bursts through the stalks. "I got lost. I couldn't find the place where the bread was left for us, and I couldn't find my way back. I was so frightened I stopped, lifted my face heavenward and prayed. I then just kept on walking, and here you are."

I can't be angry, but I am hungry. It's been decided. Tomorrow I go out to find the bread, and Itche is coming with me. Again, we wait till night has really fallen, and then Itche and I make our way to the specified place. It takes us longer than I thought it would, and Itche keeps telling me I'm headed the wrong way. I insist I know where I'm going, but Itche will have none of it.

"Necha, we're not in the right place, let's head back."

"Itche, I'm sure it's just a little bit further." And luckily I persevered, because not twenty-five meters further, there was a package in brown wrapped paper. The bread. Itche's happy enough to let me lead him back to our 'spot' and Mayer.

August, 1943. We have been debating back and forth about our next move. The wheat harvesting will be beginning and then our hiding place will be non-existent. Stanislav has given us an ultimatum, but we have nowhere to go. I decide I'm going to confront Stanislav himself and beg him to help us. I corner him on Monday morning just as he is about to leave the weekly bread, and begin my tirade.

"You were so good to our parents, and our parents to you. We have lived harmoniously and helped one another. Jadwiga risked her life to help my parents, and in the end, G-d was good to her, because she was good to us. Please, help save us from these murderers, both the Germans and the Ukrainians. We are too weak to survive the winter out in the open."

Stanislav hasn't uttered a word, and I fear I've pushed him too far. It takes him another minute and then he says, "Stay where you are; I'll come for you in four days."

Four days, and no sign of Stanislav. I wonder if he's changed his mind about coming for us, although he didn't tell me what he was planning. I just hope nothing has happened to him because of our conversation. Day five, its Shabbes; nothing, no one. Day six and at the crack of dawn, Stanislav appears. We are to come to the barn this night. We may not speak, not even whisper. We are to wait just inside until we see him or Jadwiga. The children will not be told that there are Jews being hidden. Stanislawa, fifteen, has a Ukrainian boyfriend, Pavel. Stanislav and Jadwiga both fear that if Pavel gets wind of the fact that there are Jews being hidden in the barn, he will immediately report them all.

Anxiety is making me shiver, or is it colder than usual? It is well past midnight and the three of us make our silent way to the barn. The door has been left slightly ajar, probably to keep it from creaking as we push it open. Stanislav is waiting just inside and shows us the hiding place he's prepared.

"Just before the outbreak of the war, I purchased bricks to build a silo for the wheat. The bricks have been piled here, in the corner of the barn, for the last five years, just waiting for the right moment. It's taken these last few days for me to hollow out the center, fortify the ceiling, and recreate just a pile of bricks." Stanislav shows us where he has left a crawl space for us to enter, and how he has prepared some camouflaged cracks for passing in food. He again warns us that the children are unaware and we will have to be very quiet and careful.

Mayer is the first to enter, then it's my turn, and finally Itche. Stanislav then passes in a bedpan, the week's ration of bread, and a bucket of water. He bids us good night and starts bricking up the crawl space. It's pitch dark. I feel Itche and Mayer's presence, but I don't even see my hand when I hold it up in front of my face. I've always hated confined small spaces, and now I'm terrified. Stanislav has told us the space is 2.5 meters long by 1.2 meters wide and 70 cm high. I try to remember where the bucket with the water is so as not to spill it as I try to find a comfortable position. Itche and Mayer are doing the same, trying to stretch out without knocking over the water or bumping into each other or the bricks. We all finally settle down, and from nerves, I start to mumble to myself. "Be grateful, this isn't so bad; the ghetto was worse, Belzec much worse, it could have been the dogs, it could have been a bullet . . ." . ." Mayer nudges me, "Shhh, you'll get us all caught." He's right, of course; I must be strong. In silence, I will myself to believe that this is a good place to be, a good place to be. So why do I keep thinking I'm being buried and this is my coffin?

Chapter 9

*T*HE GERMANS HAVE WON. SINCE SEPTEMBER OF 1939, during the first German occupation, and then from mid-1941, I have never felt as debased as I feel now. Being bricked into this space, having to take care of my private needs, I have been reduced to animal behavior, and I think that that was the Nazi intention, to break us, to demean us. According to Itche, we've been here a week. He is our time-keeper, as somehow, he has this sixth sense and can give you the time and day, almost to the minute. Jadwiga has come today to bring the weekly bread and water and to remove the wastes. In order to do this, she removes a specific brick, behind which there is a second loose brick. Through this aperture, we pass everything out and get everything in. Jadwiga and I speak for just a few minutes, as she wants to get back to the house before Bronislaw comes out to see what is holding her up. What she's able to tell me is that the Nazis were still executing Jews up until the end of July, out in the Jewish cemetery, but it has been quiet for the last few months.

I've let Mayer and Itche know that I plan on continuing to write, and I will need the spot closest to the loose brick, which is our "window." During the noon hours, there is a sliver of light that penetrates the seams where the bricks aren't cemented, and this affords me enough illumination to make entries in my journal. Itche, who normally occupies that space, is happy to relinquish his place for an hour or two. We are careful to do all our communicating in the softest whispers, as we never know when someone has entered the barn.

Mayer and Itche are debating, if you can call it that. I hear very soft whispering, but I feel there is a tension between the two of them.

"What's the problem?" I want to know. They explain that Rosh Hashanah is just around the corner. Itche says it's next Tuesday, and Mayer is arguing that it's Wednesday. I try to do a King Solomon solution and suggest we have Yom Tov on Tuesday, Wednesday, and Thursday, so this way everyone is satisfied. Itche calls me a "dumb girl" and Mayer agrees.

"I don't think I'm so dumb; three days is better than arguing." Itche calmly explains to me that depending on when Rosh Hashanah is, that determines when we will fast for Yom Kippur. So if we are off by a day with Rosh Hashanah in either direction, we will not be fasting on the right day. The lesson I've learned is, when learned men discourse, women should not get involved.

Mayer wins out and we celebrate Rosh Hashanah on Wednesday. Mayer and Itche take turns with the davening, all done in a soft whisper. I strain to hear the words, but it is very difficult, so in my head, I try to repeat the tefillos that I remember.

> *"Avinu Malkeinu," Our Father, our King, we have sinned before You.*
> *Our Father, our King, we have no king but You.*
> *Our Father, our King, deal kindly with us for Your Name's sake.*
> *Our Father, our King, inaugurate upon us a good year.*
> *Our Father, our King, nullify all harsh decrees upon us.*
> *Our Father, our King, thwart the thoughts of those who hate us.*
> *Our Father, our King, exterminate every foe and adversary from upon us.*
> *Our Father, our King, send complete recovery to the sick of Your people.*
> *Our Father, our King, inscribe us in the Book of Redemption and Salvation.*
> *Our Father, our King, be gracious with us and answer us; though we have no worthy deeds, treat us with charity and kindness, and save us.*

I know I have missed quite a bit of the prayer, but this is all that I remember. Feeling bad that I can't remember the Avinu Malkeinu in it's entirety, I repeat it again and again, and still again, all the passages that I do remember by heart. And so our Yom Tov is spent, Itche and Mayer in prayer, and me, in my own way, praying as best I can.

*

The rains have started. I can hear it coming down on the barn roof, the part that is made of corrugated metal. At first I thought the noise was machine-gun fire, but then I realized that it was the rain. I think of it as a small blessing; hardly anyone ventures out and we don't have to be that careful about whispering. What I didn't realize as I was rejoicing over the rain was, the earth in our little 'apartment' has become damp, damp and cold. We huddle together to try and warm up that way, but it doesn't help by much. It does improve a little bit when the rains stop, as the water stops seeping into the ground.

*

I have to get out of this bunker somehow, or I'll go mad. I know . . .

Today, I'm going to Paris. I've been here at the L'vov train station for the last half-hour waiting anxiously for the international train to arrive. I see it chugging closer in the distance and my excitement mounts. This is going to be a fabulous trip. As the train is pulling in, I locate my carriage number displayed in the window, and I'm the first to mount the stairs once the train has ground to a halt. I sit back in this luxurious first-class train seat, and just relax. First-class carriages are decorated with plush velvet armchairs, brass light fittings, and high-gloss wood panelling. There is a small tray table at every seat, and the chairs are nicely spaced, to afford privacy to all the first-class guests. I make myself comfortable, as the trip is going to take just under twenty-four hours. I've come prepared with a list of sights I'm going to see once I get to Paris and I just hope I can squeeze all of the stops into this mini, four-day trip.

The train is pulling out of the station, and the people outside are waving goodbye, some with smiles, some with tears. Some are even running alongside trying to keep up with the train and their loved ones for as long as possible, and as we pick up speed, the last of the runners falls behind. I look around me and most of the travellers elude an air of importance. I start a game with myself, trying to guess who and what these people are. It keeps me occupied almost until the German border. This game also tires me, and I doze off, and awake as we pull into the Berlin 'Hauptbahnhof,' the main station.

A ticket officer, as well as a customs official, enter our carriage and commence checking everyone's documents. They are very courteous as they look at my passport and ticket, wish me a pleasant trip, and continue on their way. The train is still stationary and I use this opportunity to remove my small case from the overhead storage bin and take out some food. I have this most delicious sandwich with me. Tomatoes and cheese, and even a pickle on freshly baked bread, mmm, what a delight. There aren't any new passengers for this carriage and the train gets underway again. The time flies by and as the scenery changes, so do the cities. We've made stops in Frankfurt and Saarbruken, and are now on French soil, via Metz, the last stop before Paris. I'm amazed at how quickly the time has passed.

Gare du Nord, the main Paris station, teeming with people. I've never seen such large crowds. L'vov is a miniature compared to Paris. I've decided to treat myself to a horse and buggy and let the driver take me on a driving tour. To my luck, there are a few empty carriages just outside the station I locate a driver that speaks plausible German, and after brief negotiations, we're off. Down we fly on the wide boulevards, past huge façades, surely housing important business. First stop, the Opera House. The driver explains that it was built in 1875 and the two outer statues are real gold. He wants to know if I wish to go inside, but I tell him that today, I'll just be making a general tour. From there we head to the Arc de Triomphe, commissioned by Napoleon in 1806 to commemorate his success. The driver tells me that the dictator was ousted before it was completed, and . . .

"Stop nudging me!" Mayer has been shaking my shoulder for the last few minutes.

"Do you realize you've been crouching at our 'window' for the entire afternoon, scribbling in your silly journal? It'll soon be dark, and I'd also like to get some light and have a look out." We've found an angle in the bricks that lets us see almost to the entrance of the barn. It helps us keep track of the days and nights. Mayer doesn't realize he's interrupted my trip to Paris, and I'm not ready to tell him, as he has absolutely no patience with my writing. I unhappily relinquish my place, with much manoeuvring, and settle down to dream on.

*

Jadwiga has included a newspaper with the bread today. It's an old issue, July 1943, so it's stale news, but I'm grateful nevertheless. I didn't think they were still printing the Gazeta Lwowska, so the newspaper is a surprise and a treat. Thank you, Jadwiga.

On the front page, there is a banner announcing the Allied invasion of Sicily. The article recounts the might of the German army, and the incompetent performance of the Allied armies. The story continues to applaud the German decision to leave the island and spare the inhabitants. I've learned to read between the lines, and these last few years, I've become expert on German propaganda. It seems to me that the Germans retreated from Sicily with their tails between their legs. Itche also thinks this is a positive sign, and is hopeful that the Americans are there to stay. Itche says that once the Americans have a foothold in Europe, they will not let go. I don't know where he has his information from, but both Mayer and I are happy to believe in his vision.

Chapter 10

*I*TCHE WAS CRYING AGAIN LAST NIGHT. I TRY TO broach the topic, but he won't talk. "Just leave me be, I can take care of myself." He's become very irritable, as have we all. Stanislav has brought the cows into the barn for the winter, and the noise and stench are overwhelming. This doesn't add to our state of mind and just increases the tension between us.

*

Today I'm out in the park. There is nothing like summer in Sambor. The kaleidoscope of color is amazing. The trees, the flowers, even people are dressed in happy, colored clothing. De Mameh has dressed me in my best outfit, a pink cotton frock with little ruffles around the collar and sleeves. She spent hours ironing this dress, and has warned me not to sit on the grass. Toby and her friends were kind enough to take me with them, as de Mameh is very busy and doesn't have a chance to come. Having an eight-year-old sister in tow is not a lot of fun for Toby, so she sits me down on a bench and warns me not to move or leave till she is finished playing. I'm just happy enough to be here, so I do as instructed.

It doesn't take that long before I spy my buddy Esther arriving. We're classmates, but more than that, her father is the Rov here in Sambor and der Tateh is one of his Chassidim. I very often accompany der Tateh when he visits the Rov and I really like Esther's company. She's come with her governess, Hella, a matronly Jewish woman, and has a doll and little perambulator with her. This is turning out to be a great outing. Toby has forgotten all about me, and I her. I don't even see her in the park anymore. I'm not too worried, as I'm with Esther, having fun, not thinking about it too much.

Hella has removed a flask from her carpetbag and pours what looks like liquid chocolate into a cup. She hands it to Esther, and reminds her to make the brocha. I'm staring, and my mouth must be drooling, 'cause Esther asks me if I'd like some, too.

"Is it 'milchig'? I ate 'fleishig' before I came." All the while, I'm staring at the cup and hoping that the drink is 'parve.'

"Yes, it's 'milchig,' but how long ago was that, Necha? It must be four hours by now." What's with the four hours? Indeed, it must be four hours since I've eaten, and her father is the Rov, and if they wait four hours, they must know what they are doing, and the drink is so very tempting, and who will know that I haven't waited the six hours.

"Sure, it's longer than four hours, Esther." She hands over the cup, and I slowly sip the thick, brown liquid, savoring every drop. We play on for a while, and soon it's time for Esther to leave. Hella wants to know where my sister is, she can't leave me here on my own, yet Toby and friends are nowhere to be seen. With a sigh, Hella offers to make a detour and escort me home. De Mameh is busy at her worktable and looks up from some sewing when I enter.

"You must have had a lovely time, and did someone give you chocolate?" Is my mother a prophet, or has someone denounced me?

"Oh Mameh, I was so thirsty, it was so very hot in the park, and Esther was there, and she offered me this drink, and she also had fleishig for lunch, and she told me she only waits four hours, and how did you know?" De Mameh draws me toward her and without a word, points to some spots on the front of my pink dress.

"There are different 'minhagim' for waiting after meat dishes. Ours is to wait six hours. Necha, go get undressed so that I can soak the stains out of your dress."

Undressing in the next room, I hear a commotion in the kitchen. Toby is being told off in no uncertain terms about not being responsible, and leaving me alone in the park. With head hanging, she joins me, and seeing me, or is it the state of my dress, she bursts out crying.

"Oh, Necha, I'm really sorry, I got so involved with my friends I forgot all about you, and when I returned and you weren't there, I had such a fright. Thank G-d you're home."

I pull myself out of my daydreaming, and put down my pencil. Oy, Toby, Toby my beloved sister, and Shia and the innocent Chana. Did they shoot you? Did they put you on a train? Were you afraid?

Were you together at the end? Who will remember you? Who will remember any of us?

*

Itche is running a fever. He has a tendency to an ingrown toenail and he thinks the toe is infected and causing the fever. At our wits' end, we anxiously wait for tomorrow when the Schultzes come for our weekly visit. The night is a real nightmare; Itche's fever is peaking and he's almost delirious. I've been soaking my scarf in water and applying a compress to his forehead, but it hasn't made much of a difference. Am I going to lose Itche too?

Stanislav is at the "window" and I whisper to him that Itche is running a very high fever. Can he please give me a few raw potatoes?

"And how will that help him?" He thinks I've completely lost my senses.

"My grandmother used raw potatoes to cure lots of things. I just hope the infection hasn't gone too far, and I can't really see what's happening in here."

Stanislav promises to be right back and, indeed, he returns in a few minutes. He passes five raw potatoes to me, a small pocketknife, and a book of matches with a candle. He cautions me to be careful with the matches, not to cause a fire, as well as the light might be a security risk. He will be back in an hour to collect the candle, the matches, and the knife. Then he re-covers the "window" and we are again plunged into near darkness.

I feel around for the matches and carefully light the candle. When I see what Itche and Mayer look like, I drop the candle, and almost start a fire. They are ghostly; my brothers look like death. I am determined to try and help Itche, and that means striking another match, lighting the candle. I steel myself when I see his and Mayer's emaciated, chalky faces again.

I get busy cutting thick slices of potato. I put a large chunk on Itche's toe, which I can see is, indeed, septic. I use some newspaper to wrap up the toe and keep the potato in place. I then cut some more slices and put these on Itche's forehead, secured with my shawl, and continue cutting all the potatoes into slices. Stanislav is back to retrieve the things he's left behind, and he's brought a cup of milk.

"Here, give this to your brother." I thank him again, as he puts the brick back into place.

· 231 ·

"Babaleh, you have to intervene in the Heavenly Court, please. Please do everything you can so that Itche gets well." I wake up sweating; I'm convinced I'm running a fever. I scramble to feel Itche's head, and I am shocked to feel that it's coolish. He is breathing regularly, so he must be asleep. Mayer, too, is sleeping, as if he's got no care in the world. Tears run down my eyes as I thank the Almighty. I have a good feeling that Itche is on the mend. Thank you, too, dear Babeh, always so wise, and I'm sure you had something to do with this miracle from your place "up there."

Jadwiga comes unexpectedly. "How is your brother? And I have some news for you. The Russians have launched a huge offensive against the Germans, and they are fighting not two hundred kilometers east of here. We are going to have to be more careful because there are lots of troupes heading east and they will be passing through Sambor. The Gestapo has issued orders that everyone in town and in the village might be called on to 'host' some soldiers. Again, please be very careful."

*

According to Itche's calculations, we are celebrating Purim this week. I ask Mayer how much of the megilla he remembers off by heart, and his response "not a lot." I guess we'll have to make do. Itche has always been the business head in the family, while Mayer is the Talmid Chacham. I've had something on my chest for the longest time, and now is as good a moment as any to air my thoughts.

"Tell me something, Mayer. On Har Hamoriah, Avraham was ready to sacrifice his son Yitzchok at the Akeidah. It would have meant blood and fire. The Akeidah didn't happen, and Yitzchok was spared. Do you think that because the Akeidah never happened, the Jewish people have been persecuted with blood and fire for the last 5000 years? Do you think we still have a score to pay with blood and fire?"

"Necha, what nonsense; I now know why women aren't supposed to learn. It's not up to humans to philosophise about how the Almighty rules the world. Just stick to your cooking and sewing, and leave the thinking to the male scholars."

"Mayer, you are a real chauvinist, and I'm glad that at least der Tateh thought girls should be educated."

"Will both of you stop arguing, you're starting to raise your voices, and someone might hear you." That, coming from Itche, ends the discussion, but I wish someone could give me some answers. I'm full of questions. De Mameh used to say I ask more questions than the NKVD, which is the Russian Secret Service. I need someone to tell me why. Who's going to tell me how so much evil can emanate from such a 'civilized people,' the 'superior' Germans, everyone's example of a cultured nation, always beginning their sentences with "Bitte schön, danke schön," always so polite; how can they be such barbarians? Who's going to tell me how so many men, women, and children were marched to their death and not a sound was heard from the rest of the world? Who's going to tell me why so many countries refused refuge to fleeing Jews? Who's going to tell me where to go to mourn my mother, my father, my grandmother, my sisters, brothers-in-law, and nieces, uncles, aunts, and cousins? Who's going to tell me if I'll be buried here till eternity? Is there anyone left out there to answer my questions? Are we the last Jews on this planet?

*

The Nazis are moving onto the farm. Stanislav has quickly come to tell us that there will be two officers and six soldiers billeted in the house and that the horses will be stabled in the barn. He's brought enough bread for two weeks and by then, he hopes they will have moved on. Through our little window, I catch sight of one of the soldiers an hour later, as he leads a horse into the barn. I tap Itche and Mayer, our signal that someone is within hearing range. The soldier tethers the horse, rubs him down, and puts some hay and water out for him, then leaves. I tell Itche and Mayer quietly what I've seen, and my observation that the soldier doesn't look a day older than sixteen. They must be in bad shape to have conscripted such youngsters. I'm hoping that it's a sign that their older soldiers are either dead or invalided. The siege doesn't last too long; they are all gone three days later, headed for the eastern front.

Pesach is next week and Mayer is reminding me to speak with Jadwiga about the food. My entreaty will not convince my brothers to eat bread on Pesach. Jadwiga is very cooperative, she remembers how strict der Tateh was with all religious laws and even suggests buying a new pot and cooking us some potatoes. That sounds wonderful to me, but the boys refuse, asking if she would kindly just bring raw carrots instead of bread. Jadwiga has no problem with this idea and agrees immediately.

Pesach, 14 Nissan 5704, and our 'apartment' is all ready for Yom Tov. The bread has long been eaten up, and Jadwiga has seen to it that we have raw carrots for eight days. Itche and Mayer take turns whispering the Haggadah, and I join in when I remember the words. At some point, my mind wanders and I don't hear, or participate in the rest of the Haggadah. I'm thinking of the Jewish infants in Egypt, stuck into the empty spaces of the walls instead of mortar. I'm thinking that almost 4000 years later, nothing has changed. No matter how modern and advanced, how educated and cultured, humans are still no better than animals.

How many more atrocities have to be rained down on our people before we see the final redemption?

Chapter 11

OMBS, I WAKE UP TO THE SOUND OF BOMBS. I scramble to see through the split in the bricks, our little window, but Itche is already there before me. He whispers that he thinks the Nazis are back on the farm, we must be careful. I settle back into my place and try not to think about what is happening outside. I can make out the sounds of tanks and small weapons' fire. Wouldn't it be ironic if we were to be hit by a mortar shell? There are horses stabled in the barn again, and they have been neighing for hours. They are very restless; who's to blame them? I fall asleep to the background sounds of agitated horses, gunfire, and bombs.

It must be morning; I can hear shouting and there is a lot of activity in the barn. The soldiers have come to saddle up their horses. I'm looking out, trying to get a good angle, when I see one of the officers making his way to the corner of the barn where we are hidden in the pile of bricks. I quickly signal Itche and Mayer, and all breathing stops. I watch as the officer lifts one of the outer layers of bricks and examines it. If he should try to move the next brick, it's over for us. The next layer is cemented down and he'll surely understand that it's a bricked-in hiding place. I close my eyes waiting for the hammer to strike, when I hear Stanislav.

"Herr Oberst, can I help you with something?" I open my eyes to see Stanislav standing next to the officer, holding a bottle of wine. "I just found a few bottles of vintage wine in the cellar, and thought you might enjoy some with your meal this evening. I was coming to check whether you prefer red or white."

My mouth drops, as I watch Stanislav in action. He is better than any actor I've seen, and where did he pick up this air of "red or white wine"? He sounds like the maitre d' in a fancy restaurant. I've almost forgotten that we're at risk, but as the officer turns back toward our hiding place, I'm jolted back to the here and now, back to the danger of the situation. He takes a step forward, looks at the space where he's removed the brick, and just as I think he's going to take another brick, he returns the one he's been holding in his hand to its original place. He then turns towards Stanislav, "I'd like the red, danke schön." As he exits the barn, he calls to one of the soldiers to saddle up his horse, they'll be leaving shortly.

The Germans don't return. Instead, the Russians arrive in force, taking over the Schultz house completely, and billeting soldiers in the barn. There are bombs falling closer and closer to where we are, but we dare not leave our hiding place. The Russians are here today, but might be gone tomorrow and then we'll fall back into the hands of the Nazis. Jadwiga smuggles in our supplies while the soldiers are out, and agrees that it is too dangerous to come out of hiding yet.

Nothing is settled. I haven't slept for the last few days, since the Russians have arrived and are sleeping in the barn. They come in after their sorties, and drink the whole night through, singing and being rowdy. I remember the Poles in town, on the weekends after they'd get their wages, drinking themselves into a stupor. They'd begin from sundown Friday, straight through to Monday, when they'd try to somehow get back to their jobs. Many is the time we'd find a drunk asleep on our doorstep because his wife wouldn't let him in. The only difference between the Poles and these Russians is that every morning, they have to be sober enough to go out and fight.

Operation Bagration, I don't know what it means, but it's all I hear the soldiers talking about. They are laughing and in good spirits, so I hope they are winning the battles. On some days, the bombs are so close, I can hear the shrapnel hitting the sides of the barn. And on other days, the battle is just a rumble in the distance.

July 23, 1944, Jadwiga has just heard from one of the officers, the concentration camp Majdanek has been liberated. The Russians have liberated both the camp and the city of Lublin, and the German army is in retreat. She suggests that we remain in hiding a bit longer, just to be sure that the Nazis have been pushed back from this area.

Jadwiga comes with bad news. A Jewish family hiding on the other side of Sambor have been denounced by some Polish neighbors and have been shot by the Nazis. It is really wiser to wait until the Germans' retreat is definite.

*

Liberated . . . liberated? Liberated! Stanislav is slowly dismantling our 'apartment,' brick by brick. I wince in the sunlight, even though it's shining outside and I'm still in the barn. Stanislawa and Bronislaw are inside with their parents, staring at us in shocked amazement. They look terrified; we must be a real sight. I ask Stanislawa if I look terrible, and she says, "Not really, I'm just surprised to see you, that's all. Were you really hiding in our barn for the last thirteen months?"

Cover up. I think she's not being truthful, and I do scare her, perhaps I even disgust her. I haven't washed for . . . I can't remember the last time, and if Mayer and Itche's color is any indication as to what I look like, I'm sure I'd be revolted at my own looks, too. The four of them have to help us up and onto our feet. Mine won't carry me, and I fold down right back onto the floor. Itche is supporting himself against the wall, but is having a difficult time trying to straighten out. Mayer seems to be the most stable on his feet, and he comes back over to see if he can help me get up.

I can't get up. I don't want to get up. Where am I going? I have no place to go, no one to find. I've lost everything. I've been liberated into an abyss.

Chapter 12

WO KILOMETERS. THAT IS THE DISTANCE FROM the Schultz barn to the entrance of Sambor. It takes 4693 painful steps, 4 hours, and twenty minutes, a distance we should have been able to cover in less than an hour. The roads heading west are congested with Russian army vehicles and as they pass us, they slow down and stare. The walking dead. I walk in between Itche and Mayer, not really walking; it's more like limping, I have to be supported.

The fields, my fields. It's summer 1939 and I'm running through the fields. The fields are exploding, for miles and miles the fields are bursting, awash in yellow and green, endless rows of sunflowers, swaying in the wind to their own secret music, a silent dance.

I stand and watch the fields, those same fields, Itche prodding me on, "Come on, Necha, we'll never get to Sambor at this pace."

"Itche, how many sunflowers do you think there are in the field?"

"I don't know, and I don't really care. I don't own them, so what difference does it make if there are one hundred, one thousand or one million?"

"Mayer, how many sunflowers do you think there are?"

"Like the stars in the heavens, and the sand on the sea shores . . . too many to count."

True to form, the businessman has given me his answer, and the Talmid Chacham, his.

Can it be that war has raged back and forth over these fields for five long years, and the sunflowers are still growing? Can it be that after five long years of a war waged against them, I will still find Jews in Sambor? I quicken my pace, shrugging off the support of Itche and Mayer and hurry on my way, past the barbed wire, past the stream, back to the Blich, back the way I came fourteen months ago.

The houses on the Blich are deserted. Mortar shells have hit many, and others have been burnt out. The glass is gone from the windows, the doors hang open on their hinges. We pick our way slowly past the houses on our street and come to a stop in front of our own building. Images flash past in my mind: Goldie, with her embroidered Star of David; old Yoel Genuth being thrown out the window; Izzy, hair white as snow, waving his last farewell; de Mameh, bent over the stove, trying to feed the hoards of refugees; Babeh Reizel ordering Mayer to eat; der Tateh, asking me why his nightingale isn't singing.

My legs won't carry me an inch further, and I collapse against the façade. Itche, and Mayer too, overwhelmed by their own memories, slip down next to me. We are barely here a few minutes when we see some people in the distance, and they are coming our way. It's hard to make out who or what they are, and we sit in nervous silence, hoping that it's not Ukrainians. The Schultzes have warned us that in many of the liberated towns, the Jews who have managed to hide throughout the war are killed by Ukrainians when they leave their hiding places. I sit here thinking how sad that would be for us, but I don't have the strength to move.

Watching the people moving closer, I see that there are two of them. As they get even closer, I see two tall, erect people, what look like a man and a woman, dressed in potato sacks, sunburnt and strong, and they are just about parallel to us. I have a problem craning my head to look up at them.

"Itche, is that you?" the man addresses us.

"Oyzer? Oyzer Orlander?" Itche is trying to rise to his feet, and I follow suit. I come almost face to face with Yitta. She is taller than I am by a head, and while she is standing erect, I am a hunched wreck.

"Yitta, oy Yitta," falling on each other's shoulders, five years worth of tears erupt from me. Yitta isn't crying, she just stands here embracing me, trying to console me. Pulling myself together, I straighten up as best I can, and search out her eyes. Words don't pass between us, but I know, I feel and I know, she has lost Berish, her child.

Together, our rag-tag group, the three invalids, and the two "peasants" dressed in tattered potato sacking, make our way out of the Blich and toward the newer part of town. Lelova 8, our house, occupied now by Poles. There is a boy in the doorway, staring at us, but when his mother sees the group just outside her home, she pulls her son into the house and slams the door. That's when it hits me. This is not our city any longer. We have to close the door. We have to move on, otherwise our survival is at stake, and I mean close the door both literally and figuratively.

Slowly, we walk toward the Begleiter Shul at the end of the road. It's still standing, minus doors and windows. Looking inside, we realize it was converted into a stable, to house the Nazi horses. There are still droppings and souring hay everywhere, any trace that this was once a holy place of worship, gone. Mayer, not one to give up, starts sifting through the hay. He goes from pile to pile, looking for . . . I know not what. We all humor him; let him look. We aren't late for any appointments, so what does it matter. Yitta and I find a spot out back to sit, a stone's throw from the door, and in the sunshine.

It doesn't take five minutes and there is a commotion inside, Mayer shouting he's found something. The three men rush out into the sunlight to examine what looks like a sefer. It is, it's a sefer, and it's the Zaide, Reb Menachem Efraim Treiber, the Maggid's sefer, *Shemen HaMor: Mafteach Bais Dovid.* Of all the hundreds of seforim, of all the furnishings and fixtures, the only thing that remains is this sefer. Mayer's face has become reanimated. "The Almighty is sending us a sign." We leave the Shul in better spirits, with hope.

Yitta and Oyzer are going to need clothing. "That would be nice, but I haven't anything to purchase clothing with, no money and nothing to barter," Yitta says without a trace of self-pity. I am quick to remove my backpack from my back and I pull out the pouch of jewellery that has fallen to the bottom.

"Yitta, I have some dollars here. Why don't we go and see if we can get you something to wear; your brother, too. Yitta stares at the bulging pouch, and at my patchwork backpack. "What other treasure do you have hidden in there?"

I don't answer Yitta. How can I? How can I tell her I'm carrying Jewish history in my bag, my story, the story of the people nearest and dearest to me? The story of my neighbors and friends; the story of the holy Rabbonim and Dayanim; of the simple people; the story of innocent infants and children; of pregnant women, and of old grandmothers. The story of Galician Jewry.

The story of how the world stood by, turned a blind eye to the mass-murder of millions of our people. Clouds of Jewish ashes hanging over cities, and the world stood silent.

There is Tonya's heroic story of Tach VeTat, as well as Freya's story of the dark times of the Inquisition, and Dina, survivors of the English massacres. A legacy . . . you might call it. A "gravestone," finally erected for all those who perished, and were never buried. That is what I have in my backpack

Epilogue

IN 1939, ABOUT 25,000 PEOPLE WERE REGISTERED IN SAMBOR, of which 8,000 were Jews. In August of 1944, approximately thirty Jews came out of hiding in and around Sambor, the remnants of Sambor's Jews. Necha, one of those survivors, was my mother, and *her* story, as recounted above and continued here, is true.

The first weeks were very emotional for all the survivors that returned. Every cobblestone, every doorstep, held memories of loved ones, family and friends. Dazed, the thirty or so *nefoshos* camped out in the shell of the Begleiter Shul, but at the end of August, most Jews agreed that remaining under Soviet rule was not a good idea. The Soviets in combination with the Ukrainians equalled trouble for the Jews. It became known that the Russian officer in charge of the city Tarnow, which was not too far from Sambor, was Jewish, and perhaps more sympathetic to the refugees' plight. Most of the group made their way to Tarnow, among them Necha, Yitta, Oyzer, Itche, and Mayer. They spent the entire winter, through Pesach, in Tarnow.

By June 1945, Tarnow was teeming with Russian soldiers and Jewish refugees from all parts of Galicia. Among those refugees was the Family Reich: Reb Chaskel; his wife, Malia; their two sons, Efraim and Shmuel; their two daughters, Hanya and Ruchel; Hanya's husband, Reuven Wolf; and his father, who also happened to be Malia's brother. This amazing family survived the war in their home town of Dembitz, hidden in an attic by the local doctor and his wife. There was an immediate click between the Orlanders and the Reichs, and especially between Necha and Hanya. Necha and Hanya became inseparable, and a bond was forged between the

Reichs and Orlanders that has, so far, spanned sixty-five years, and five generations.

Itche received an offer from the Agudah to leave for Paris and oversee orphaned Jewish boys. Mayer chose to remain in Tarnow, as he was offered a post as Rabbi. Oyzer declared his intention to marry Necha, when they got out of Poland, and found a more permanent existence. With the good wishes of both of her brothers, Necha, Yitta, and Oyzer, together with the Reich clan, board a train. Final destination: Palestine.

The plan was as follows: travel through Czechoslovakia then into Hungary with a final destination of Grosswardein (Nagy-Varad) Romania, where counterfeit Greek passports were available, and these would enable them to get to Greece and from there, on to Palestine.

Many Jews fled to Grosswardein, Romania, and the local population wasn't too happy with these particular refugees, these Galician Jewish survivors that had arrived with some money in their pockets. Jealousy and mistrust festered between the Romanian Jews and these Galician refugees. Oyzer and Reb Chaskel were summoned by the head of the local Jewish refugees' office and told to either leave Grosswardein or face Russian imprisonment. Reb Chaskel and Oyzer immediately gathered the rest of the group and caught the first train out of Grosswardein, a coal train, headed via Hungary for Austria.

The group hopped on and off the freight trains until they arrived in Salzburg, Austria. There, at the beginning of February 1946, the Reich and the Orlander parties sadly parted ways.

Oyzer, Yitta, and Necha, determined to find a town that had a serious Rov and a kosher mikvah, made their way to Fürth, Germany, where the kehillah was under the auspices of Rav Shapira, the Fürther Rov. The old town Fürth was home to one of the oldest kehillahs in Germany, and there was still a kosher mikvah in the old Shul, albeit one that was built hundreds of years ago.

There, on Friday, March 1, 1946 with the Fürther Rov officiating, Necha Lamet married Oyzer Orlander.

Author's note

THERE WERE PROBABLY HUNDREDS, IF NOT THOUSANDS, OF Dinas, Freyas, and Tonyas all through the ages; but they are, indeed, fictitious persons. The story of Necha, however, is real.

Necha's story is my mother's. The only fictionalized part is that there never was a journal. This was my way of writing the stories my mother recounted to me as I was growing up. Some of the names and the time frame might not be 100% accurate.

The Babeh Reizel, my real-life great-grandmother, was even more imposing than portrayed.

Fraide Pesel, Necha's mother, was a saint and heroine, and actually did choose to martyr herself for the sake of saving many others' lives.

Mordechai, Necha's father, was a chassid in the true sense.

Yitta was a pure soul, never had more children after Berish passed away. She retuned her soul to her maker in 5770, 2010, at the age of 103. She always attributed her long years to the Ostilla Rov's brocha. (For more details on Yitta's life during the war years, see the following section.)

Oyzer was instrumental in refurbishing the mikvah in Fürth and inspiring many of the engaged DPs to have kosher marriages. He was also the shochet for the DP camp in Fürth and surroundings cities. True to his and Necha's upbringing, their home was open to scores of displaced persons, whom they mentored and fed until August 1949, when the couple left for the United States. Oyzer continued his shechitah until 1960 and their home was open to the needy until their passing.

Itche, true to form, became a very successful businessman in the

States; his story was portrayed accurately, but the names of his wife and sons, fictitious.

Mayer still going strong at age 94, B"H, has republished the Maggid's seforim, *Shemen HaMor* and *Mafteach Bais Dovid*.

Family Schultz was honored in a ceremony at Yad Vashem, proclaimed as "Righteous Among the Nations."

May his name be erased, Rokita was tried for war crimes in Nuremburg.

I ask forgiveness from you, my dear mother, Necha. I have attempted to put myself into your skin, by remembering all your stories of "how it was back in the 'alte heim'" and your experiences during the war. I remember sharing *Mila 18* by Leon Uris with you when it first came out. It was the story of the Warsaw Ghetto uprising, and as we both read it, Mammy, you kept saying, "I should really write a book." I was too young at the time to encourage you. For that, too, I beg your forgiveness. There is no way I can really know what or how you felt, I only know that what I write is through the pain I received from you by osmosis.

—Toby Orlander-Thaler

Yitta's Story: 1939–1945

This is by no means an afterthought, but you might be wondering about Yitta's story. Yitta, my dear aunt, who was a major player in my life, and influenced me almost as much as my mother. Yitta was a true princess, in deed and in spirit. She carried a heavy burden, never again having children after the loss of her Berish, but never questioned the Almighty's ways. She returned her pure Neshama to her maker at the age of 103.

In September of 1939, after the German invasion, the Ostilla Rov, Reb Pinchas Twersky, together with his Gabbai, were guests of Reb Shloime Zalman Orlander's. This was the Rov's "stantzia," hospitality house, on his many visits to Sambor. During the Friday night seudah, heavy, running footsteps were heard on the stairs, and loud banging on the doors . . .

"Aufmachen, schnell, aufmachen." All present looked to the Rov for direction, and he pointed to Yitta. "Go and see what the soldiers want. You speak German, ask them what they need. And pull your scarf further down on your forehead."

"I'm scared, no, I'm terrified."

"Don't be; I promise you, you'll be fine. Nothing will happen to you."

Yitta went to the door. The Nazis were looking for someone to direct them to a tavern. Yitta answered their questions, and they went on their way. She was safe.

Unfortunately, her husband was less lucky. When the Nazis returned to Sambor in 1941, Yitta's husband, Yossel Billet, was one of the first casualties. He was hung in the town square by the Germans.

In 1942, during the Shavuos *Aktzie* of 5703, Yitta, together with her young son, hid in a bunker shared with approximately twenty other people. Her brother-in-law, holding the small Berish as he slept, heard the Nazis enter the room overhead. To keep the child from crying out, he covered his mouth and unintentionally suffocated the little boy. Yitta was now alone, without husband or child.

A few days before Rosh Hashana, rumors spread through Sambor of terrible massacres in Dobromil, and the Ostilla Rov asked Yitta to smuggle herself into that town and verify the facts. He chose Yitta, as she was fair-skinned and could pass for a non-Jew dressed in peasant clothing.

A day passed, then two; soon, three days had passed and it was almost sundown of Rosh Hashana, but Yitta had not returned. The Ostilla Rov refused to begin the Yom Tov prayers until he had word of Yitta's safety. From afar, they saw her pitiful silhouette. From exhaustion, she was almost crawling her way back into town. The story she finally told about the happenings in Dobromil was more horrific than anything they had heard previously.

Yitta's father, Reb Shloime Zalman, her mother, Taube Billet, and her sister, Chaya, were murdered in Belzec on 9 Cheshvan, 1943. Her brother Naftali Hertz was killed in the suburbs of Sambor, Sivan 1943, and her brother Ahron was shot in Radlowitz in Iyar 1943.

In June of 1943, knowing that the ghetto was to be liquidated, Yitta and Oyzer broke through a wall in the ghetto, cut through the barbed wire, and swam across the river to safety. Having no money, nor jewellery, nothing to pay off the Poles with, they spent the next fourteen months hiding in tunnels they were able to dig, in the forest, in abandoned shacks, in barns, staying out of sight of the farmers. They lived on raw potatoes, roots, and berries, and anything they could find in the fields and forests. They knew not to trust the Ukrainians, the Poles, and certainly not the Germans. What kept them going morally was overhearing two Poles one night as they were lying in a trench.

"Did you hear? They say the 'Wunder Rabbina' passed through Sambor last night on his way to Hungary." The Poles were speaking among themselves of Reb Aron, the Belzer Rebbe zt"l.

The tears rolled down Oyzer's eyes as he told Yitta, "The Rebbe is rescued; there is something to live for."

Good Poles were few and far apart. One farmer found them hiding under the hay in his barn, and told them they would have to leave. Oyzer somehow begged the farmer to let them stay on one more night, as it was the Passover. The Pole agreed, left, and returned a short time later with bread. Oyzer told Yitta she was allowed to accept and eat it, as it was Achron shel Pesach, the last day, and in Israel, the Passover was over; people in Israel were already eating bread, so she should, too. His one request was that she saves a small piece for him for tomorrow night. Yitta didn't eat the bread until the next evening when she shared it with Oyzer.

May 1944 and Oyzer and Yitta found refuge in a cornfield. They would go to the nearest stream at night to drink water, and then again return to their hiding place in the stalks. After a week, there was a bucket of fresh milk at their watering hole. Every night, they would drink the milk, return to their corn stalks, and the next day again, and again find a bucket of milk. This scenario was played out until the liberation. Obviously, the farmer knew there were Jews hiding in his fields and he wished to help them. Lying under the warming sun, being nourished by the cream-rich milk, Yitta and Oyzer's bodies healed. The Russians liberated them in August of that year.

Dedication

IT'S ALL ABOUT SPECIAL WOMEN . . . I'VE BEEN VERY FORTU-
nate on this journey called life to have encountered some very
extraordinary women. Of course, my mother and grandmother,
whose stories you've just read; the incredible Rebbetzin Zehava
Braunstein, who was my English Lit. teacher and encouraged me to
write; Rebbetzin Zoberman, my high school teacher, who, in spite
of my incorrigible behavior, always assured my mother that I would
amount to something. There were many great women who have
crossed my path, but few of them have touched my heart as did my
dear friend Goldi Wolf-Lowy a"h.

There is no such thing as "chance" in the Jewish believers'
lexicon, and when Goldi married into the Reich clan, it was just
another stitch in the tapestry that was the Orlander-Lamet/Reich
saga; a continuation of the Necha-Hanyu link. It was obvious from
the moment I met Goldi that she was not ordinary – her generous
spirit, her selflessness, her pure joy in sharing, her happiness in the
good fortune of others in spite of having to weather many hardships
herself. Goldi never complained, never lost her "Bitachon, never
asked, "Why me?" In her last very difficult years, suffering ever-in-
creasing pain and incapacitation, she bore her illness with dignity,
like the true princess she was.

During these last few years of Goldi's life, her husband, Lezer,
in sheer selflessness, sacrificed his business, his social life, and his
every waking hour to tend single-handedly to Goldi's every need.
On her shloshim, Lezer consoled me with the following thought:
"Oh Death, you are nothing but a door; for when we go through
you, you are no more."

Dedication

My dear Goldi, it was an honor knowing you, and although it is impossible to catch the essence of you on paper, I dedicate this book to you. You will always remain in my heart and thoughts, a shining example of a true "Woman of Valor."

Acknowledgements

IN THIS WORLD, NOTHING IS RANDOM; NOTHING "JUST HAP-
pens." It's all part of the greater plan of the Almighty.

I thank the Creator with every breath I take for giving me such exceptional parents, may their souls rest in peace; for rescuing them from the purgatory of Galicia and giving them the strength and courage to begin life anew.

I thank the Creator for guiding my parents out of the accursed Europe, to the "goldene medina," America, where they were able to raise their three children in relative peace and comfort.

I thank the Creator for giving my parents the gift of grandchildren and great-grandchildren, who brought joy to their old age.

I thank the Creator for sending me a "one-in-a-million" husband, a partner who has stood by my side every step of the way, even during some of my hair-brained "detours."

I thank the Creator for the special bond I have with my daughters, and their "real" better halves, and my sons, together with their respective wives. Each of you has found your true "ezer k'negdo" and you have made us very proud parents and in-laws. A special thanks to my daughter-in-law Esther Reiner-Thaler from Lakewood, who, as the first reader, devoured the original manuscript and was extremely encouraging. To Miriam Segal-Thaler, Boro Park, for her amazing Hachnosas Orchim, always hosting us in a very warm and welcoming way. A special thank-you to my daughter Rachel Thaler-Konig for her unwavering support, and to my granddaughter Perla Cohen-Gros for pushing me to keep writing my poetry, which was the launching pad for this book.

I thank the Creator for an amazing and colorful bouquet of

special grandchildren and great grandchildren. May they never experience the horrors of war nor hard times.

I thank the Creator for the excellent relationship that I have with my brothers, Shloime and Duvid, and their respective wives, Ruchi and Pessie. I thank the Creator for some very dear cousins: Freida, Vivian, Ann, Rachel, and the very special 'newcomer,' Mickey. Mickey, who sowed the seeds with a simple statement: "There's so little reading material out there for Charedi girls" – and this book was born.

I thank the Creator for my mentor, Rebbitzen Miriam Sternbuch. She's an inspiration, and guides me in her unassuming way.

Not to forget my nephew Moyshe Silk, who was and is invaluable with the book contract and lots more, and my nephew Benjamin Seror, who steered me in the right direction with this book.

I thank the Creator for sending me a circle of the most wonderful friends. He has replaced the sister I never had with an entire "sisterhood": How fortunate was I that the Creator sent Hilda Freund-Rosenbaum to befriend me when I arrived as a young bride to a very foreign Antwerp. We were as inseparable, as two peas in a pod.

Dear, dear Claire Reicher and Esther Elevitsky, my soul mates . . . what a great troika we are – "the Golden Girls." Claire, a special thank you for rescuing this book in the eleventh hour by making a very valid observation.

And where would I be without Goldie Baum, my "big sister," and Jackie Schwarz-Fischler, my "little sister," or my very special colleague and friend Marleen! I am truly thankful for all those friends who complete the circle of the sisterhood: Adina, Anita, Ayala, Basya, Bella, Betty, Chavie, Clary, Clarisse, Esther, Esti, Faigy, Gaby, Gitty, Hedy, Illa, Judy, Kathy, Malvine, Micheline, Miriam, Nina, Pearl, Perla, Ricky, Rifkie, Rita, Sarah, Shoshana, Tzivi, Vera, just to name a few.

I thank the Creator for sending Renee Landau my way. Your friendship is invaluable, and thank you for the patience to proofread.

I dare not forget my colleague Koen Devos, whose amazing eye for detail and knowledge were truly helpful.

I thank the Creator that Tzvi Mauer of Urim took the risk of publishing a first-time author, and for Sara Rosenbaum, my editor. I thank the Creator, Sara, for your astute editing, and the sensitivity to understand my intentions and direct me in getting my message across. As I have never published before, I am sure that I have to be especially thankful to the Creator that you, Sara, have been extremely quick and professional in editing, and haven't kept me dangling.

I thank the Creator for all the constructive criticism that Judit Schechter and Denise Weiss offered on the manuscript.

And last, but certainly not least, I thank the Creator for my dear, dear "buddy" Joan Feldheim, without whom this book would not have made it past chapter one. I know that you, Joan, are still hoping that someone will publish my poetry. I think that you and I have both seen that one should "never say never," so, maybe one day . . .

I thank the Creator that He has given me the gift of achieving this goal, and I pray with all my being that our generation will be the one to merit the final redemption.

Glossary

Acharon shel Pesach   The last of the eight days of Passover

Aktzie   Nazi sanitized term for mass round-ups and killings; from the German, *Aktion*, meaning "campaign."

Alte heim   The old country

Aufmachen   "Open!"

Balaboste   Skilled housewife

Bal'ahguleh   Wagon driver

Bircat Hamozon   Prayer after meals

Bitachon   Trust in the Almighty

Bleishtift   Lead Pencil

Book of Eichah   Book of Lamentations; written by the prophet Jeremiah about the destruction of both Temples

Chazzan   Cantor

Chevra Tehillim   A group for reciting Psalms

Davening   Praying

DP camp   Displaced persons camp

Ezer k'negdo   Suitable marriage partner

Verdammte Jude   "Damned Jew"

Fleishig   Meat- or poultry-based foods

Gabbay   Rabbi's personal assistant

Galus   Diaspora

Hashem Lukach   God has taken

Hashem Nosan   God giveth

Kaddish   The mourners' prayer

Kittel   White robe worn by men on their wedding day, holy days, and eventually used as their own shroud

Klugerins   Professional mourners (female) hired to wail, and pray at gravesites

Kohanim   Priests; direct male descendants of the Biblical Aaron.

Lashon HaKodesh   Hebrew of the Scriptures

Lechu Neranena   Friday night prayer (lit. "let us sing for joy")

Ma Nishtana   Passover song, traditionally sung by the youngest able child at the Seder.

Melamed   Religious instructor or teacher

Milchig   Dairy items

Neshama   Soul

Oznayim la'kotel   "The walls have ears"

Pan   Mister (in Polish)

Panie   Mrs. (in Polish)

Parve   Foods that are neither meat nor dairy

Pesach   Passover

Pikuach nefesh   A term often used to refer to the obligation to save a life in jeopardy

Seder   Ritual service and meal, when referring to Passover.

Seforim   Holy books

Shamesh   Beadle

Shavous   Festival of Weeks

Shehechiyanu   A blessing to offer thanks to the Almighty for new or rare experiences, and for the joys of the Holy days.

Shloshim   Thirty days from time of burial, which ends the mourning period for a spouse

Shema   Prayer said twice daily: morning and night

Siddur   Prayer Book

Sterntechel   Traditional woman's ornamental head covering.

Succot   Feast of the Tabernacles

Tallis (pl. Talleisim)   Prayer shawl

Yom Kippur   Day of Atonement

Zohar   A mystical work of commentaries on the Torah, written in Aramaic; a key Kabbalistic text.

About the Author

Toby Orlander was born in Furth, Germany after the Second World War, the child of Holocaust survivors. While she was still in her infancy, her parents were fortunate enough to leave Europe and start anew in the USA. She spent her childhood in Pittsburgh, and in the 60s, the family moved to Brooklyn, New York. There, Toby attended Bais Yaakov High School and Seminary, and after graduation, used her teaching skills at the Achi Ezer school in Flatbush.

Toby came almost full circle when she married her husband, Jacob Thaler, and moved back to Europe, residing in Antwerp, Belgium. She is a mother, grandmother and great-grandmother, and still finds time to pursue a full-time career in business, and work part-time as a *shadchanit*.

To contact the author, please email her at byfirebysword@gmail.com.